Tribal Peasant Unrest:

A Paradox in Welfare Administration

Tribal Peasant Unrest:
A Paradox in Welfare Administration

Chhatish Chandra Dhal

2012
Kaveri Books
New Delhi - 110 002

First Published in 2012
ISBN: 978-81-7479-130-6

Published by
Kaveri Books
4832/24, Ansari Road
New Delhi-110002 (India)
Tel: 011-23288140, 23245799
Fax: 011 2328 8140
E-mail : kaveribooks@vsnl.com
kaveribooks@gmail.com
Website: www.kaveribooks.com

Typeset in Baskerville BE Font at
Delta Book World, New Delhi - 110 002.

Printed at
G S Offset Printers, Delhi

PRINTED IN INDIA

Dedicated

To My Esteemed Father

Banabihari Dhal

who is no more with us

Foreword

There were two different systems of governance prevalent in India during the colonial period – one in the territory directly ruled by the British and the other in the Princely States which had accepted the British suzerainty. There were very large princely states like Mysore, Hyderabad and Kashmir and also very small princely states equal in area to a village. The Princely States of Orissa were medium or small in size, equal to a district or a sub-division or an Assembly constituency, both macro and micro level studies of the Princely States have been made in Orissa as well other states. Micro level studies are justified because of the fact that the nature of governance in a princely state depended upon the attitude of the ruler and local milieu.

Mayurbhanj, at present a district of Orissa, having four sub-divisions was the largest Princely State of Orissa, with a predominantly tribal population. It came under the British suzerainty soon after the British occupation of the *Mughal bandi* districts of Balasore, Cuttack and Puri. After some transitional arrangements, along with other Princely States of Orissa, from 1818 to 1922, Mayurbhanj remained under the control of the Commissioner of Orissa division who was also designated as the Superintendent of feudatory states of Orissa. In 1906, subject to the control of the Superintendent, the post of Political Agent was created for the supervision of princely states. In 1922, the Political Agent was made independent of the control of the Commissioner of Orissa division and was designated as Political Agent and Commissioner of Orissa Feudatory States. In 1933 the princely states were brought under the direct control of Government of India. That year Eastern States Agency was created, consisting of 26 Orissa Princely States and 14 states of Central Provinces, which was to be supervised by a Resident under the control of the Political Department of Government of India.

Mayurbhanj State had the benefit of enlightened rule from the later part of the nineteenth century onwards. Maharaja Krushna Chandra Bhanjadeo who ruled the State from 1867 to 1882 tried to modernize the administration of the State. He donated Rs. 20,000 to the Cuttack which was afterwards named after T.E. Ravenshaw. After Krushna Chandra's untimely death in 1882, Mayurbhanj remained under Court of Wards for ten years. In 1892 Shriram Chandra, Krushna Chandra's son became the ruler of the State, on attaining adulthood. Shriram Chandra had proper education unlike his father. He was educated at Ravenshaw collegiate school and Ravenshaw College of Cuttack under the guardianship of the English couple– Mr. and Mrs. H.B. Kiddell. He undertook a through reorganization of the state administrative system, introduced light railways and allowed the Tata Company to exploit the iron ores of the State.

After Shriram Chandra's accidental death in 1912, the State again remained under the Court of Wards till 1920. Purna Chandra, the elder son of Shriram Chandra became the ruler. Due to Purna Chandra's death, caused by tetanus infection at Bombay in 1928, his younger brother Pratap Chandra became the ruler. Both Purna Chandra and Pratap Chandra were well-educated and progressive rulers. During Pratap Chandra's rule the merger of Mayurbhanj with Orissa took place. His rule saw the rise of the Praja Mandal Movement which resulted in the formation of a state legislature and a responsible ministry in December 1947. When in December 1947 at Cuttack, the Union Home Minister, Sardar

Vallabhbhai Patel asked the rulers of Orissa states to sign the merger agreement. Maharaja Pratap Chandra could avoid signing on the plea that he could not do so without consulting the popular government. But when the popular government failed to manage the State, the Government of India appointed a Chief Commissioner for the State. Finally, the Government of India merged Mayurbhanj with Orissa with effect from 1st January 1949 while assuring the unwilling tribals that their interests would be properly safeguarded.

Dr. Chhatish Chandra Dhal who himself hails from Mayurbhanj had made a commendable effort to write the dissertation covering the period from 1882 to 1949 when the State underwent profound socio-economic and political transformation on the basis of data, collected from local sources, Orissa State Archives, National Archives of India and Nehru Memorial Museum and Library. He has particularly highlighted the popular movements in the first half of the twentieth century. I hope the work will be appreciated by the scholars as well as the general readers.

Prof. Atul Chandra Pradhan
Former Professor of History
Utkal University, Vani Vihar
Bhubaneswar (Orissa)

Preface

Mayurbhanj was one of the twenty four Princely States which were merged with the Province of Orissa after independence. In size, population and natural resources Mayurbhanj was the first among the equals and its ruling Chief had a dynastic history of one thousand years prior to the British conquest. The geographical location of Mayurbhanj being of strategic importance as the intervening territory between Bengal and Madras; Bengal and the Central Provinces, it had attracted the attention of the Bhonsles of Nagpur in the 18th Century and that of the East India Company in the 19th Century. The Princely State with its Headquarters at Hariharpur and Baripada was coveted by both the Marathas and the British because they wanted to use it as a land bridge for military expedition against each other. On account of the special position of Mayurbhanj, the British formulated the Ring Fence Policy and treated the state as a spring board in their political move to occupy Orissa. While signing the treaty engagements in 1804 the East India Company treated Raja Damodar Bhanj's successor Rani Sumitra Devi with special honour. The close proximity of Mayurbhanj to Bengal was an advantage for the Rani who maintained close and cordial relationship with the Company's establishment in Calcutta and was rewarded by their protection and support whenever occasion so demanded.

Mayurbhanj had a series of benevolent Rajas whose administration was both benevolent and progressive. This became quite evident from the reign of Maharaja Krushna Chandra Bhanj (1867-1882) who modernized the State administration making Mayurbhanj the Premier Feudatory State of Orissa. Not only her superiority was acknowledged by the Orissa States, but also she was exhibited as a show piece on several occasions by the British authorities for her welfare oriented administration. The Rajas of Mayurbhanj followed the British rules and regulations and adopted the noble principle of Rule of law in the State despite the fact that they were free to rule the state as they liked and the British Government followed a policy of non-intervention in their internal administration. How the Rajas deviated from the well-trodden path of feudal aristocracy and with what results is the quintessence of this work.

The History and Culture of Mayurbhanj has drawn the attention of many scholars earlier which justified the reason why Mayurbhanj was a deviation from other Feudatory States of Orissa. Arjun Joshi's History and Culture of Khijjingakotta (Calcutta, 1983), Prabodh Kumar Mishra's Archaeology of Mayurbhanj (New Delhi, 1996), Balram Srivastav's Art of Khiching (1986), R.P.Chanda's Selections from official letters and Records (Calcutta, 1942), Notes on the History of Mayurbhanj (Calcutta, 1949) and D.M.Praharaj's Tribal Movements and political History in India (New Delhi, 1988) are some of the relevant works which have dealt with the various aspects of history and culture of Mayurbhanj. The present work differs from the above publications in giving more focus on the benevolent administration of the Rajas, the people's movement led by the Prajamandal Organisation and the tribal resistance against the State's merger with Orissa. In doing so many records available with the Mayurbhanj Collectorate Record Room at Baripada, Nehru Memorial Museum and Library, New Delhi, Orissa State

Archives, Bhubaneswar and personal records of Sunaram Soren, the Tribal leader who was about to give a turn to the history of Orissa in 1948-49 have been utilized. Another significant primary source of reference was the oral records collected through interview of important personalities who played memorable roles in the Prajamandal and Tribal movements during 1939-49. Some of them are dead and gone, but some are still alive to describe the saga of political developments of a crucial phase of national history.

The Bhanja rulers inherited a rich legacy of enlightened administration since 1867 and the same tradition was further enriched by Maharaja Sreeram Chandra Bhanj (1892-1912) and his two illustrious sons Maharaja Purna Chandra (1920-1928) and Maharaja Pratap Chandra (1928-1947). All of them made significant contributions to the political, social and intellectual progress of the State as well as the Province. Apart from introducing a modern government they sponsored the new tradition of involving the people in day-to-day administration by devolution of powers to representative, Agencies whose members were partly elected and partly nominated. They brought railways, telegraphs and modern hospital facilities for rapid economic change as well as public welfare. They extended support to the Utkal Union Conference which was the only politico cultural organisation aimed at the unity of the scattered Oriya speaking tracts under one province and the progress of education. Their liberal contributions to the Ravenshaw College for a building, for a power house, to the Medical and Engineering Schools and for the publication of Oriya Encyclopedia in several volumes made them immortal figures of history. The lasting benefits they granted inside the state as well as outside earned for them deserving accolade and deep gratitude of the posterity. It is in this context the author proposed to undertake the present study to evaluate the material and moral progress achieved by the leading Princely State of Orissa notwithstanding the shackles of colonial rule.

The majority population of Mayurbhanj consists of tribals. They belong to Santhal, Kol, Bhumij, Dharua, Lodha and Kharia group. They have their own language and identity which is quite different from the nontribals. The tribals live mostly in the subdivisions of Bamanghaty, Kaptipada and Panchpir. Their main occupation is agriculture, animal husbandry, labour and collection of forest products. In the Bamanghaty area the iron ore mines and the steel mill of Tatanagar also provide them employment. Education has no priority in their life. In the recent years they have evinced great interest in education to seek jobs in the public sector. In the 19th and 20th centuries there were many occasions when the tribals resorted to rebellion. They, however, did not join the Gandhian movement of freedom in large number. Their outlook is always clannish and their living standard is poor. They have often been subjected to economic and cultural exploitation on account of their simplicity and ignorance. Though the British Government had specific policies for the tribals they preferred to remain loyal to the Rajas. Distinguished historians like Harekrushna Mahtab held the view that the absence of a legitimate Raja in Mayurbhanj had been the cause of tribal uprising in Mayurbhanj and Keonjhar. This hypothesis needs to be substantiated by facts. But it is true that by nature the tribals are different from the non-tribals. They are often provoked by injustice and economic exploitation. The alien rule in the 19th and 20th centuries did not understand the basic grievances of the tribals, nor it adopted adequate measures for their redressal.

The society of Mayurbhanj being a synthesis of tribal and non-tribal customs and way of living, presents a strange paradox. Is it conducive to law and order and nonviolence? The history of Mayurbhanj throws interesting light on this aspect of human behaviour. There is both social and political stability on account of continuous rule of the Bhanja dynasty extending over a period of about one thousand years. The State presents a rare continuity in her history that has helped to shape her political personality and social cohesion.

The present work is an humble attempt to record the history of Mayurbhanj of the first half of the 20th century which witnessed traumatic experience in Indian history in the form of final chapter of the colonial rule, the Gandhian struggle for independence, the Prajamandal movement to end feudal aristocracy and the policy to integrate the Princely States with the Indian Union.

The work has been divided in to six chapters. Chapter one, deals with the origin of the Bhanja dynasty and their achievement till the advent of the East India Company. The demographic composition of Mayurbhanj, her potentialities in the form of natural resources have been discussed to realize the background against which the history of Mayurbhanj developed though many vicissitudes of time. Another relevant aspect of the study is the conquest of Orissa by the East India Company, the nature of early British rule in the Feudatory States of Orissa and the relation between the state vis-à-vis the Paramount Power.

In chapter two the administration and achievements of the Rajas from 1882 to 1947 have been elaborately discussed throwing light on its benevolent aspect. The factors, which influenced modernization of the State administration along with its liberal aspect have been analyzed in great detail. It was unfortunate that the State had to be placed under the Court of Wards on two crucial occasions (1882-1892 and 1912-1920) during the minority of the Heir Apparent, but that indirectly provided administrative stability in a difficult phase of colonial history.

The history of the Prajamandal movement or Peasants movement in Mayurbhanj has been discussed in Chapter three showing its area and magnitude of operation. Why the peasants unrest developed in Mayurbhanj notwithstanding the benevolent aspect of the rule has been given due weightage. The differences between the Congress agitation in the British Provinces and the Prajamandal movement have been brought under focus. There was violence in the Prajamandal movement of Talcher, Dhenkanal and Ranpur, but that of Mayurbhanj was peaceful. That time the relationship between the Chief and the Prajamandal leaders was cordial all through giving no chance to violence has been substantiated by facts.

Though the Prajamandal organization formed a popular responsible government in Mayurbhanj, its functioning was not smooth. After some initial success in ensuring people's welfare through irrigation and education, the Prajamandal Government was confronted with insurmountable problems which led to its failure. How political development gradually led to the merger of Mayurbhanj with Orissa is the subject matter of Chapter four.

In chapter five the tribal rebellion of Mayurbhanj during 1948-49 showing resistance against merger with Orissa has been discussed in its national perspective. The situation had to be firmly dealt with by the Government of Orissa well supported by the States Ministry is the main focus here. The attempt to keep Mayurbhanj separate as a political unit in the Indian Union did not succeed because it was incompatible to Sardar Patel's scheme of integration.

Finally, chapter six contains some conclusions drawn on the basis of the contents of the above-mentioned chapters.

The present work is a new approach to review the historical events of Mayurbhanj during 1882-1949 and to integrate them for a holistic picture of the Premier Feudatory State of Orissa in the context of Post 1947 drama.

The materials used in writing this book have been collected from Mayurbhanj Collectorate Record Room, Baripada, Mayurbhanj District Library, Baripada, Jubilee Library, Baripada, MPC (Auto) College Library, Baripada, Orissa State

Archives, Bhubaneswar, Record Room of Orissa Legislative Assembly, Bhubaneswar, National Archives, New Delhi, Nehru Memorial Museum and Library, New Delhi and personal interviews with many leading figures who either participated or witnessed the events of the period under review.

I would be failing in my duty if I do not record my deep gratitude to Professor Atul Chandra Pradhan, Former Head of the Department of History, Utkal University who kindly supervised my work and brought it to its present shape. In spite of his busy schedule he showed me profound sympathy and support in going through the manuscript and suggesting changes wherever required. I acknowledge gratefully my indebtedness to him for his meticulous care and patience.

Finally, I wish to thank my wife Mita and two sons Nilank Pratik and Nishant Pratik for bearing with me the hardship and giving me their willing support without which the work could not have been completed.

I take this opportunity to record my thanks to Mamata Singh who typed out the manuscript with much care and diligence.

Chhatish Chandra Dhal

Contents

THE MAP OF MAYURBHANJ

The History of Mayurbhanj

1 Introduction

Mayurbhanj is presently one of the thirty districts of Orissa. Under colonial rule it was a Princely State, linguistically, culturally and administratively linked with directly administered Oriya-speaking tracts. From 1818 up to 1922 the Commissioner of Orissa Division was the Superintendent of Oriya-speaking Feudatory States including Mayurbhanj. In 1933 the Princely States were placed under the direct control of the Political Department of Government of India. In 1936, the new province of Orissa was created headed by a Governor who served as the ceremonial head controlling the native princes through a Political Agent with headquarters at Sambalpur.

Geography

Mayurbhanj is geographically located between 22° 33' 45" and 21° 17' 0" north latitude and between 85° 42' 30" and 87° 17' 15" east longitude. Before its political integration with Orissa in 1949 apropos the national policy of integration in the post 1947 scenario, it was a powerful and prominent native state of Eastern India. It occupied an area of 6240 square kilometers in the 19th century. Today its area is approximately 10,418 square kilometers[1].

The State was bordered in the north by Seraikela State and the districts of Singbhum and Midnapore; on the south by the state of Keonjhar and Nilgiri and the district of

Balasore; on the east by the districts of Midnapore and Balasore and on the west by Singbhum and Keonjhar. The geographical location had a great advantage for which the East India Company regarded it "as the most valuable of Orissa Feudatory States". Due to the strategic location the state played a very crucial role in 1803 when the East India Company occupied Orissa.

According to the Census of 1941 the population of Mayurbhanj was 9,90,977. The State once upon a time abounded in inaccessible forest tracts, hills and perennial rivers. The major hill range is known as the Simlipal hill, which forms a part of the Eastern Ghat. Today Simlipal has been given the status of a National Park claiming international recognition for the biodiversity; it possesses many varieties of flora and fauna. Long ago in 1872 W.W. Hunter described the native state in the following words -

> "The hitherto almost unexplored mountains of Mayurbhanj heaped upon each other in noble masses of rock from 3300 feet to nearly 4000 feet high, sending countless tributaries to the Baitarani on the south and pouring down the Burhabalanga with feeders on the Suvarnarekha on the north. The peaks are densely wooded to the summit and except at regular passes, are inaccessible to the beast of border[2]."

Mayurbhanj has been divided in to three distinct natural divisions, the hill tract in the middle covered by the Simlipal range and the undulating plain in the west and the east. The state has four revenue divisions Sadar in the plain area, Kaptipada adjacent to the district of Balasore, and Panchpeer and Bamanghati in the hilly upland adjacent to Singbhum and Keonjhar[3].

Flora and Fauna

The richness of flora and fauna of Mayurbhanj is a gift of the Simlipal hill, which is famous all over the world for its biodiversity. There are to be found evergreen forests with a large number of tree species common to tropical forest. The rulers were aware of the various animal species and varieties of birds and insects. The Elephant and the Royal Bengal tiger occupy a pride of place. Such a wonderful world of nature has been attracting inland tourists for whose convenience facilities have been created. There was a time when adjacent places of Baripada like Krishnachandrapur and Betnoti were visited by wild beasts making it possible for the State Government to arrange hunting expeditions for the visiting dignitaries. Among birds most commonly to be found are peacock, parrot, hill myna, pigeon, dove, oriole, bulbul, skylark, and robin etc. The Wild Life Conservation Department and the Forest Department are careful to prevent unscrupulous poaching for which the Tiger Reserve and the Core Area of the National Park have been declared inaccessible and no human settlement is being allowed there[4].

Demographic Features

The State Government conducted Census in 1931 under an officer specially designated for the purpose. The state had a population of 8,89,603. During the next decade the figure increased by one lakh. There are two groups of people living in Mayurbhanj, the tribals and the non-tribals. The former are called the *Kalapithias* for their dark complexion and the latter are known as *Hatuas* for their business activities in the weekly *Hats*. Among the non-tribals are people of castes like Brahmanas, Karans, Khandayats, and Chasas or peasants. There are some Marwaris and Gujratis who came as businessmen and contractors in the late 19th century or early 20th after the Railway line was opened in 1905. Among the tribals are found the Santals, Kols, Bhumija, Bathudi, Bhuyan, Ho, Gond, Saunti, Kharia, Lodha, Mankidia, Munda, Oraon, Saora or Sabors and Mundari group. They were 5,60,954 in number and they spoke their own languages, which was different from oriya. Dalton in his 'Descriptive Ethnology of Bengal' States "there is a tradition that the Kharras with another tribe called Purans were the aborigines of Mayurbhanj, one of the Katak Tributary Mahals". They lived in homogenous groups in their own villages and sustained either on forest products, agricultural labour or marginal farming[5].

The tribals constitute about 62% of the total population living in the subdivisions of Panchpir, Bamanghati and Kaptipada. They have adapted to cultivation and animal husbandry as supplementary source of income. Education has not been able to make much head way among them for various reasons, though they are not unwilling to avail upon its advantages. They had very close ethnic affinity apart from respect for tribal traditions. The history of Mayurbhanj records several tribal apprising caused by their clannish outlook, problems of acculturation, percolation of non-tribal value systems, exploitation by non-tribals and the imposition of alien rules and restrictions[6]. A study of these uprisings will reveal the consequences of changing British policies and the backward tribal groups' spontaneous effort to assert themselves against social, economic and political injustice. Their nature of protest was always violent because they knew no other way to moderate their view points[7].

The number of Muslims was insignificant. During the early part of the twentieth century they were given a plot of land near the market place at Baripada to build a mosque. They adopted tailoring and goat business as their main occupation. Some were appointed by the Revenue Department for collection of revenue. In the history of Mayurbhanj there was no example of communal disharmony[8].

The Christians came to the State in the last part of the 19th century for missionary work in the tribal tracts. The State Government permitted the Roman Catholics to have their Missionary Church at Nangalkata with adequate forest and cultivable land. The permission was granted by Maharaja Krushna Chandra Bhanj in 1879. In 1880 the Missionaries set up a new settlement naming it as Krushna Chandrapur as a tribute to the Maharaja. The second missionary was set up at Baripada by Miss Allanby of the Evangelical Missionary Society in 1902 during the reign of Maharaja Sreeram Chandra Bhanjdeo. They were allotted 4.68 acres of land opposite the Court building in the town where a Church building shortly came up to pursue the missionary activities. They sponsored a Leper Assylum at Sreeramchandrapur in close vicinity of the town[9]. The Maharaja was also equally patronizing to he Brahmo Samaj as he had respect for the religion due to emotional reason. However, a small community of Bengali speaking people who had their colony near the school built a Prayer Hall in 1926 to facilitate the Brahmo movement[10]. The Brahmos had a prayer hall at Karanjia as well where from they shifted their activities to Baripada in 1905.

Another group of people who are distinctly separate from the above mentioned beliefs are called the *Kumbhipatias* who adopted the faith founded by Alekh Gosain[11]. Their number is small.

Mayurbhanj is a tribal dominated district now having ten constituencies for the State Legislature open to nine tribal and one General candidate. Among the tribals the Santals, Kols, Bhumij and Bathudi are most numerous. As per the 1961 Census the Santals constituted 35% of the population[12]. The tribals lived mostly in the rural areas in their own villages.

With regard to the languages spoken by the people of Mayurbhanj, it may be said that while the non-tribals speak oriya, the tribals speak Munda group of languages consisting of Santali, Ho, Mundari, Bhumiji, Mahali, Kera, Karmali and Karua. As per the 1951 census figure 23 languages were enumerated which increased to 24 in 1961 census. About 20,171 persons spoke Bengali as the mother tongue. The Kurmis speak a mixed language of Hindi, Bengali and Oriya and they are good agriculturists[13].

The tribals adopt a patriarchal family structure. They are governed by the Hindu law in matters of family, partition and succession. In some cases they follow their own customs of marriage, divorce and disposal of the dead. The dowry system of 'Pana' is followed by some where the bride groom's party gives dowry or presentation to the bride. Taking possession of a bride by force is an approved custom in the tribal society. After putting vermilion on the forehead of the girl the abductor takes her to his home as a legal wife. The tribal women are free to divorce or remarry after the husband's death. It is a free society with least inhibition[14].

In religious belief the tribals are found to be Nature worshippers having no scripture. They follow certain rituals to appease the deity and accept the *Dehuri* as the village priest. The Santals call their supreme deity as 'Thakur Jiu' or Sin Bonga. They believe in spirit, ghosts and many superstitions, while some tribals cremate the dead body some bury it. In recent times there is rapid detribalization on account of the spread of education. The tribal society is breaking up like ninepins and there is rapid social elevation through the process of acculturation. Their food, dress, language, living style and economic life are fast undergoing changes. They have shown interest for education and Government employment to enjoy the benefits of reservations. Except in the interiors of Simlipal hill it is difficult to see an aboriginal living on roots and fruits of the forest. Their customary dance form and intoxicated drink called *Handia* are still there, but the rapid force of changes are not difficult to notice[15].

Historical background

Mayurbhanj had a unique distinction of having been ruled by one family called the Bhanjas who enjoyed continuous hegemony over the tribal land from 10th century to 1947. Though they had three different seats of Government, Khiching in the ancient period up to 1361 A.D, then Haripur in the medieval period from 1400 to 1803 and finally

Baripada up to 1947, the Bhanja rulers left behind them an unbroken legacy of welfare Government which made them successful and famous in the pages of history. A brief summary of their history will make this point clear.

Ancient Period

The ancient name of Mayurbhanj was Khijjinga-mandala with its capital at Khijjingakotta. It formed a part of the land called Utkala in the Puranic literature. N.N. Vasu has identified modern Khiching with the ancient Khijjingakotta, the capital of the Bhanjas from the 10th century to 1361 A.D. when it was destroyed by Sultan Ferozeshah Tughluq[16] .

There were three branches of the Bhanjas who ruled at different places and had issued their separate copperplate grants showing their separate identity.[17] The matter has been elaborately discussed in Senapati and Sahu edited *Orissa District Gazetters on Mayurbhanj* (1967) in pages 47-91.

The Vinaya Pitaka, a Buddhist Text mentions about a tribe called the Bhanna inhabiting the region called Utkala who could be the ancestors of the Bhanjas of Mayurbhanj. In the post Gupta period the process of state formation had resulted in the establishment of numerous independent tribal states whose Chiefs were elevated to the Kshatriya caste of Hinduism by a process of acculturation or Sanskritization.[18] Khijjinga Mandala was one such tribal state which has extended over Mayurbhanj and Keonjhar. Among the earliest rulers mention may be made of Satrubhanja of the Asanpat Stone Inscription and Disabhanja of the Sitabhinji Rock paintings. Satrubhanja of the Asanpat Stone inscription[19] was the ruler of Vindhyatavi and as a powerful ruler had conquered up to Nepal in the North offering sacrifice at Gaya and donating cows and lands to large number of Brahmans. Raja Disabhanja of Sitabhinji paintings[20] has been shown moving in a royal procession of elephant followed by attendants. Both could be the ancestors of the Bhanjas of

Khijjingamandala who were subordinate rulers of the imperial Bhaumakaras of Utkala as has been proved by the use of Bhauma era in their copper plate grants[21] .

On the basis of literary, epigraphic and archaeological sources the ancient origin of the Bhanjas appear quite convincing. The Bhanja inscriptions provide an uniform account of their legendary origin. What ever Surendra Nath Sen describes about Jai Singh, a member of the Jaipur Raj family of Rajputana having come to Puri on pilgrimage had conquered Mayurbhanj and was the progenitor of the ruling family does not bear scrutiny. Because Jai Singh, the founder of Jaipur was a man of the 18th century and he can not be assigned to an earlier period. [22]

The Copperplate Charters give us a legendary account stating that Adi Bhanja, the first Bhanja ruler was born out of the egg of a peahen. After his birth he was taken care of by sage Vasistha in his heritage – Kottyasrama. After giving him proper education Vasistha gave him 80,000 villages to constitute the new kingdom on which Adibhanja began his rule. This legendary account narrates the story of acculturation or Sanskritization in the process of which a tribal Chief was brought up under the guidance of an Aryan hermit named Vasistha. The Copperplate description corroborates the social elevation of the tribal Chief by Sanskritization. A combined effort of the Aryan social tradition and tribal reality was at the root of state formation in the Post Gupta period in Orissa.[23]

The Copperplate Charters of the Bhanjas of Khinjalimandala (Baud-Sonepur region) also give an identical account about the origin of the progenitor from the egg of a peahen. The peacock is a sacred bird in Mayurbhanj and else where and the name of the Kingdom in later period who changed to Mayurbhanj associating peacock with the Bhanjas. Bird is a Totem worshipped by the tribals. So the early Bhanjas were tribals and sage Vasistha representing Aryan culture baptized the tribal Chief by Hindu religion and Brahmanical social system. The Kshatriya elevation of Adi bhanja was done by Vasistha, the Brahman sage whose presence in the court of Khijinga Mandala and Khinjalimandala was a symbolic presentation of the impact of Sanskrit culture. All the Copperplate Charters of the Bhanjas was in Sanskrit language indicating thereby the profound influence of Brahmanas on Bhanja polity.[24]

Pandit Binayak Mishra and JD Beglar (of the Archaeological survey of India) have associated the Bhanjas with the Maurya dynasty of Magadha to justify the association of Mayura with the Bhanjas. Since the word 'Maurya' can not be assumed as a derivative of Mayura, the above theory does not appear tenable. [25]

The origin of the dynasty as narrated in the Copperplate grants of Khijjinga Kotta and the one preserved in the Raj family of the modern times are identical which leads one to conclude that the Khijjinga Kotta line maintained its continuity till recent times when the dynastic rule was brought to an end in 1947-48. This has led noted historian like R.C. Mozumdar[26] to believe that the modern ruling Chiefs of Mayurbhanj are linked to the ancient Bhanja family of Khijjingakotta. Thus the ancient and the modern Bhanjas formed one continuous royal line which had ruled for over one thousand years in unbroken succession. This is a rare phenomenon in Indian history making Mayurbhanj proud of its royal heritage.

The sober history of the ancient period culled from archaeological -source reveals that Kottabhanja was probably founder of the capital town Khijjingakotta (modern Khiching). The epigraphs provide us names of Narendra Bhanja and Ranabhanja who ruled successively. They were subordinate to the Bhaumakara Kings of Utkala and used the Bhauma era in their charters. Ranabhanja was succeeded by his son Rajabhanja. Though a devout Saiva, Rajabhanja patronized

Buddhism. The colossal image of Avalokitesvara, now preserved in the local museum at Khiching was sculpted by Dharanivaraha and his wife Kirtii[27].

Khijjingamandala continued to remain under the political suzerainty of the Somavamsis and their successor dynasty the Imperial Gangas from 950 A.D. to 1361. During the above period Khijjingakotta flourished as a cultural center of Jainism, Budhism and *Panchopasana* of Hinduism. Several monuments and art objects recovered from the vast ruins of modern Khiching bear testimony to its glorious cultural heritage[28].

The Bhanjas had to bear the brunt of two external invasions during the imperial Ganga period, once during King Chodaganga's rule and again in 1361. The first invasion was by the Kalachuris of Ratnapur in modern Chhatisgarh who were at loggerhead with the Gangas[29]. In 1361 Sultan Feroz Shah Tugluq invaded Jajnagar- Orissa enroute Khijjingakotta and caused terrible devastation to the township destroying the monuments and forts. Being exposed to Islamic expeditions the Bhanjas abandoned Khijjingakotta and moved on to a safer place in the East. Raja Hariharbhanja established the new capital at Hari Pur in 1400 A.D. on the banks of fertile river Burha Balang, a perennial stream helpful to agriculture and commerce.

The archaeological wealth of Khijingakotta are now preserved in the local museum in the form of images, coins, copperplates, sculptures and various other artifacts. These were excavated by excavation conducted at Viratgarh, Chaulkunji, Itamundia, Sankhuarajar garh, Vasulisal and other ruins. The temple of Kutaitundi is a silent witness to the monumental art and architecture of the glorious past. They are examples of the cultural pursuits of the Bhanja kings and the great impact of India's pluralistic culture[30].

Medieval Period

After leaving Khijjingakotta, the fugitive Bhanja King had a transit camp at Bahalda wherefrom they proceeded Eastward in search of a safe region away from the Muslim invaders. The imperial Ganga dynasty was unable to guarantee their safety due to its own declining state of affairs. In 1435 a military coup led by Kapilendra Dev Gajapati occupied the throne ushering a new era of political changes. During his reign the threat from the Muslim Nawab of Bengal became increasingly menacing and the Northern part of Orissa became vulnerable to Islamic invasion[31].

Haripur Garh

Haripurgarh, the new capital of the Bhanjas was unable to escape from the predatory activities of Nawab of Bengal. Sulaiman Kararani, the Afghan Nawab of Bengal defeated the Gajapati King Mukundadev with the help of his general Kalapahad in 1568 and occupied Orissa including Mayurbhanj[32]. The crossfire that ensued between the Mughals and the Afghans, Orissa found hereself in an unenviable position, not to speak of the plight of Mayurbhanj. In 1575 Daud Khan, the Bengal Sultan took shelter in Hariharpur in order to escape the wrath of the Mughal army compelling Baidyanath Bhanja to escape to Rayagada for safety. Baidyanath Bhanja took resort in spiritual pursuits by accepting Vaishnavite philosophy of Srichaitanya which preached of peace and love. His preceptor was Rasikananda, the disciple of Srichaitanya. A beautiful Gaudiya temple of bricks and terracotta was built at Hariharpur in honour of Guru Rasikananda. The period was agog with the message of Vaisnavism in the vast region of Eastern India[33].

In 1592 Orissa along with Mayurbhanj came under the rule of the Mughals. The Bhanja king acknowledged the supremacy of the Mughals and paid tribute to Raja Mansingh. At that time the territory of Mayurbhanj had extended from

Midnapore in the north to river Vaitarani in the south. The Raja was the lord of twelve zamindari and eighteen forts. During the war of succession following the illness of Emperor Shah Jahan, Krushna Bhanj adopted an aggressive policy for occupation of more territories. He followed an oppressive policy to collect money. In 1660 Emperor Aurangzeb had sent Khan-I-Dauran as subadar of Orissa. The meeting between Raja Krushna Bhanj and the subadar was tragic for the Raja who was killed for his offensive attitude. His successor Trivikram Bhanj maintained cordial relation with the Mughals. The Mughal control over Mayurbhanj continued up to 1751 when it was transferred to the Marathas[34].

The Marathas were famous for their policy of extortion. Mayurbhanj was a victim of Maratha depredations very frequently during 1751 to 1803 on account of which the Raja abandoned Haripurgarh and took shelter in the nearby jungles. Raja Raghunath Bhanj, Chakradhar Bhanj and Damodar Bhanj who ruled successively from 1751 had to bear the brunt of the predatory Maratha army. In 1761 the East India Company took possession of Midnapore as a part of its conquest of Bengal. This brought the East India Company in close contact with Raja Damodar Bhanj of Mayurbhanj and vice versa. As a protective measure against the Marathas' limitless demand for money, Damodar Bhanj considered it wise and desirable to remain friendly with the East India Company. As a gesture of friendship he wrote two letters to Henry Vansittart, the Governor General. He also allowed James Rennel to conduct a map survey of Mayurbhanj and the adjacent area. This gesture made Vansittart quite happy and in reciprocities the Company assured help in times of need[35].

East India Company and Damodar Bhanj

Mayurbhanj and the East India Company came in contact with each other much before the British occupation of Orissa in 1803. The strategic location of Mayurbhanj as an intervening territory between the two hostile powers – the Marathas and the British made such contacts inevitable. But mutual contact was at first restricted to commerce only. When the East India Company established a trade center of Hariharpur the agents found out that Mayurbhanj produced the largest and best quality of tassar in the whole country[36]. During the rule of Raja Damodar Bhanj (1761-1796) negotiation began for establishing political relationship. The President at Midnapore wrote to Governor Harry Verelst that,

> Mayurbhanj was so advantageously located that with a very little assistance from the British, the state of Mayurbhanj would be able at any time to prevent the Marathas from entering Bengal from Southward direction[37].

Considering the magnitude of the Maratha menace the Company and the Raja began to usher in mutual trust against the common enemy. Both had to adopt a policy of restraint and diplomacy to befriend each other despite provocative and unpleasant situation[38].

The cordial relation between the East India Company and Mayurbhanj continued even after Raja Damodar Bhanj's death in 1796 when Rani Sumitra Dei assumed rulership. In fact the company advised the British Collector at Midnapore to ensure safety of the Rani against any adverse circumstance. The friendly relation was encouraged by Lord Wellesley, the Governor General who was planning an expedition to conquer Orissa from the Marathas when his negotiation with the Bhonsle of Nagpur failed[39]. The British successfully brought about a rapprochement between the Rani and her contender Raja Trivikram Bhanj of Keonjhar state. In response to this gesture Rani Sumitra rendered all possible help for the smooth movement of troops in 1803 during Orissa campaign[40]. The Company's Government honoured her with a *Khilat* as she had acted as a friend in Wellesley's military adventure. When the conquest of Orissa was over in October 1803, no treaty or engagement was immediately signed with

Mayurbhanj. After the death of Rani Sumitra in 1811 Raja Trivikrama Bhanja became the new ruler of the state[41]. The company's respect for the honourable status for Mayurbhanj continued unhampered till 1829. In 1816 Charles Dawes the Magistrate of Midnapore wrote to the Government that "I wish to be perfectly understood by the Right Honourable, the Governor General in Council that Mayurbhanj Zamindar is in a great measure an independent Raja"[42].

The successor of Trivikram Bhanj was Jadunath Bhanj who ascended the Gadi is 1829 and signed a treaty of friendship with the East India Company. He was honoured by the Company's government with a *Khilat* for rendering important services in quelling the tribal rebellion in 1830 in Bamanghaty area. The disturbances created by *Sarvarkar* Madhav mohapatra, the Chief of the Dharua tribe could be neutralized by the Raja most tactfully[43].

Jadunath Bhanj ruled up to 1863. He had entered in to treaty engagements with the Company in 1829 acknowledging their paramountcy and expressing his submission and loyalty[44]. He was granted *Khilat* again twice for his laudable conduct and cooperation. His loyalty for the British Government was tested in 1857 when his son-in-law Arjun Singh, the Raja of Porahat was involved in a Kol rebellion. The Government exerted pressure upon Raja Jadunath Bhanj to persuade his son-in-low to surrender so that law and order could be restored in the Bamanghaty region. After the surrender of Arjun Singh a *Khilat* was bestowed upon Jadunath Bhanj consisting of a pearl necklace, a silver mounted sword and other gifts. The exemplary conduct of the Raja earned him the title of Maharaja Bahadur[45] in 1860. He died at Cuttack three years later.

Maharaja Jadunath Bhanj was a distinguished ruler of Mayurbhanj who never wavered from the path of loyalty and remained steadfast in ensuring the welfare of the people. He was kind, enlightened and profoundly loyal, for these sterling qualities he was held in high esteem by the Company and the Viceroy. His long reign of thirty five years was one of crucial test for a subordinate Chief that ended with pride and success[46].

But the decade following the death of Jadunath Bhanj witnessed many developments including the emergence of a new approach to administration. He died leaving behind two sons, Srinath Bhanj and Sitanath Bhanj[47]. As successor to the throne, Srinath Bhanj ruled over Mayurbhanj up to 1867 with total incompetence and failure. The critical situation caused by tribal uprising as reaction to official tyranny and the devastating famine of 1866 warranted a change of ruler and method of governance[48]. TE Ravenshaw, the Superintendent of Tributary states being personally present in Bamanghaty to quell the revolt took away the management of the state from the hands of Srinath Bhanj appointing his nephew Krushna Chandra Bhanj as the new ruler instead[49]. He also transferred Bamanghaty to the care of the Deputy Commissioner of Singhbhum for better administration of the tribal dominated region with sympathy and understanding. The transfer order was reversed in 1878 when the government observed the high sense of maturity, and modernization in state administration[50].

British Policy towards the Feudatory States and Mayurbhanj

The Princely States located in the hilly tracts of North and North Western Orissa were a separate entity from the viewpoint of administration. In October 1803 with the conquest of the coastal tract extending from Balasore to Ganjam the East India Company's Joint Commissioners for the affairs of Cuttack province (John Melville and Colonel Harcourt) signed treaty engagement, in two phases. In the first phase treaty and engagement was signed with eleven states, viz. Atharh, Baramba, Dhenkanal, Hindol, Khandpara,

Narsingpur, Nayagarh, Nilgiri, Ranpur, Talcher and Tigiria. In the second phase Baud, Daspalla, Keonjhar, Mayurbhanj and Athmallik accepted the treaty engagements[51].

The above Garjat States were paying fixed annual tributes to the Bhonsle of Nagpur. In return the Marathas adopted the policy of non-interference in the internal affairs of the states. In 1803 the Garjat states were known as Tributary Mahals. After signing the treaty engagements with the Joint Commissioners, the Chiefs not only acknowledged British paramoutcy, but also promised friendship and loyalty to the Company besides agreeing to pay fixed annual tributes[52].

The Commissioners acknowledged the annual tribute as fixed in perpetuity and promised no further enhancement on the Tributary states[53]. In view of the inaccessibility of the states and the rough nature of the tribal inhabitants, the British Government treated them as a separate entity and kept them under formal control and supervision. The British laws and regulations were not applicable to them. The Chiefs enjoyed full freedom in their internal administration. As per Regulation XIV of 1805 the Judge–cum Magistrate of Cuttack was entrusted with their formal supervision[54].

The Chief of the Tributary Mahals remained as subordinate allies of the Company.

In 1807 Robert Ker, the Judge Magistrate of Cuttack failed in his effort to extend British regulation to the Tributary Mahals. The Company was happy when tribute was paid regularly and absconding offenders were surrendered besides other cooperation for law and order. The higher authorities did not accept the suggestion of Ker[55].

In 1814 Lord Moira, the Governor General established the office of the Superintendent for Tributary Mahals to check the misconduct of the Rajas[56]. The crimes and offences of the Rajas were subject to the supervision of the Superintendent. The first incumbent in the office was Edward Impey who received a salary of Rs.500/- per month. This ensured effective supervision of the Garjats[57].

Edward Impey was in favour of introducing uniform system of administration and to civilize the inhabitants. But the fear of adverse reaction among the tribals forced the Government to reject the idea[58]. They merely transferred the power of collecting tributes from the Collector of Cuttack to the Superintendent[59]. John Richardson, the Settlement Commissioner in Cuttack was of the view that to leave all powers in the hands of the Chiefs was "highly objectionable and loudly forbidden by humanity and good policy[60]. But the Government stuck to their policy of non-interference. Even the British criminal laws could not be extended for tear of reaction[61].

However, in the Regulation XI of 1816 the Superintendent was empowered to hear and try all claims to the right of inheritance or succession in the Tributary Mahals. Appeal against his decision could be heard by Sadar Diwani Adalat with in a period of three months. The Government had no intention to reduce the influence of the Rajas over the peasantry. The Superintendent was cautioned not to be hyper active as otherwise the Government would abolish the office. So the management of the Mahals was left at the mercy of the Rajas. The Superintendent remained helpless[62].

The Regulation V of 1818 created the office of the Commissioner for Orissa Division for better administration of the three districts - Balasore, Cuttack and Puri. The Commissioner was made the Ex-officeo Superintendent of the Tributary Mahals. Robert Ker, the first Commissioner took over the charge of the Tributary Mahals. His successor was William Blunt who joined in 1820[63]. Blunt's proposal to introduce police and criminal regulations was turned down for fear of serious reaction[64]. The avowed policy of non-interference continued. The only change was the creation of the office of the Assistant Superintendent.

In 1829 George Stockwell, the successor of Blunt suggested the extension of Regulation X of 1793 by which the territory of a minor Chief could be brought under the Court of Wards to secure the payment of annual tribute[65]. This, Stockwell said would guarantee safety to the people and the chief. Appreciating the suggestion, the Government introduced the system of Court of Ward in 1831. The events in Athgarh, Dhenkanal and Narsinghpur justified the decision[66]. To quell disturbances and to check the misconduct of the Chiefs the Government justified its decision to assume direct control of management. However, the general policy of non-interference did not change. They said, the Superintendent

Would interfere as little as possible in matters either of civil or criminal justice with the people of those Mahals[67].

The administration of AJ Mills (1840-1846), the Superintendent ushered in a period of vigorous action in the affairs of the Tributary Mahals. It began with the attachment of Nilgiri in 1840 in the event of a peasants uprising caused by the Rani's maladministration. Same year Mills confiscated Banki for the atrocious conduct of the Raja. He also recommended his banishment from the state[68].

Mills found it essential to formulate a set of rules to guide the conduct of the Rajas. In 1848 the Government had to take strong action against the Raja of Angul leading to confiscation of the state[69].

Mills was succeeded by F. Gouldsbury in 1847 who was in favour of enforcing British rules in the Tributary Mahals, particularly in judicial administration. But the Bengal Government informed him that the prevalent system "did not call for any material change at present"[70].

On the eve of the mutiny of 1857 the efforts of British officers to enforce uniform rules and regulations in the Tributary Mahals proved futile. The chiefs remained absolute in their possession. During the Mutiny the Chiefs proved their sincere loyalty to the paramount power. They served as "breakwaters in the storm which would have swept over us in one great wave"[71] said Lord Canning. He made the Home authorities realize the importance of the native states as bulwark against emerging forces of nationalism. Appreciating this attitude the Queen's proclamation in 1858 stated,

> We shall respect the rights, dignity and honour of native Princes as our own[72].

From 1858 the Government of India decided to maintain good relationship with the ruling chiefs. The Viceroy reviewed the situation periodically and conferred upon them new sanads. The Rajas were allowed to enjoy the right of adoption. In the new sanads issued in 1862 the word 'Mahal' was substituted by 'States' which remained unchanged till 1947[73].

On 25 November 1874 Sir Richard Temple, the Lieutenant Governor of Bengal issued revised sanads to the Oriya Chiefs on behalf of the Viceroy at Darbar held at Cuttack conferring upon them the hereditary title of Raja[74].

In his address to the chiefs the Lieutenant Governor said,

> "Keep your affairs in your own hands and under your own eyes, and do not leave too much to your Ministers and Agents. Continue to make moderate and equitable settlements with your ryots. Educate your people. Open out roads, foster local trade between your states and the fertile delta of Mahanuddy. Build boats on your rivers, which navigate canals now under construction. Exchange the products of your native hills, the timber, the oilseed, the lac the resin, the iron-ore-for the products of other lands... In

all things follow the advice of your excellent commissioner whom you may always regard as your best friend[75].

It become clear from the above address that in formulating a new policy towards the states, the British Government accepted the moral responsibility for good government, peace and security in them. It was also made apparent that in case of oppression, injustice, disputed succession, political turmoil, and conflict between two neighbouring states the government would not hesitate to interfere. K.M. Pannicker rightly observed that though territorial conquest ended in 1858, the paramount power slowly aggrandized upon the powers of the Rajas by restricting their freedom through watchful Residents, loaned officers and nominated Dewans[76].

In 1888 a significant decision given by the Calcutta High Court defined the position of a Feudatory state vis-a-vis the British administration. It ruled that the seventeen Feudatory States of Orissa did not form a part of British India. According to this decision the government had to revise the Sanads given to the Rajas defining their status, powers and position[77]. The new Sanads provided definite limitations on the exercise of criminal and civil powers by the Rajas. In all matters of administration the chiefs were found to consult the Superintendent and to comply with his wishes[78].

In 1891 the government further decided that the Superintendent of Orissa Tributary States would exercise the power of a Political Agent under the Chapters IV and V of the Foreign jurisdiction and Extradition Act XXI of 1879[79].

Administrative Reorganization, Classification and Policy during 1903-1939

Sir Andrew Fraser, the Lieutenant Governor of Bengal (1903-08) had evinced great interest in the affairs of the Orissa states. He strongly recommended the appointment of a

Political Agent for the Tributary States of Orissa like that of the Chhatisgarh Division. He would be a friend, adviser and colleague to the Chiefs and would make them realize their responsibility and help them to tone up their administration. In 1906 LEB Cobden Ramsay was appointed as the first Political Agent for Orissa states. He and the Chiefs were placed under the official supervision of the Commissioner of Orissa Division[80].

As a reaction to this, the Chiefs submitted a memorial to the Viceroy urging upon him to revise the provisions[81]. Accordingly, revised Sanads were issued in 1908 by Lord Minto revising the limitations with liberal clauses. All the Tributary Chiefs were now recognized as the Feudatories of the British Government. They were required to conform to the advice of the Commissioner on all important matters. The Political Agent was placed under the control of the Commissioner to supervise and regulate the twenty-six Chiefs of Orissa states. In 1922 the power, position and status of the Political Agent were enhanced assigning him with the designation of Political Agent and Commissioner of the Orissa Feudatory States[82]. In protocol he was ranked at par with the Commissioner of Orissa Division.

The Political Agent-cum-Commissioner was to see that the Chief's administration aimed at inspiring the subjects with a sense of appreciation of the British rule. He would convince the Chiefs about his attitude of non-interference. He was to monitor the administration in the line of fairness and justice. The Chiefs would rule according to their own ideas and own influence.

In 1928 the British Government appointed the Buttler Committee to ideal with the administrative reforms of the Princely States of India[83]. The Maharaja of Mayurbhanj, the Raja of Hindol, Nilgiri and Talcher deposed before the Commission in Bombay on 15 April 1928 on the issue. The Committee recommended for the formation of Eastern States

Agency which came in to existence on 1 April 1933 comprising all the twenty six Feudatory States of Orissa and fourteen States from the Central Provinces. This step was vehemently criticised by the Oriya nationalists[84].

The Governor General of India as the Crown representative exercised control over the Eastern States Agency through the Agent to the Governor General stationed at Ranchi. Under him were two Political Agents, one for the Twenty-six Orissa States with headquarters at Sambalpur and the other for the fourteen States of Central Province stationed at Raipur[85]. Subsequently, when Tripura and Cooch Bihar were added to the Eastern States Agency, the headquarters was shifted from Ranchi to Calcutta and the designation of the Agent to the Governor General was changed to Resident[86].

The Orissa States Agency having 26 States were divided into three classes– A, B and C on the basis status, size and sources of income. The Resident stationed at Calcutta was controlled by the Political Department of the Government of India. This arrangement continued till the British rule in India came to an end in 1947[87].

The Sanads of 1937 were the last in the process of defining the status and responsibilities of the Orissa Chiefs. Though they were recognized as 'autonomous rulers of their own principalities with defined criminal jurisdiction, in reality the Paramount Power did not hesitate to intervene in the affairs of the State under various pleas like–'Good Government, and disputed succession. The Chiefs were not permitted to cede, sell, exchange or part with their territories to other states without the approval of the Paramount Power[88]. The Chiefs were periodically reminded to remain loyal to the Crown and faithful to the terms and conditions of treaties, engagements and grants. The Sanad was an one sided contract imposed by the British on the Chiefs without committing any obligation as granter of Sanad[89]. The Sanad was a deed of grant by the Sovereign power and the states were the recipients enjoying an inferior and subordinate position. That was their position, which determined their relationship with the British Government[90].

References

1 M. Laeequddin, *Census of Mayurbhanj State,* 1931, Vol.I, Report, Calcutta, 1937, p.1.

2 N. Senapati and N.K. Sahu, *ODG, Mayurbhanj,* Cuttack, 1967, pp.5-6

3 Ibid. pp.7-9 and p.4.

4 Ibid., pp.19-30; P.K.Mishra, *Changing Pattern of Political Culture,* New Delhi, 2002, Pp.127-135. The Biosphere Reserve laid down by the CNPPA (Commission on National Parks and Protected Areas) laid down in clear terms, "The area should perpetuate in a natural state, preserving samples of physiographic regions, biotic communities and genetic resources and species in danger of exploitation, to provide ecological stability and diversity".

5 Senapati and Sahu, op.cit., pp.92-127

6 K.Majumdar, *Changing Tribal life in British Orissa,* Delhi, 1997.

7 B.M.Das,(ed.) (i) Souvenir on Socio-economic life of the Tribals of Orissa during 19th and early part of 20th centuries, 1981.(ii) Praharaj, D.M. *Tribal Movement and political History of India,* Delhi, 1988 Mishra, P.K.(ed.) Souvenir on Problems of Detribalisation in Mayurbhanj and Keonjhar, 2002.

8 Senapati and Sahu, op.cit., p.128. In 1931 their number was 5350.

9 Senapati and Sahu, op.cit., p.128.

10 Ibid., pp.128-129.

11 Ibid., p.129

12 Senapati and Sahu, op.cit., p.103, see the Table pp.102-103

13 Ibid., p.106 and p.113.

14 Ibid, p.p129-148

15 Ibid., For Economic changes See pp.305-336. For Socio Cultural life see p.135ff.

16 N.N. Vasu, *Archaeological Survey of Mayurbhanj* (1911) p.5. and P.K. Mishra, *Archaeology of Mayurbhanj* New Delhi, 1997, Preface.

17 Srigdha, Tripathy, *Inscriptions of Orissa* Vol.VI, (1974) see the Introduction.

18 P.K. Mishra, *Evolution of Orissa and Her Culture* (Calcutta) 1984, pp. 3-4

19 Orissa Historical research Journal, XIII No.2, pp. 1-8. Also see A. Joshi, *History & Culture of Khijjingakotta*, p.31.

20 K.C.Panigrahi, *History of Orissa* (1981) p. 139.21 S.Tripathy, op cit.

22 Senapati and Sahu, op.cit. pp.138-139.

23 P.K.Mishra, op.cit. p.5 and S.Tripathy, op. cit, pp.1-48. There were atleast ten copper plate charters giving similar description of the legend.

24 Senapati and Sahu, op.cit pp.64-65 W.W.Hunter, *Orissa* (1872) Vol.I, pp.308-09.

25 Senapati and Sahu, op.cit. p.64

26 R.C.Mazumdar, *The Age of Imperial Kanauj*, Bombay 1984. p.74.

27 The epigraph on the image reads "rajye sri rayabhanjasya lokeso bhagavanayam Sri Dharani varahanasaha kirttiya vinirmitah". Archaeological survey of India, 1922-23, pp.27-28.

28 Orissa Historical research Journal, XIII, No.2, pp.4-5, and A-Joshi, op.cit. p.31.

29 R.P.Mohapatra, *jaina monuments in Orissa* (1986) pp. 115-116

30 R.P.Mohapatra, loc. Cit. ASI, 1922-23, p.127 and Ibid p.87 N.K.Sahu, Buddhism in Orissa (1959) p.214. JBORS – IV pp.172-77. R.P.Chanda, *Bhanja Dynasty of Mayurbhanj and their ancient capital Khiching.*

31 Senapati and Sahu, op.cit, pp.65-67. Haripurgarh is in ruins. Excavation by the Archaeological survey of India has exposed the royal place, temples in ruined condition and the walls of the rectangular fort.

32 H.Blockman, (Tra) *Ain-I-Akbari*, vol. I, p.375.

33 For details see P.K.Mishra, *Archaeology of Mayurbhanj* (1997) pp. 19-33. and *History and culture of Mayubhanj* (Oriya) 2000, pp.27-29.

34 Senapati and Sahu, op.cit. p. 69.

35 Ibid p. 70

36 P. Acharya, *Studies in Orissan History, Archaeology and Archives*, (1969) pp. 216-217 and 219-20.

37 P.Acharya, "Two centuries of British connections" published in Mayurbhanj Chronicle (Baripada) 1936.

38 The issues of Midnapore, Nayabasan and Amarda were a few examples enough to stake their friendship. For details R.P.Chanda, History of Mayurbahnj, 1949. p.53 ft.

39 Senapati and Sahu, op.cit. pp.71-72.

40 Mohammad Laeequddin's Report 1937. p.20 and Chanda (ed) SOLRI 186, p.188

41 Consequent upon the death of Rani Sumitra on 8 April 1811, the Gadi was offered to Yamuna Devi, a younger Rani of Late Damodar

Bhanj. She invited Trivikram Bhanj from Keonjhar to become the Raja, Trivikram had been adopted by late Damodar Bhanj before his death. R.P.Chanda, Op.cit. 1949 p.128

42 B.C.Ray, *Foundations of British Orissa*, 1960, pp.14-15 and Chanda(ed) SOLR p.188.

43 The khilat consisted of an elephant costing Rs.1000/-, a horse costing Rs.300, a pair of shawls costing Rs.100/- and a set of royal dress costing Rs.225 SOLRI, 304, p.425.

44 R.P.Chanda, *Notes on the History of Mayurbhanj,* p.17.

45 Senapati and Sahu, op.cit. p.-74.

46 Chanda(ed) *SOLR* no.656, p.544.

47 Senapati and Sahu, op.cit. p. 74.

48 *Report of the Famine commission,* 1866 (Calcutta) vol. I, p.21.

49 Ibid p.101, para 302. Srinath Bhanj died on 10 Nov. 1867. He was issue less. So his nephew was anointed as Raja.

50 Senapati and Sahu, op.cit. pp.76-77.

51 LEB Cobden Ramsay, *Feudatory States of Orissa* (Reprint, Howrah, 1950) pp.24-25.

52 C.U.Aitchison, *A collection of Treaties, Engagements and Sanads* relating to India and Neighbouring countries, vol.I, pp.188-190.

53 Ibid.

54 Proceedings, Bengal Judicial (civil) no. 34 5 September 1805, Regulation XIV of 1805.

55 Ibid and letter dated 18 February and 26 February 1807 Registrar of Sadar Diwani Adalat to the Government dated 14 February 1807.

56 Ibid No.29, dated 26 July 1814.

57 LEB Cobden Ramsay, op.cit. p.25.

58 Ibid.

59 Proceedings, Bengal Judicial (Civil) No.29, 26 July 1814 Superintendent of Tributary Mahals to the Government. And No.30, 26 July 1814, Government to Superintendent of Tributary Mahals.

60 Bengal Revenue Proceedings No.29, 18 March 1815, Richardson to Government, 20 December 1814.

61 Ibid.

62 Proceedings Bengal Judicial (Civil) No.33, 5 December 1839.

63 He enjoyed office from 1820 to 1828.

64 Proceedings Bengal Judicial Civil no.21. 10 August 1821, Government to Blunt, 10 August 1821.

65 Ibid. No.7, 29 November 1831.

66 Ibid.

67 Proceedings Bengal Judicial (criminal) No.48, 5 December 1839 Secretary to Government of India to Secretary to Government of Bengal 25 November 1839.

68 Ibid, No.55 of 14 April 1840. Mills to Government 20 February 1840 Ibid, No.34 of 27 October 1840. Mills to Government, 6 October, 1840.

69 Proceedings Bengal Judicial Political No.1348 17 November 1848.

70 Letter of the Government to F.Gouldsbury 29 September 1851 Proceedigns Bengal Judicial Political No.186.

71 K.M. Patra, op.cit. pp.315-16.

72 White paper on Indian states, Government of India, Ministry of States, New Delhi, 1950. p.12 and p.15.

73 The Feudatory and Tributary States of Orissa Division, and the Rules Applicable to them, part – I (Calcutta) 1907, p.2.

74 Proceedings of the Lieutenant Governor of Bengal, General Department (Political) December 1874. Government of Bengal to Government of India No.4516 9 December 1874.

75 Ibid.

76 K.M.Pannicker, *Introduction to the study of the Relations of Indian States with the Government of India* (London) 1927, pp.35.37.

77 The ruling was given in a case of murder committed in Mayurbhanj state. The offender was given death sentence by the Deputy Commissioner of Singhbhum. The decision was challenged in 1881 by Raja Krushna Chandra Bhanj who claimed that Mayurbhanj was not a part of British; hence the High Court had no jurisdiction to try the case. It was a full bench decision of the High Court which ruled that Mayurbhanj was not a part of British India. In 1888 the Secretary of State in Council decided that 17 Tributary Sates of Orissa did not form a part of British India... x'.

78 *Bengal Administration Report*, 1901-02 p.59.

79 Proceedings, Bengal Judicial (Political) April 1892 no.72 Notification by the Government of India Foreign Department no.1363-1 dt 26 March 1891.

80 *Bengal Administration Report*, 1905-06, pp.4-5.

81 The memorial was drafted by Madhusudan Das, the leading Oriya Advocate of Cuttack. N.K.Sahu. (ed) *Utkal Divas Souvenir*, 1969, p.11.

82 C.U. Aitchison, op.cit. Vol.II, p.321.

83 On the basis of an exclusive engagement between the Raja of Mayurbahnj and East India Company in 1829 Mayurbhanj submitted a memorandum and was admitted to the Chamber of Princes.

84 The Samaj. 4 January 1933.

85 The Samaj, 10 January, 1934.

86 In 1936 the Eastern States Agency was divided in to three different Agencies under the same Resident, (1) Bengal States Agency with Cooch Bihar, Tripura and Mayurbhanj; (2) Chhatisgarh States Agency with 16 States (including Kalahandi and Patna) and (3) The Orissa States Agency having 23 States. (Athgarh, Athmallik, Bamra, Baramba, Boud, Bonai, Daspalla, Dhenkanal, Gangpur, Hindol, Keonjhar, Kharswan, Khandpara, Narsinghpur, Nayagarh, Nilgiri, Pallahara, Rairakhol, Ranpur, Sareikela, Sonepur, Talcher and Tigiria.

87 Orissa State 'A' Class (Mayurbhanj, Sareikala, Patna, Kalahandi, Keonjhar, Gangpur, Dhenkanal, Sonepur, Bamra, Nayagarh and Baud. 'B' Class (Athgarh, Athmallik, Khandpara, Kharswan, Narsinghpur, Baramba, Bonai, Daspalla, Hindol, Nilgiri, Rairekhol, and Talcher. 'C' Class (Pallahara, Ranpur, Tigiria) The Samaj, 10 January, 1934 and V.P.Menon. The story of the Integration of Indian States (1961), pp.144-151.

88 Foreign Political Department Nos. 179-83 December 1938.

89 Sambalpur University Archive, Memorandum on the Treaties, Position and Status of the Feudatory States of Orissa, p.16.

90 Lee Warner, op.cit., p.378.

2 Dynastic History:

Rajas of Mayurbhanj: 1882-1947

The year 1866 was a turning point is the history of Orissa, also in the history of Mayurbhanj. While millions were dying in the coastal districts of Orissa Division on account of the unprecedented famine of 1866, Mayurbhanj was in turmoil on account of a tribal uprising in the Bamanghaty area which necessitated the presence of T.E. Ravenshaw, the Commissioner on the spot to quell the rebellion because Srinath Bhanj, the Raja of Mayurbhanj was a weak and incompetent ruler. Along with Ravenshaw was present Krushna Chandra Bhanj, the nephew of the Raja whom the Commissioner liked as a promising young man with the prospect of succeeding Srinath Bhanj to the *Gadi.* The rebellion was quelled in 1866 followed by the death of Srinath Bhanj in 1867 which facilitated the succession of Krushna Chandra Bhanj to the throne of Mayurbhanj. The close association of Krushna Chandra with TE Ravenshaw was to bear fruitful results in toning up the administration of the state and in retrieving the people from the precipice of anarchy and instability[1].

Krushna Chandra Bhanj was the Raja of Mayurbhanj from 1867 to 1882. Though he did not have any formal education he had a broad outlook and farsighted vision. It is believed that Ravenshaw and the contemporary utilitarian philosophy had a profound impact on the young chief[2]. The administrative measures adopted by Raja Krushna Chandra

Mayurbhanj State Palace of Baripada

ushered in an era of modernization in the administration of the state. His government marked a departure from the past and precipitated the beginning of enlightened rulership.

Process of Modernization

The typical tribal population of Mayurbhanj with its strong affinity to tradition was a challenge for the Commissioner-cum-Superintendent of Orissa Tributary States. It was difficult to break with the past and start a new era without the spread of education and leadership of educated personnel. The accession of Krushna Chandra Bhanj and his close association with TE Ravenshaw was a happy augury for Mayurbhanj to break away from the tentacles of tribalism and superstition by encouraging education and inducting educated person from Bengal in state service. The Maharaja initiated a process of modernization in the form of enlightened and welfare oriented government which had far reaching results in making Mayurbhanj an ideal state. In doing this he was well supported by the elite group of officers he selected judiciously for implementing his policies.

Belgadia Palace of Baripada

1. Krushna Chandra Bhanj

Krushna Chandra Bhanj (1867-1882) was handsome, intelligent and a youngman of pleasing manners. Having been endowed with the qualities of head and heart he wisely heeded the advice of T.E. Ravenshaw in bringing about series of administrative reforms[3]. After overcoming the initial period of court intrigue of some officers the deceased King and the Rani he set down with sincere real to promote the welfare of the state.

His first bold step was to modernize the administration. He created every department essential to grease the administrative machinery while setting up the civil and revenue courts and appointed Special Officers to take care of their charge. For the first time a recorded administration was setup with provision to keep all orders systematically in a record room. In judiciary all case records were maintained, plaints written, statements and deposition of witnesses along with judgment of the magistrates were ordered to be written on paper. The tradition of using palm leaf came to an end. In the record room the documents, papers and registers were kept carefully under the custody of responsible person. The establishment of a registration office with a Sub-Registrar to function under the collector resulted in keeping records on death, birth, mortgage, sale etc. The Maharaja himself acted as the appellate court disposing of cases after hearing the judgement of lower courts[4].

Maharaja Krushna Chandra laid the basic framework of the police department. In each Pargana the Sardar was

Maharaja Krushna Chandra Bhanj Deo

bestowed with the power of investigating crime and adopt preventive measures as and when necessary. The Sardar was equivalent to a modern Sub-Inspector who dealt with minor offence and crimes. Since in Bamanghaty and Panchpir the tribals were more in number and they were of volatile temper steps were taken to set up Police Station at Joshipur which was equidistant from both. The new police station had one Sub-Inspector and some Constables. The state saw its first Prison or Hazat for under trial prisoners and convicts. It was located at the centre of the town which now accommodates the daily market. To cook food for the prisoners a Brahmin cook was appointed. The convicts were kept engaged in physical activities like gardening, building roads and houses[5].

The Maharaja had to take up land revenue administration as a permanent source of income for the state treasury. There were certain malpractices like leasing out land without record of measurement. The unscrupulous *Pradhans* or Tax Collectors imposed tax on their free will. There was necessity of proper land settlement and classification. The system of taxation had to be rationalized. The state was divided into districts and Parganas. Each Pargana was placed under a Sardar for revenue collection through the *Pradhans.* The Sardar deposited revenue in the State Treasury. Legal action was taken against default as for non-payment of land tax by filing rent suits. The Sardars and the *Pradhans* were also accountable for lapses if any[6].

The State established a department of public works with J.L. Atkinson, the engineer who supervised the construction of road and public buildings. As roads and bridges were essential for communication in the context of law and order and efficient administration, the Maharaja completed highways from Baripada to Balasore in the east and Bahalda in the north. Among important public buildings mention may be made of the Palace, School, police station, post office, jail, and the rest house at Baripada. The Public

Works Department also started the construction of an irrigation project in the Rasunia Pargana[7].

The Maharaja was eager to promote education for which the Department of Education was established under Dr. HC Bowzer. For the school at Baripada an English knowing teacher and Sanskrit Pandit were appointed. To provide free elementary education in the rural areas several *pathsalas* under Oriya *Avdhanas* were also setup. His friend T.E. Ravenshaw as the Commissioner of Orissa Division had been instrumental in establishing an Intermediate College, an engineering school and a medical school at Cuttack besides doing various other significant works. The college was later named after T.E. Ravenshaw which in course of time developed as the Premier Educational Institution of Orissa. The Maharaja contributed a huge sum of Rs. 27, 000/- for the construction of a permanent building for the college[8].

The state took care of the health and hygiene of the public of Mayurbhanj. Therefore, Dr Bowzer organized a Charitable Dispensary at Baripada. At first the Dispensary started functioning in the Palace in a separate room. The Doctor prescribed western medicines to a people who were sceptic about its usefulness. Out of disgust Dr. Bowzar resigned[9].

The Maharaja had realised the significance of a Printing Press in spreading education. So he setup a printing press at Baripada which not only printed forms and documents, of the Government, but also a news letter called 'Mayurbhanj Fortnightly' Magazine. To promote reading habit among his people he set up a Public Library and a beautiful public garden called Golapbag as a recreational facility for the citizens[10].

All these measures facilitated the dawn of a new era of welfare-oriented administration. The traditional royal prerogative sponsored enlightened government putting an end to medieval oligarchy. Well educated Bengali officers like Diwan Nund Kumar Mukherjee whom the Maharaja appointed proved not only loyal and efficient, but also helped him to expedite the development of internal resources for economic growth. Other notable officers who contributed immensely in this effort were Prasanna Kumar Ghosal, the Diwan, Durga Prasad Das, the Settlement Officer and Artatran Mahapatra, the Treasury Officer. The development of the state being unprecedented, the Maharaja earned the deep respect and love of his people[11]. His popularity for good works and benevolent Government found special mention in the Government records[12].

Maharaja Krushna Chandra Bhanj's prematured death on account of small pox at the age of 34 (29 may 1882) was a rude shock to the state administration. For a short period the state was disoriented on account of many aspirants for the *Gadi*[13] and as the Crown Prince Sriram Chandra was a minor. The late Maharaja before his death had requested the Bengal Government to assist him by sparing a British Officer. The lieutenant governor of Bengal did not like the management of the state to pass on to the younger brothers of the deceased Raja. The Lieutenant Governor selected Mr. H.P. Wylly, the Superintendent of Canal Revenue, Cuttack for the purpose. In recommending his name, the Governor argued that during the next eight years (1882-1890) till the Crown Prince attained majority and assume the rulership of the state, a good European officer would be able to introduce an enormous amount of improvement in every branch of the state administration so that Mayurbhanj should be a model to other states[14].

Therefore, the management of the state was entrusted to Mr. H.P. Wylly who managed everything on behalf of the Court of Ward. He managed it efficiently till 1892 when Sriram Chandra Bhanj became the ruler[15].

2. Sriram Chandra Bhanj Deo (1892-1912)

The alertness of the British Government saved Mayurbhanj from plunging in to a war of succession or Court Intrigue after the sudden death of Krushna Chandra Bhanj in 1882. Those days small pox had no treatment and there were frequent tragedies in the Bhanj family on account of the Killer disease. Krushna Chandra Bhanj had three sons–Sriram Chandra, Sri Shyam Chandra and Sridam Chandra. The second son Sri Shyam Chandra became the adopted son of the Raja of Nilgiri and Sridam Chandra lived till 1946 acting as the Chief of the Maharaja's household which was known as the domestic department.

Maharaja Sriram Chandra Bhanj Deo

Sriram Chandra was born on 17 December 1871 and was a minor of eleven years old when his father died. On account of his minority, the state came under the Court of Wards or direct control of the Superintendent of Tributary Mahals who appointed H.P. Wylly as the Manager of the Estate in December 1882. The request of Brundaban Chandra and Gokul Chandra, two brothers of late Maharaja Krushna Chandra for accesion to the Gadi was rejected. The Government's intention was to make Mayurbhanj an ideal state by effecting allround progress through good management[16].

The early education of Sriram Chandra had begun at Baripada from where he was shifted to Cuttack in 1884 with Govind Chandra Mahapatra as his guardian. At Cuttack the young Prince was kept under the guardianship of HB Kiddell and his wife who remained together in the Mayurbhanj House at Chouliaganj for six years. Both Mr. Kiddell and his wife while taking good care of the Prince, inculcated in him the essence of truthfulness, humility and other laudable virtues of humanism[17].

Sriram Chandra was a voracious reader of books who took special delight in literature, General studies and history. In 1888 he passed the Entrance examination of Calcutta University from the Ravenshaw Collegiate School and the Intermediate examination two years later. He read up to BA with Science and Mathematics but could not take the University examination due to pressing engagement at home. He returned to Mayurbhanj in 1890 after attaining majority. At Baripada his private tutors were Mr. Kiddell and Sri Mahini Mohan Dhar MA, BL who taught him Science and Mathematics in which he had deep interest[18].

As the Maharaja of Mayurbhanj Sriram Chandra assumed full control of the administration from 15 August 1892 and switched over his interest to the study of Philosophy and Law. He was an admirer of English law as its cardinal principles were equity and justice. From the beginning of his rulership he laid emphasis on liberalism and humanism as the guiding features of his Government. Mayurbhanj was geared up to follow the path of benevolent administration under the benign care of the Maharaja[19]. The results of liberal administration were appreciated by the people and the Government soon after a couple of years of their introduction.

The Maharaja himself assumed the reins of Government and started the popular measures by establishing Mayurbhanj State Council and the Judicial Committee with himself at the helm of affairs. The Council was setup in 1892 with the Diwan, the State Judge, the Superintendent of the Police and the State Engineer. There were two non official members nominated by the Maharaja; one was Brundaban Chandra Bhanjdeo and the other was Ramjhari Jit Babu. The following matters are looked after by Council:

(i) The Annual Budget estimate;
(ii) Legislative matters;
(iii) Administrative rules for all the departments;
(iv) Taxation,
(v) Annual Reports of all Department;
(vi) Any other matter which would be referred to by the Maharaja[20].

According to the Regulation-II of August 1892. Seven Acts were passed including the Indian Penal code, the Criminal Procedure Code, the Civil procedure Code, and the Evidence Act. The Acts were binding on all Courts of the State. The Judicial Committee was first of its kind in Orissa to function as the High Court. The State Council was empowered to hear appeals even against the orders of the Maharaja exercising casting vote in the Council as its President. All laws relating to Criminal, Civil and Revenue matters like Revenue settlement regulation, Land Acquisition Laws, Forest and Excise rulers were enacted by the Council with Maharaja as the President.

By making a thorough reorganization of the Tenancy system he gave the Tenants in 1896 for the first time, the right of occupancy over their holdings. The tribals were given special protection by abolishing–*abwabs*[21].

The introduction of the reforms was to follow organizational changes. He divided the state in to four Sub-divisions, Sadar, Kaptipada, Panchpir and Bamanghaty. He followed the British rules and regulations while establishing Courts in the Sub-divisions. He held charge of the Sadar Sub-division himself delegating similar powers to Sub-divisional officers of the outlying Sub-divisions. The Sub-divisional offers were endowed with adequate judicial powers to deal with law and order issue. In Sadar Sub-division, a Collector was appointed with Magisterial powers. The Maharaja was the Chief Executive of the State controlling the police, public works, forest, education and medical services. The Dewan was delegated with full powers in revenue matters. As head of the Revenue Department, he looked after Settlement, Agriculture and zamindari matters[22].

The State Government gave priority to the police system. Though the traditional system of chowkidari was retained for watch and ward in the villages, a new system of police stations and police out posts was introduced for the detection and control of crimes. The number of police station in Mayurbhanj by 1910-11 was 13 police stations and 10 out posts. The state maintained a strength of 65 officers and 272 constables. This added sophistication to the criminal administration in the state[23].

The Maharaja was very particular about enhancement of state revenue. As the state had adequate forest wealth, he wanted to explore the potentiality to utilize the revenue for the development of the state. He was allowed the sale of liquor and narcotics to earn revenue. The states having majority tribal population, their life style demanded the use of liquor, tobacco and ganja type of narcotics. Therefore, the Maharaja did not discourage the production or sale of liquor which was a part of utilizing forest products like Mahua and toddy extracted from palas trees[24].

Mayurbhanj was rich with iron ore at Badampahar, Garumohisani and Suleipat. The quantum and quality of deposit was surveyed by Pramath Nath Bose, an eminent Geologist and leased out to the Tata Iron and Steel Company[25]. The above mines led to rapid growth of industrialization in south Bihar (Mordern Jharkhand) giving employment to thousands of tribals in the adjacent area. There was perceptible change in the income of the state as well.

Regulation II, 1908

In 1908 the Mayurbhanj State Council passed three important legislations, viz. (i) The Mayurbhanj Emigration Regulation, which prevented the emigration of tribals as labourers to the Tea gardens of Assam; (ii) The Regulation for the exclusion of the undesirables which was passed to empower the Maharaja with certain arbitrary powers to expel any person from the state without assigning any reason and ask the persona non grata to leave the state within twenty four hours. The law was popularly known as "twenty four hours law"[26]. Maharaja Pratap Chandra had also applied it to expel a notorious Prajamandal leader of Rajaloka named Minketan Dash on 5 March 1947[27]. Another Prajamandal leader to suffer similar fate was Baikunthanath Sadual, the Paik leader of Panchpir[28].

It is presumed that the prevailing political situation in Bengal following the partition in 1905 had set the spirit of anti imperialism ablaze. The British Government had to adopt measures of repression to stifle the rising voice of nationalism. As a loyal Chief the Maharaja had to introduce the Draconian law of expulsion to keep his state peaceful. The British Government in Bengal and Punjab had resorted to take expulsion of extremists like Bipin Chandra Pal, Lajpat Rai and

Ajit Singh as per the provisions of Regulation III of 1818[29]. This Regulation had been passed to deal with the Pindari menace, who were a threat to India's law and order situation[30]. The Maharaja might have followed the British Government in introducing the Regulation II of 1908 in order to throw out undesirable persons from the state. But during Sriramchandra's reign the law was never misused, as Mayurbhanj did not produce any ultranationalist.

Administration

The Maharaja had the wisdom to separate the Executive and Judiciary of the state. The Dewan was the head of the general Executive administration while the State Judge controlled and supervised the Judicial Department. The Sub-divisional officers of Bamanghaty and Panchpir exercised both executive and judical powers because of the sensitive nature of the Sub-divisions. But they were under the Dewan for civil administration and under the State Judge for judicial matters. As has been said before, the Maharaja in imitation of the High Court of British India as the highest court of appeal had setup the Judicial Committee. The Judicial Committee was formed by the Chief as the President and two members of the State Council. This was the apex Court of the state[31].

Petition to revise the Sanad of 1894

Sriram Chandra had submitted a memorial to the Viceroy on 14 July 1896 stating that Mayurbhanj be treated a special status different from other Tributary Mahals which would bestow upon him greater powers in criminal administration. The Superintendent had forwarded the petition to the Lieutenant Governor with the views as mentioned here[32]

The Raja personally superintends the administrative works in all its Departments and has appointed properly qualified officers in each department. Babu Mohini Mohan Dhar, State Judge is the head of the Judicial Department, Mr.

Kiddell of the Police and Jail Department, the Dewan of the Revenue Department, Mr Martin of the Public Works Department, Mr. Webb of the Forest Department and the Assistant Surgeon of the Medical Department. Through the agency of these officers and under the supervision of the Raja, the administration of the state is carried on much in the same style and under the same system as obtain in British Orissa and with a degree of efficiency and care which reflect credit as the enlightenment of the young Raja.

While admitting a slight distinction in the early days between his (Mayurbhanj) state and other Mahals by separate special mention of Mayurbhanj in Regulation XII of 1805 and as no engagement was made with its chief till 1829, the petition was turned down by the Government of India as they did not like to encourage other Rajas to imitate Mayurbhanj claiming revision of Sanad for special status[33].

Irrigation

The land reforms initiated by the Maharaja aimed at improving the lot of the peasants. Apart from giving them the right of occupancy, the state permitted them to sell, mortgage or transfer their holdings. The Settlement Department carefully prepared the Record of Rights which specified the area of holding and the annual dues to be paid to the state. The area of land under cultivation was increased by authorizing the peasants to clear jungles and reclaim more land for cultivation. This was known as the permission to enjoy *Amalnamas*. The Maharaja was aware of the importance of irrigation to increase production of land. Two irrigation projects at Haldia and Baldiha were completed at a cost of Rupees Six lakhs. It was an outstanding work of great utility for the peasant population. The above two projects brought about 12, 000 acres of land under cultivation. The state established granaries or paddy store houses at different parts of the state which gave paddy on loan to needy farmers at low rate of interest. Other steps to improve agricultural production were; (i) agriculture loans (ii) land improvement loans, (iii) loans to purchase seeds and tools to help the farmers[34].

The peasants had to be protected from exploitation by the moneylenders. It was ordered that no moneylender was allowed to extract any amount of interest which would be more than the principal amount. The state introduced Credit Cooperative Society to provide easy loans. Though it was a good system, the Credit Cooperation System did not work well due to poor response and poor management[35].

The state encouraged Tassar culture in specific areas where mulberry trees were in plenty. This helped to supplement income of the tribals who could make use of the peripheral forest areas to adopt scientific rearing of silk worms. Another experiment the state undertook was the cultivation of cotton. This could not be successful as Mayurbhanj did not have black cotton soil. It was Mr. Danial Hamilton who pioneered the cultivation of cotton. He also introduced mango orchards in vast areas adjacent to Baripada with selected varieties of mangoes brought from other places. The Gardens are still there at Palbani, Takatpur close to Baripada town and Rajabasa. Hamiltan also experimented with the plantation of rubber, but failed to make much headway[36].

Jail Reforms

During the time of the Maharaja some reform measures were introduced to improve jail administration. In 1885 the Baripada Jail had been established in the center of the township. In 1908 a huge Jail building was constructed away from the town keeping in mind the needs of health and sanitation. The cost of the building was rupees one lakh nineteen thousand five hundred and fifty. In 1908 September the prisoners were shifted from the old jail to the new one. The old jail building was transformed to a permanent market and was handed over to Baripada Municipality for maintenance. It was agreed upon by the Municipality authorities to give the state half of the profit earned from the market[37].

The Maharaja was no less interested in promoting education among his people. In 1892 the Middle English School at Baripada established by his father was elevated to the status of a High English School. For a decade or so the students did not pay any fees. In 1904 Sir Andrew Fraser, the Lieutenant Governor of Bengal during his visit to the state suggested the Maharaja to collect fees. In Maharaja Krushna Chandra's time Mayurbhanj had 44 schools of various categories. The number increased to 231 by 1910-11[38]. The growth of schools led the Inspector of Schools in that year to observe the laudable effort of the Chief in spreading education among the tribal children. The student strength of Mayurbhanj was far in number than all the Tributary Mahals taken together. The Inspector also noted that Mayurbhanj was spending 1/24 of its total revenue on educational progress. It was much higher than what the British Government was spending in India[39].

The state did not neglect the traditional Tols where Sanskrit was being taught by Pandits. Sreeram Chandra established two Sanskrit Tols to promote Sanskrit learning. In order to have trained teachers, he established the Teachers Training School at Baripada giving scope to learn Basic education like gardening, handicrafts etc[40]. The prevalence of Purdah system was an impediment for female education and not much could be done to overcome the problem. The Lower Primary Schools were opened to the girls but not higher classes[41]. In January 1899 the Public Library at Baripada was established to cater to the public demand. It was known as the Victoria Diamond Jubilee Public Library. Now it is known as the Sreeram Chandra Public Library. It was first of its kind in Orissa[42].

Baripada Municipality

In 1905 a pioneering step was taken to establish the municipality at Baripada to maintain sanitation and hygiene in the town. A regular Constitution was drawn up in the model of other leading towns where Municipal Act was in vogue. The state setup a Municipal Committee with a Chairmen and fifteen Councilors among whom six were officials and nine non-officials. The state conservancy department was merged with the Municipality. A cousin of the Maharaja named Lal Saheb Harish Chandra Bhanj Deo was appointed the first Chairman of the Municipality[43].

Gopabandhu Das

The Maharaja was a protagonist of Oriya nationalism. His love for young educated Oriyas became evident when he appointed Gopababndhu Das as the state pleader in 1910[44]. He was soon appointed, as the member of the state council giving him full scope to express his free opinion in legal matters. He was also made the Vice Chairman of Baripada Municipality. He was opposed to the imposition of Court fees because he thought it would discourage the poor people to seek fair justice. He suggested increase in the budgetary allocation for education. By comparing Baroda and Mayurbhanj he could point out that while the Raja of Baroda was spending 10% of the revenue on education, Mayurbhanj was spending only 3.5 % of its annual income. Gopabandhu was quite vocal in presenting his own attitude and judgement. He stayed in Mayurbhanj for a short period of two years only, is 1910-12[45].

Mayurbhanj Light Railway

Mayurbhanj being rich in minerals and natural resources like timber and many other forest products, there was no infrastructure like railways for transport and easy communication. The first requirement was that of a Light Railway for which an agreement was signed with the Bengal

Nagpur Railway Company and land was alienated in their favour for the construction of the railway lines[46]. No compensation was claimed by the state for the raiyats who lost their land[47]. Permission was also granted by the Government of India for the opening of a Telegraph Line from Baripada to Baripada Road (Rupsa).

The first phase of the Mayurbhanj Light Railway connected Rupsa (Baripada Road) with Baripada in 1905 whose initial planning was done by Arnold Mortin, the State Engineer. This line gave Baripada access to Howrah-Madras Main line. Its inauguration was done on 2 December 1904 by Sir Andrew Fraser. The distance was about 50 kilometers. The entire cost of approximately Rupees Six Lakhs was borne by the State. It gave opportunity to traders of Calcutta to take advantage who rushed in to the virgin market of Mayurbhanj. Large number of Marwaris and Gujerati traders arrived at Baripada as contractors and traders[48]

Very soon it was realized that the Railway line should be extended up to Bangriposi and Talbandh to reach the unlimited resources of Simlipal hill. M/s B Barooah and Company of Calcutta showed interest in buying the precious timber of Simlipal hill whose huge Sal forest was found most suitable for the new railway tracks of Assam and Bihar. The scheme of extension upto Talbandh was under consideration of the Government for quite some time. The distance was 75 kilometers and expenditure for the whole project was estimated to be Rupees eleven lakhs. As per the terms and condition the state was given a membership in the Board of Directors of Barooah Company[49].

Medical Facilities

Sreeram Chandra was very much concerned about the welfare of his people. During the Court of Wards Mr. Wylly the Manager had engaged the service of Dr. Purnachandra Gupta by appointing him as the Head of the

Medical Department. He continued to serve the state till 1903. The Maharaja increased the number of Charitable Dispensaries from one to three. On 14 May 1906 a separate outdoor facility was created at the Baripada hospital. Other necessary changes were also introduced at the Baripada dispensary. An extension of the hospital building was completed in due time. The state took measure against the spread of epidemics like Cholera and Small Pox. The benefit of Western Medicine was thrown open to the people by appointing good Doctors[50]. The Chief also helped the Government in setting up a medical college at Cuttack which today bears his name[51].

Other Benevolent Measures

By increasing the revenue of the state in a most unprecedented manner through sale of minerals and forest wealth the Maharaja explored various ways of development. In this context he mooted the brilliant idea of harnessing the waterfall of Bareipani in Similipal hill for the production of hydroelectricity. Though the project could not be implemented due to his sudden demise in 1912, the vision with which the Maharaja completed the survey and estimate work were commendable[52].

The Maharaja's modern outlook and priority for industries and growth of agriculture were no doubt the results of his world tour of Europe, USA and Japan where he witnessed the remarkable changes through science and technology[53]. While visiting these countries he made it a point to meet cross section of the people and even students to observe the rapid economic changes of the countries and factors responsible for that. The British ambassador from Tokyo writes.

I have been much struck, as have the Japanese, by the intelligence, tact and modest good sense displayed by this young Native Chief (referring to Sreeramchandra). He has a perfect command of the English language and has evidently read and studied much of all the Native Chiefs who have visited Japan during the past ten years, the Maharaja is certainly the one who has done most credit to his English upbringing[54].

Oriya Nationalism and Utkal Union Conference

In 1903 Madhusudan Das organized the inaugural session of the Utkal Union Conference at Cuttack in December with a view to unite the Chiefs and leaders of the Oriya speaking tracts in a common platform to forge them together for administrative amalgamation of the scattered tracts under the province of Bengal. The Organizing Committee invited Sreeram Chandra Bhanj Deo to preside over the inaugural session. It was a well deserving honour to the Maharaja who had a soft corner for Oriya nationalism and interest in the development of Orissa. The Maharaja gave an inspiring speech to the assembled representatives emphasizing upon major issues which concerned the progress and well being of the Oriya speaking people. In his address he touched upon issues like;

(1) rapid development of the industrial potentiality of Orissa,
(2) amalgamation of the scattered Oriya speaking areas;
(3) the spread of general, technical and female education,
(4) social reforms,
(5) development of agriculture on scientific basis,
(6) spread of scientific knowledge for agriculture and animal husbandry, and united effort in all fronts.

The Chairmanship of the Utkal Union Conference was a unique honour to the Maharaja giving recognition to his leadership, stature and nationalist outlook. On his suggestion an affiliated Association was setup to sponsor Oriya students of merit to go abroad for advanced technical education and training[55].

Philanthropic and Cultural Works

Maharaja Sreeram Chandra was a great humanist. Among the important social works, he did mention may be made of a Leper Assylum near Baripada, Charitable Dispensaries, Public Library, Public Park, spacious play ground, a hostel for the high school named after Sir Andrew Fraser[56]. He had given new life to the Chhow dance of Mayurbhanj by availing international recognition.

As a benevolent ruler with progressive outlook and farsighted vision he not only endeared himself to the people but earned deep respect among the higher authorities. He always gave priority to the interests of the people and the state over his own. At an early age he lost his married wife named Lakhsmi Kumari and a daughter who died of small pox. To commemorate the sad and sacred memory of Maharani, the Lakhsmi Kumari Dharmasala was founded at Baripada in 1906. It is a fine and commodious building and affords shelter to all travelers and strangers to Baripada. A beautiful garden was laid out and named Ranibagh in her honour[57]. He did not marry Sucharu Devi, his beloved and the daughter of Keshab Chandra Sen, the Brahmo leader because his people resented it. He maintained a very simple and austere life to avoid burden on the state. For these sterling qualities of head and heart and the enlightened government he set up in Mayurbhanj, the British Government conferred upon him the title of Maharaja and made the title hereditary. He was granted a Khilat in March 1903 on the occasion of the coronation ceremony of Emperor Edward VII and a Sanad was invested upon him by Sir A Bourdillon, the Lieutenant Governor of Bengal. The citation in the Sanad read[58].

"I am glad to know that you worthily play the role of the leading Chief in the Garjat States of Orissa, and not only in public but in private life you set an admirable example which your fellow Chiefs would do well to follow. The Government are proud to have had during your minority so apt and satisfactory a pupil under their charge. Since you have assumed the control of Mayurbhanj State you have ruled it wisely and well, while the liberality, which you have shown beyond the borders, has been generous and enlightened. Your farther was created the Maharaja at the Delhi assemblage in 1873 and it is a sincere gratification to myself and to your many well wishers that the same title was bestowed upon you upon a similar but more splendid occasion. May you live long to enjoy it."

Death

But the Maharaja did not live long enough to enjoy the good wishes. His eventful career was abruptly snapped on 22 February 1912 due to a shooting accident caused during a hunting expedition with some of his guest and relatives. On 31 January he sustained injury from the splinters of a bullet to which he subsequently succumbed[59]. The sudden death of the Maharaja besides cutting a brilliant career suddenly plunged the state to deep mourning. The loss was irreparable which gave a serious jolt to the developing state. Though he was survived by two sons, both were minor and the state had to be placed under the Court of Wards till 13 November 1920 when Purnachandra Bhanj, the Heir Apparent attained majority and assumed full powers as the Chief of Mayurbhanj State[60].

3. Maharaja Purnachandra Bhanj Deo (1920-28)

The two sons of Sreeram Chandra were Purnachandra and Pratapachandra, both students of the Prince Mayo College at Ajmer when the tragic accident occurred. As Purnachandra was only 13 years of age, the Government took over the state administration placing it under the Court of Wards. It was managed by three ICS officers, viz. Mr. CL Philips, Mr. Scot and Mr. Peak as the Superintendents of the state. They were

Maharaja Puranchandra Bhanj Deo

competent and fair minded officers who took good care of the state. Purnachandra completed his graduation in 1917 and was married to the Princes of Wankaner in Kathiawad[61].

Santal Melee

In May 1917 Mayurbhanj witnessed a Santal rebellion the immediate cause being the British Governments attempt to recruit the sturdy tribals for the Labour Corps to work in France where the World War was going on. Purnachandra had whole heartedly supported the Government Policy persuading the tribals to join the Labour Forces. Two Sardars–Gopabandhu Pattnaik of Muruda and Madanmohan Mohanty of Majhalbhag were compaining for the recruitment drive. They explained to the tribals the advantages of joining the Labour Corps in support of the Government. But the unfavourable climatic condition of Europe prompted the tribals to resist. They also had strong traditional superstition against crossing the sea. Hence, the compulsion with which the Government imposed the recruitment was opposed by them. There were instances of oppression resorted to by the Recruiting Agents whose natural consequence was resistance[62].

The first phase of the tribal rebellion was witnessed in May 1917 confined to the Sadar Subdivision. In the second phase, the rebellion spread to Bamanghaty and Panchpir Sub-divisions. The santal rebellion resulted in assault against officers of the state engaged in recruitment works, looting the Bazaar, and damage to the Railway lines. But the Government quickly restored order by swift armed action and limited number of Infantry soldiers who rushed in from Calcutta. Mr. CL Philip, the Commissioner and political Agent visited the state during disturbance supervising the Police action. It did not take much time for the Government to quell the rebellion[63].

But it was a temporary agreement with certain assurance given by the Government to the Santals regarding their deployment. Since the Santals were not convinced fully with the assurance, they again organized themselves for rebellion. Since rebellion or melee against the state was punishable under the Regulation VII of 1892 the tribals reacted violently in June 1917. This time the area of disturbance was Bamanghaty Sub-division. The rebels looted the shops of Rairangpur and resorted to arson. One State Police constable was killed by them leaving the Government with no alternative but to resort to military action. In this connection the Commissioner and the Political Agent, the Superintendent of the State (Mr. Peak) undertook strenuous journey though the deep forests dissuading the tribals to take up arms and disturb peace. Their efforts ended with success and the rebellion was quelled before rainy season began. In this operation the Government had to incur heavy expenditure of Rupees 84,002.[64]

Though the rebellion of 1917 was short lived, it was a very trying moment for the state administration. As may as 1118 person were put under trial, of whom 141 got acquitted, 977 got convicted and punished. From among the arrested persons 712 were charged with major offences and 406 for minor offences. While some Police officers like Janaki Ballav Das, SP Mayurbhanj, Srikarishna Mahapatra, SP Balasore, Anukul Chandra Roy, SDO Sadar, Akshay Kumar Chatterjee SDO Kaptipada and Satakadi Chatterjee, SDO Panchpir exhibited exemplary courage, maturity and tactfulness. They were commended upon by the Government for their deligence and careful handling of sensitive situation. Among the Judges who conducted trial mention may be made of LTR Lucas, Special Judge and Haridas Bose, the State Judge. Death sentences were pronounced upon four accused, 33 were sentenced to transportation for life, one was sentenced to RI for life and 13 was sentenced to 14 years transportation. After the rebellion the Government gave cash compensation and bonus to some families for their maintenance[65].

The Heir Apparent – Purnachandra took great interest in soothing the temper of the tribals. He supported the War Policy of the Government by rendering active service in Europe in the rank of a lieutenant in the Royal Air Force and when peace was restored was entitled to nine gun salute[66].

The Lieutenant Governor of Bengal and Orissa announced the formal accession of Purnachandra to the Gadi at Cuttack on 20 November 1920. During the short rule of eight years the young Maharaja bestowed upon the State of

Mayurbhanj a progressive and benevolent administration keeping in line with the high ideals of his illustrious father Maharaja Sreeram Chandra[67].

Before his formal coronation Maharaja Purnachandra as a loyal Feudatory Chief had contributed Rupees 27,000 for the purchase of an aeroplane, for War service and Rupees 12,000 for a motor Ambulance[68]. The state contributed Rupees 21,50,378 to the War loan and Rupees 16,845 as donation for the war[69]. He played a very active role in pacifying the agitated tribal communities[70].

Coronation

On 13 November 1920 Maharaja Purnachandra Bhanj Deo was installed on the throne. Two years later he was made an Honorary Lieutenant for the personal War service he had rendered. He was made ADC to the Prince of Wales (Later Emperor Edward VIII) during the latter's visit to Patna in 1921.

Administration

Maharaja Purnachandra Bhanj Deo was a benevolent and enlightented ruler. This becomes evident from his achievements. He had inherited a state whose annual in come was rupees 28, 53,090. He introduced several development and welfare measures. He established the Judicial Committee which was the highest Court of appeal in the State. For the Baripada town he introduced electricity and drinking water facility. He made financial provisions for the improvement of the Secretariat and Court buildings, construction of irrigation projects, and extension of the Mayurbhanj Light Railway from Bangriposi to Talbandh for easy transportation of timber. He contributed personally to create a reserve fund of Rupees Two lakhs, the interest amount of which was utilized for digging tanks, wells and bandhs in the state to promote agriculture[71].

The Maharaja intended to make the peasants community happy and prosperous through effective agrarian reforms. The sale and transfer of land by a tribal to a non-tribal required specific permission of the State Government. Such permission was equally mandatory when a non-resident of Mayurbhanj wanted to purchase land. In case of transfer of fragmented holdings the consent of the state was obligatory. In all cases of Lakhraj tenures the prior permission of the Maharaja was binding. The right over Lakhraj[72] tenures was governed by the Lakhraj control order which specifically laid down that all Lakhraj tenures were deemed to be held subject to the conditions of good behaviour and loyalty of the holders and any serious breach of the conditions would entail the forfeiture of these rights. The state imposed such restrictions to control indiscrete sale or liquidation of Lakhraj holdings[73].

Improvement of Agriculture

Since agriculture was the main prop of state economy the Maharaja did his best to help the farmers. He advanced loans to needy farmers, loans for improving the land, loan for building house, and other essential loans for social obligations. Granaries or Hamars gave loan of paddy for sowing and in times of drought or famine. During the scarcity of 1919 the state advanced paddy loan of 36,254 maunds to effected person[74].

Culture

During the rule of Maharaja Sreeramchndra initial steps had been taken by NN Vasu and Kamakshya Prasad Bose to reveal the archaeological potentiality of Mayurbhanj. The new Department of Archaeology was created for the purpose. In consequence NN Vasu had brought out a pioneering work entitled "Archaeological survey of Mayurbhanj" (Calcutta, 1911) vol.I[75]. The second volume could not see the light of the day due to the sudden demise of the Maharaja in early 1912. But a beginning had been made in the right direction. Vasu had identified Khiching village with the ancient town of Khijjingakotta. A large number of precious antiquities had been collected by Kamakshya Prasad Bose, the Sub-divisional Officer of Panchpir[76].

Maharaja Purnachandra BhanjaDeo visited Khiching in 1920 to pay homage to the tutelary deity of the Bhanja family whose shrine was located there. On his request Rama Prasad Chanda a noted archaeologist from Calcutta came down to Khiching to continue with the unfinished work of NN Vasu. By excavating a few sites be brought to lime light several antiquities of the ancient Bhanja dynasty and suggested that a Museum be located at Khiching to preserve the same. The Department of Archaeology created by Maharaja Sreeram Chandra in 1905 was revived and the foundation of a local Museum was laid by Maharaja Purnachandra. He had appointed Paramananda Acharya as the State Archaeologist and Sailendra Prasad Bose as his Assistant[77]. Acharya was deputed to Calcutta and London to collect archival records of the Bhanja kings. Sailendra Prasad Bose stayed at Khiching to organize the site Museum. He was also entrusted to do the excavation and conservation of Haripurgarh, the second capital of the Bhanja kings who ruled from 1400 AD onwards up to 1803 when they shifted to Baripada[78]. Under the patronage of the Maharaja. Bose successfully completed the conservation work of Haripurgarh. From 1927 he shifted to Khiching to work for exploration and excavation of the area. But the sudden death of the Maharaja in 1928 halted the progress of archaeological department.

Maharaja Purnachandra Bhanj Deo's interest in promoting culture was evident in several steps he took during his rule. The publication of Oriya Encyclopedia was funded by him. Its volume I edited by Gopal Chandra Praharaj could see the light of the day. Other projects and institutions, which received liberal financial support were numerous[79]

General Administration

The Maharaja scrupulously exercised the enormous powers bestowed on him. But instead of arbitrarily taking any decision he delegated most of the executive and judicial powers to the Dewan and the Judicial Committee respectively. He had final say on matter determining principles and policies of administration. The Dewan was assisted by a Secretary to implement executive orders. He also coordinated and controlled the administration of various Departments[80]. He did not hesitate to involve the people in the mechanism of administration. Emulating his illustrious father the Maharaja introduced the system of election in the Baripada Municipality. The strengthening of the Department of Archaeology facilitated the preservation of ancient monuments. Professor RD Banerjee of Banaras Hindu University took up the compilation of the History of Orissa in two volumes giving due weightage to the history of the Bhanjas of Mayurbhanj[81]. The state initiated action to restore the ancient monuments of Khiching[82].

Sir Henry Wheeler the Governor of Bihar and Orissa addressing a Darbar at Baripada said,

"Mayurbhanj takes the lead in area and very easily in population and revenue, and in modern times its progress has been continuous. Its ruling family has the advantage of a long and distinguished historical tradition and modern ideals of administration have been steadily persued with conspicuous success."

Maharaja Purnachandra had gone to Bombay to attend the Buttler Committee's meeting to depose as a member of the Indian Chamber of Princes where he died on 21 April 1928 due to Tetanus Infection. He was only 29 years old and had no issue. Therefore, the government anointed the younger brother Pratap Chandra Bhanjdeo as the new Chief of Mayurbhanj[83].

4. Maharaja Pratap Chandra Bhanjdeo (1928-1947)

The younger brother of Maharaja Purnachandra Bhanjdeo though not expected to ascend the throne of Mayurbhanj, destiny had decided otherwise. After the dead body of Purnachandra reached via Rupsa at Baripada and placed in the balcony of the ground floor of the Place for public Darshan, the custom in the family was to order for its cremation by the new Raja. So Pratap Chandra was made the Raja on 23 April 1928 and performed the funeral rites as was the custom. His reign was quite eventful witnessing the freedom movement leading to India's independence and the Praja Mandal movement leading to the setting up of a popular Government in Mayurbhanj is 1947 on the eve of independence. Finally, there was the merger of Mayurbhanj with Orissa Province on 1 January 1949 bringing an end to the long reign of the Bhanja Kings. Rajtantra or Monarchy was replaced by Loktantra or democracy.

Early Life and Education

Pratap Chandra was educated at Mayo College, Ajmere and did his graduation in Science at Muir College, Allahabad. For a couple of years during the rule of Purnachandra, he was the Chairman of Baripada Municipality[84]. He was married to Premkumari, the daughter of Sardar Singhji of Shahpur State in Rajputana. He had twice visited Europe. The funeral ceremony of the deceased Maharaja was attended by many ruling Chiefs of Orissa Feudatory States, Raja of Bastar and his Rani, Rajas of Wankaner and Shahpura and Mr. JE Scott., the Political Agent and Commissioner of the Orissa States[85]. The Political Agent gave the formal recognition of the Government of India to the new ruler's accession on 16 June 1928[86].

In view of the enlightened administration of Maharaja. Sreeram Chandra and Purnachandra, the Government of

Maharaja Pratap Chandra Bhanjdeo

India did not like to impose any restriction on the new Maharaja. They granted him the right to exercise full powers in internal administration in March 1931. Same year Maharaja Pratap Chandra was nominated as a Member of the Chamber of Princes under Article 2A(ii) of the Constitution of the Chamber of Princes[87]. The Viceroy in his letter dated 9 March 1931 observed,

"It (Mayurbhanj) is by far the largest among the Orissa States which have as yet no permanent member in the

Chamber. With an area over 4000 square miles and revenue of some Rupees Thirty lakhs, it is obviously fit to stand among the larger Indian states; and I have satisfied myself that its administration is efficient, enlightened and progressive. I have, therefore, with the concurrence of the Bihar and Orissa Government, cancelled the specific restrictions in the Mayurbhanj Sanad, which would prevent its being considered a state with full internal jurisdiction and have decided to summon the Maharaja for the forthcoming Chamber session as a full member[88]."

Therefore, with effect from 1 April 1933, Mayurbhanj was placed in direct political relation with the Government of India through the Agent to the Governor General designated 'Agent to the Governor General Eastern States Agency. Later on from 1st December 1936, Mayurbhanj, along with Coochbehar and Tripura formed a separate Agency called as 'Bengal State' with headquarters at Calcutta. The state's annual tribute was fixed at Rupees 1067-11-9 paise and the Maharaja was allowed to enjoy permanent salute of 9 guns[89].

Maharaja Pratap Chandra was a fine sportsman, a connoisseur of fine arts like music, painting and dancing. He was also a skilled pilot. In view of his contributions to the War efforts during the World War II, the King Emperor made him a Honorary Flight Lieutenant in the Royal Air Force on 22 February 1943. Earlier to that he had been bestowed with the title of Knight Commander of the Most Eminent Order of the Indian Empire (KCIE) on 1 January 1935. In 1944 when the new Utkal University was established, he became the Pro-Chancellor[90].

State Administration

Maharaja Pratap Chandra Bhanjdeo followed the footsteps of his predecessors in giving the people of Mayurbhanj a welfare oriented administration endearing himself to the subjects as an ideal ruler. He received accolades from his contemporaries who had first hand knowledge about his sagacity and administrative acumen. He appointed Dr P.K. Sen, Bar-at-law, Khitis Chandra Niyogi and Major Bindheswari Prasad Pande as his Dewan during 1928 to 1947. They helped him to modernize and democratize the administration of the state[91]. Though there were public criticism that deserving Oriyas did not get any appointment in the state, the Maharaja ignoring such allegations appointed highly qualified persons as Dewan, State Judge, Assistant State Judge, Secretary, State Engineer, State Medical Officer etc. in order to have sound advice end experienced administrators with progressive outlook. A Congress leader and nationalist of the stature of H.K. Mahatab had complained the favour being shown to the Bengalis. But such allegations were naive, because capable persons in state service were given good positions after 1947 when the State merged with Orissa. For example, Shyam Chandra Tripathy became the Director of Public Instruction, G.C. Satapathy Additional Director of Public Instruction, Radha Govind Das, the Collector of Cuttack, Ramchandra Das, Inspector General of Police, Orissa, Paramananda Acharya, the Superintendent of State Archaeology etc[92].

His selections were based on merit. For example, After the reversion of E. Mcleod Smith ICS from the post of Dewan (1922-1929) to the Government service as Deputy Commissioner, Angul, the Maharaja held the charge himself till the appointment of a suitable person. The first appointment as his Dewan was Dr. PK Sen MA (cantab) LLD. Bar-at-law who served him for a year or so. He became the State Judge in 1933 and toned up the organization of the High Court. In April 1933 he was deputed to England to depose on behalf of the Indian Chamber of Commerce before the Joint Parliamentary Committee on Indian Constitutional Reforms[93].

After Dr Sen relinquished his office on 17 June 1925 Khitis Chandra Niyogi MA, B.L. Advocate of Calcutta High

Court was appointed as the Dewan. He was a former member of the Indian Legislative Assembly. He remained a good friend of the Maharaja even after 1940 when he left the state[94]. The Maharaja often consulted him on matter of important legislations. It may be mentioned here that Niyogi served the Nehru Cabinet after India's independence in the capacity of Minister, Planning. After him Major B.P. Pande, B.A., LL.B, FRES (London) took over charge of 16 August 1940. He was a leading Advocate of the United Provinces who had attended the 3rd Round Table Conference in 1933 as a representative of the Princely States[95].

The above-mentioned Diwans assisted the Maharaja in improving the state administration. Many new departments were created for Industrial and Economic Survey, Cottage Industries, Agriculture, and Cooperative Societies. The Industrial Institute at Baripada was given a new look to train personnel for the professional jobs[96]. The State Press was modernized and Mayurbhanj State Gazette was published under the care of a Public Relation Officer who highlighted various development programmes and projects of the State Government. The Maharaja organized the State Secretariat, the Praja Sabha and Kendra Parishad with a view to provide efficient administration in which there was increasing participation of the people[97].

How the Maharaja gave Mayurbhanj a benevolent Government will be clear from the following facts. Though the bureaucracy was kept under the watchful eye of the Maharaja who treated corruption as a crime and adopted drastic measures of punishment, he allowed the state employees to enjoy the benefits of provident fund. They were governed by a Service Code. The establishment of Mayurbhanj Kendra Parishad was a land mark in the history of the state which involved the people in the administration[98].

The Maharaja provided the facilities of electricity and telephone to the general public. From March 1929 the area covered by Baripada Municipality enjoyed the advantage of electricity. Power was supplied to 73 State Offices and 50 private buildings. From June 1929 telephone facilities were provided at Baripada. The administration was made transparent as all its policies and activities were published in the State Gazette and Annual Reports on Administration for public information. The Mayurbhanj State Gazette was a bilingual and fortnightly publication. It started its appearance from 1936. The Oriya edition of the Gazette was entitled as 'Bhanja Pradeepa)[99]. By this publication the Maharaja met the need of people's right to information, which is valued today as a very important right of the people. All laws, regulations, orders, notifications on leave, appointment, promotion, transfer, changes etc, relevant information on weather, crop conditions, epidemics, tour of the Maharaja and Dewan etc were published in the State Gazette giving a complete picture of the administration[100].

Organization of the Secretariat

It was KC Niyogi, the Dewan who initiated steps to organize the Secretariat. The Departments of Government were divided between the Maharaja and the Dewan. Necessary Gazette notification was issued on 1 April 1936 giving hints about the shape of things to come. All Departments were amalgamated together under the nomenclature of Secretariat thereby the State administration was Unified under the supervision of the Dewan. The post of Chief Revenue officer was created with effect from 1 April 1936 to look after the revenue matters, Settlement, Excise, Income Tax and Zamindaris[101].

Special care was taken to streamline the State Budget as per the procedure followed in British India. PN Mukherjee, a retired Audit and Accounts officer was appointed to overhaul the financial rules and procedure. He framed the Manual of Budget procedure and made it effective from 1 December 1936. Hereafter the Finance Department of the Secretariat prepared the annual statement of estimate and expenditure. The preparation of the Budget Manual and adoption of the Budget procedure was a milestone in Mayurbhanj State administration[102].

Census operation was an essential feature of modern administration. Mayurbhanj State first undertook the measure in 1931 by appointing Mohammed Laeequddin as census officer. He worked for five years to give shape to the matter and the first Census Report was published in 1935 in two volumes. The report contained data on population, history, physical features of the State, mountains and rivers, climate, flora and fauna, mineral resources, forest wealth, tribal population, their life, emigration and immigration, manners and customs and cultural life etc. The job was done with great care and labour[103].

The Maharaja had a firm grip over administration as he always insisted upon timely feedback. Through open public meetings held at the Darbar hall of the Palace he used to gather information relevant to all matters. When any officer was on leave the charge of the department was assumed by the Maharaja himself. His frequent visit to rural areas was an effective method to keep contact with the common men[104]. The villagers were persuaded to present their grievances freely without any fear. To eradicate corruption from the bureaucracy the Royal order dated 15 November 1938 had been promulgated prohibiting acceptance of bribes or gifts by the State Employees[105]. The order specifically mentioned summary dismissal of corrupt employee, if detected. Any body was free to report either to an officer or to the Dewan either verbally or in writing if there was any case of complains against corruption[106]. As a keen sportsman himself, he wanted the sports activities in the state to develop. To promote sports he selected Brajasundar Dash, a noted football player as Games Teacher in the School. Under his care many good sportsmen were trained to play outside the state. The

Mayurbhanj Athletic Association was set up to organize annual soccer Tournaments in which Mahanbagan, East Bengal and many reputed teams participated. This Association conducted competition for two tournaments. Sreeram Chandra Meemorial and Sree Purna Chandra Memorial for senior and Junior players respectively. The Baripada club was established in 1932 for the relaxation of elites and officials of the town[107].

Personal Involvement

Maharaja Pratap Chandra was a thorough bread administrator who spared no pains on getting himself involved whole heartedly in administration and all sundry activities of the state. He would work regularly in the office from 10 Am when an officer was on leave or on tour outside the state. He would visit construction sites as and when a project work was in progress or a road being repaired. During the War time there was short supply of many essential commodities like sugar, cloth and kerosene oil. The Maharaja himself worked in the capacity of Civil Supply Officer issuing Ration Cards to genuine citizens assessing their needs. The presence of the Maharaja was a morale boosting factor to administration and gave great contentment to the people[108].

Democratization of the Government

Maharaja Pratap Chandra's greatest contribution to Mayurbhanj was the introduction of some democratic principle in the process of Government. He created the institution called 'Praja Sabha' or Community of the subjects whom he gave a share in the day-to-day administration. An order called the Praja Sabha Order was passed on 23 November 1938 by which five Praja Sabhas or Committees of people was established, one each in the subdivisions and the fifth one at Baripada[109]. In these Sabhas complete freedom was given to the people to discuss their problems and the Policies of the State. Whatever was the consensus, the

Maharaja did not hesitate to implement to respect the popular view points. On 14 March 1945 he established the Kendra Parishad (Central Legislature)[110] with right to make laws for all people, all places and all Courts within Mayurbhanj. The matters relating to the members of the Royal Family were beyond the jurisdiction of the Parishad. Similarly, matter relating to the position of the state vis-a-vis the Paramount Power was also excluded from the jurisdiction. However, the Kendra Parishad order came in to force on 9 December 1945 and it was a milestone in the history of Mayurbhanj.

State Bank of Mayurbhanj[111]

The objective of industrialization through Small Scale Industries being one of the programmes of the Maharaja, he set up the Mayurbhanj State Bank on 2 May 1938 notifying its rules and Regulations in an Extraordinary issue of the State Gazette dated 1 May 1938. The notification stated the Bank as a part of the Department of the state under the general control of the state authorities. The state clearly made it a point that the State Bank could not go in to liquidation without the approval of the Maharaja. Thereby the State Government stood as the Guarantor for the Bank to assure the persons doing business as creditors and debtors. A branch of the Bank was opened at Rairangpur on the 25 July, 1938 which had great business prospects due to its close proximity to Tatanagar. The State Bank granted loans to potential entrepreneurs in order to promote their economic interest[112]. For all transaction outside the state, the Bank had established agency connection with the Central Bank of India Ltd. And the Imperial Bank of India.

Khiching

The ancient town of Khijingakotta (Modern Khiching) was the center of Bhanja kingdom from the 9th century to the 1361 AD. When they shifted to Haripurgarh. The archaeological findings of the place had to be preserved for the posterity. The

Archaeology Department started by Maharaja Sreeram Chandra in 1905 was in a moribund state after his sudden death in 1912. Whatever steps Maharaja Purnachandra had taken after 1922 by engaging R.P. Chanda and Sailendra Prasad Bose to conduct excavations and conservation of Khiching and Haripurgarh had been stalled by his sudden death in 1928. But he had promised the people to restore the ruined temple of Khijjingeswari at Khiching as she was the Tutelary deity of the Bhanja dynasty. In 1929 the Maharaja ordered for the large scale conservation of Haripurgarh through Paramananda Acharya, the State Archaeologist. The work was completed by Sri S.P Bose who was then shifted to Khiching to excavate the site and conserve the Kutaitundi and Chandrasekhar Temples. He also prepared a plan for the preservation of the Great Temple at Khiching. After rejecting the plan prepared by J. Page of the Archaeological Survey of India, the Maharaja approved a plan and an estimate prepared by S.P. Bose whose idea about the new temple found identical view of the Maharaja. The construction of the new temple was started in 1935 and was completed in 1942 at a cost of Rupees 80,000. The temple now stand there as a replica of Orissan temples and the place is visited by hundreds of pilgrims everyday. The Maharaja also took interest in completing the Museum building which became a store house of antiquities of the ancient period[113].

Education

The Maharaja did not neglect the growth of education in Mayurbhanj. He was aware of the tribals and their lack of interest in English education. In an address at the Baripada High School in 1938 he had said,

"No one would be more pleased then I, if the backward people will come forward in large number to take advantage of educational facility provided by the state[114]."

He provided funds for the construction of a New Hostel to accommodate one hundred borders besides completing a Free Hostel for Baripada High School. The state completed two more Hostels and named then after the two sons of the Maharaja. But the Maharaja showed no interest for college education as there was no scope to employ the highly educated youths. He did not want to produce Babus. This view was reflected in a report of the Dewan which said.

"Higher education, however important it may be else where is not a pressing problem in Mayurbhanj[115]."

Instead, he was of the conviction that

"A well grounded knowledge of the 3 Rs. together with a knowledge of some productive industry, art or occupation such as will make them self-reliant striving units of the society is what your subjects require for their prosperity and happiness[116]."

Probably, the above view of the Dewan was endorsed by the Chief. The Dewan furthers wrote.

"To bring up a class of young men whose intellectual equipment cannot be other than that of matriculates at the highest but who consider it beneath their dignity to make a living of any sort by manual labours, is bound to be disastrous in the long run to them and to the society. To obviate such a catastrophe, the schools have sooner or later to be recast so as to be able to give the younger generation a suitable training ground for intelligent bread earning occupation[117].

The above views reflected a negative attitude of the Government towards higher education. In his address to the Senate of the Utkal University the Maharaja as the pro-chancellor and president had said that –

"Modern Universities have produced great and distinguished men, but on the other hand, it is found that very often people come out of the University as the products come out of the Factory. I do not claim to be an Expert on University education. Therefore, keeping in view the dangers and pitfalls which are inherent in University education, we must make our educational policy more result oriented[118]."

The Maharaja was in favour of an education which would enable the people to earn their bread. So, though he liberally donated for the educational progress of Orissa, he showed aversion to higher education in his own state, as there was no scope of employment. The Public leaders of Mayurbhanj time and again urged upon the Maharaja to start a college, but in vain. He would retort to the entreaties by saying[119].

"Do you want me to produce monkeys by such college". How liberal was his support to higher education outside the state is evident from the fact that, (1) he instituted a Gold medal in Utkal University to be awarded to the Best Graduate; (2) he deputed GC Satapathy to Utkal University for five years to work as the Registrar; (3) He donated Rupees Eight lakhs for the University; (4) An annual endowment of Rupees 18,000 was made to the Benaras Hindu University for the promotion of Sanskrit learning; (5) A professor chair was established there in the name of his father Sreeram Chandra Bhanja Deo; (6) He funded the publication of a series of Sanskrit works to be entitled 'Mayurbhanj Sanskrit Series' (7) the state funded the equipments of the physics Department of the Ravenshaw College, Cuttack and (8) Full financial support was given for the publication of the Oriya Encyclopedia of Gopal Chandra Praharaj of Cuttack[120].

The Maharaja was an advocate of Vocational education and training for which he established the Purna Chandra industrial institute on 16 July 1931. The Dowager Maharani Takat Kumari had also donated money and land to the Institute. The School gave training in weaving, dyeing, calico printing, bleaching textiles, carpentry and making of furniture. The Maharaja's Dhoti was always supplied by this Institute.[121]

Another aspect of deep interest of the Maharaja was to encourage social service, adventure and sports through the Boy Scouts. Whenever there was a natural calamity like flood, famine epidemic Cholera and arson the Volunteers were chosen from the Boy Scouts. By attending the Governor's rally in 1938, the Boy Scouts of Baripada High School received the prestigious Kanika Shield. In 1947 the Boy Scouts attended the World Jamboree in France[122]. Inspired by the contemporary events, the Maharaja encouraged spread literacy campaign through Night Schools opened at various places. The state granted scholarships to meritorious students to go out side Orissa for technical and professional education like Mining, Veterinary Science, and Medicine. He also bore the expenditure of Dr. Krushna Chandra Panigrahi for Post Graduate education in Indian History and culture at Calcutta University, of Paramanand Acharya in Geology in London and of Ramchandra Dash at Scotland Yard, UK in Police training[123].

Judicial Administration

Since the first Dewan Dr. P.K. Sen Bar-at-Law was a legal luminary a bold step was taken in toning up the State Judiciary. The independence of the Judiciary was respected. His faith on the Judges and the full proof Judicial system did not give the Maharaja any scope or opportunity to interfere. The Magistrates and Judges acted without fear. In selecting his judges, the Maharaja was very discrete and upright and he saw no reason in interfering the way they dispensed with justice. The rule of law prevailed and the State Judiciary earned high reputation for its impartiality. The Civil and Criminal Courts followed the Rules and Regulation in their letter and spirit. Any appeal against this decision was heard by the Judicial Committee. The State Judge supervised the activities and judgments of the Lower Courts presided over by the Magistrates, Munsifs, Sub Judges and Sub-divisional officers[124]. The Mayurbhanj state established the High Court on 10 April 1933 with the Dewan as the Chief Judge. Two other Puisne Judges and the State Judge. By establishing a High Court, the Judicial Committee was abolished. The High Court became the Apex Court to hear all appeals and revisional matters. Dr. P.K. Sen was the first Chief Judge of Mayurbhanj High Court the publication of 'Mayurbhanj law Reporter', a quarterly law journal was an important feature of Judicial administration. The Journal helped in knowing about judicial cases of other states which made coordination easier. It was of great help to the State Bank and the State Police Department as guidance. In this connection another significant decision was to build a High Court building which now stands as a monumental heritage. Masons and artisans were brought from Calcutta to build the Indo Saracenic architecture without any folly[125]. Mayurbhanj Judicial administration was admired everywhere as a progressive step among the Feudatory states of Orissa.

Promotion of Agriculture

The economic condition of the people of Mayurbhanj was totally dependent on agriculture with peasants forming the bulk of population. The Department of Agriculture encouraged scientific farming. As a model farm the State had sponsored scientific cultivation at Shamakhunta which received water for irrigation from the Baldiha Irrigation Project. Not only different varieties of paddy were cultivated there, but through annual exhibition the Government wanted to showcase increased production through better farming. The annual exhibitions coincided with the Birthday celebration of the Maharajas who rewarded the best Cultivator and the best Horticulturist. Even fruits and vegetables of better quality and size were exhibited for others to emulate[126].

The peasants were assured of their rights over their agricultural holdings. Land revenue collection was fair and equitable. There was a standard approved rate on the basis of quality of land. There was a Settlement Department to measure and classify land and to fix revenue. Those who enjoyed the facilities of irrigation were to pay higher rate of revenue. Whenever there was resettlement of the land the rate of revenue enhancement was made in a moderate scale. Whenever there was any natural calamity, the state had the provision to grant relief. To overcome crisis of scarcity the state had opened Hamaras or Grain Golas to give paddy on loan to needy farmers. The rate of interest was low. Even for improvement of agricultural land loans were provided. There were Cooperative Credit Societies as well to help the needy farmers[127]. Two marketing offices had been appointed to conduct market survey of the agricultural products. It was a touring job collecting price data from all the subdivisions for preparing the report.

The exploitation of farmers by unscrupulous moneylenders was a long experienced factor in economic life. In 1938 the state passed the Agricultural Debt Relief order on 19 September to protect the agriculturists from the Moneylenders who often gave loans keeping land as mortgage. In case of default the farmer had the opportunity to sell his land to the state to repay loan and then take the land back from the State as a Share Cropper. Though there was difference in the status of ownership of land of the farmers, he was not running the risk of loosing it to the Moneylender. As a share cropper he could cultivate his land as before. This was good for the farmer[128].

During the Second World War there was scarcity of food grains in the market. The scarcity intensified due to the Bengal Famine of 1942. In this context the state launched the Grow More Food campaign in which the Revenue Officers were engaged in educating the people about the campaign. The Revenue Department sanctioned Taccavi loans in cash and paddy to assist the agriculturist. All available state lands were brought under cultivation so that production would increase. Since water supply was essential in cultivation, all possible water sources were exploited. The success of the Grow More Food campaign was dependent upon adequate water supply. Therefore, a Chief Engineer was appointed to control and supervise Irrigation schemes and an Irrigation Committee was setup to help him. The result was expansion of the Haldia bundh and extension of canal net works[129].

Revenue

There were several officers to take care of revenue matters. They were headed by the Chief Revenue officer. The Sub-divisions have their own Sub-divisional Officers for day to day functioning. An officer was especially designated to take care of settlements. The Income Tax Officer and the Excise Deputy Collector were also under the control of the Chief. Revenue Officer. For collection of land revenue there were Sardars in each Pargana. Two other Revenue Officers were the Tahsildar and the Naib Tahsildar. The number of Sardars in 1941-42 was 17 and that of Tahsildar was II[130].

Mining and Geology

Mayurbhanj was rich in mineral resources. This awareness had facilitated the work of Geological Survey in 1903 which indicated rich deposit of iron ore. It was in the time of Maharaja Sreeram Chandra Bhanj Deo that mining lease of Iron ores was granted to Tata Iron and Steel Company. After thirty years the lease was renewed by Maharaja Pratap Chandra and a regular Department of Mining and Geology was started in December 1936 to ensure further survey and regular inspection of the mines. The survey conducted in his time revealed heavy deposits of vanadium in the Bamanghaty Sub-division[131]. To regulate and control the procedure of mining the Maharaja issued the Mayurbhanj State Mining Order on 14 November 1936 which provided for inspection of mines, control of mining operation, fixing of minimum hour of work, safeguard against accident and to ensure medical help in case of accidents[132].

Welfare Measures

The Maharaja was aware of the new developments and changes in Western Medical Science. As a benevolent ruler he gave priority to the health and welfare of female patients by establishing a Ladies Hospital close to the Charitable Hospital at Baripada. The Maharani inaugurated the Zanana Hospital on 6 September 1938[133] in the presence of nearly 2000 ladies of the town. The building had cost Rupees seventy thousand with proper facilities of electricity, water supply and sanitation. The Ayurvedic Dispensary was shifted to its new building in the Sanskrit Tol campus and Kaviraj was appointed[134]. The main Hospital was provided with a Tuberculosis Ward and an X-ray machine was installed in the main hospital[135].

Sports, Aviation and other Activities

Maharaja Pratap Chandra Bhanjdeo being a great lover of sports and a sportsman himself played volley, tennis, billiad in the Palace courtyard and the club at Baripada. As a lover of football he used to attend the final competition of Sreeram Chandra Bhanj memorial tournament. He played host to the two teams who contested on the final. His patronage and personal interest induced many leading teams of Bengal and Bihar to participate in the tournament[136].

As a lover of music, the Maharaja learnt flute from Kalicharan Patnaik, a noted Odisi dancer and sitar from Ustad Jadu Rao who was a veteran musician. The revival of Chhau Dance was an outstanding contribution of the Maharaja. Mayurbhanj Chhau was famous since the time of Maharaja Sreeram Chandra in the early 20th century. But on account of his sudden death and the long duration of Court of Wards the dancers had been disorganized. During the brief rule of Maharaja Purna Chandra Chhau Dance could not be long sustained. But Maharaja Pratap Chandra took it to its climax of glory by organizing the dancers as two teams Uttara Sahi and Dakshina Sahi and by organizing annual competitions regularly in the Palace. The teams gave demonstrations in Calcutta and Delhi to earn praises. The Maharaja infused new ideas and items in Chhau to make it more fascinating and popular. He allowed the introduction of Hindustani music to make Chhau more universal[137]. He was responsible for the induction of foreign musical instruments too. The state gave special grants to the Parties for their dress, rehearsals and training under renowned ustads[138].

For the entertainment of the people, the Maharaja organized a forty member Brass Band Party with a Russian Band master who played Indian and western music regularly once a week at the Children's park. On ceremonial occasions the Band party played at the Police ground in ceremonial dresses[139].

The Maharaja was an ace pilot. There were special Planes of the state for his use. Two aircrafts were purchased, named "Vega Gull" and the "Leopard Moth". An aerodrome had been built at Rajabasa, few kilometers away from Baripada. R.P. Dangalkar and KM Mukherjee were appointed as State Pilot and Ground Engineer respectively. During the War period the Planes were placed for use of the Viceroy[140].

The Second World War was an unprecedented event in the history of the world when the Imperial Government sought help from the native Chiefs. In response to the request, the Maharaja setup a War Effort Committee with 41 members drawn from all sections of people with a small Executive with the Dewan as the President. There were Sub-Committees in the Sub-divisions gathering information on the food front and security matters. In 1943-44 the state contributed a sum of Rupees thirteen lakhs to the War Fund. In 1943-44 again an additional sum of Rupees three lakhs and seventy thousand was contributed. The state placed three planes costing about three lakhs at the disposal of the Viceroy. In addition the state supplied free timber as and when required by the army. Those who served the Defence Forces were given free education for their children. Their families were taken care of. The Chhau team was entrusted to entertain the Air Force personnel apart from football and cricket matches. The officers from New Zealand, Canada and Allied Countries were hosted lunch and dinner at the State Guest House while on their way to the Burma Front[141].

The Maharaja allowed his houses at Calcutta, Chandipur, Cuttack and Puri for use by the army. Inside the State all Inspection Bunglows and Guest Houses were placed for the convenience of the Army officers. When Italy surrendered before the Allies on 10 September 1943 the State declared a holiday to celebrate the victory. These efforts endeared the Maharaja to the Viceroy who invited him to the National Defence Council as a representative of the Indian States and the Honourary title of Flight Lieutenant in the Royal Air Force was conferred on him[142]. The total contribution of Mayurbhanj to the War fund was Rupees Twenty four lakhs twenty thousands[143]. All these resulted in Lord Wavell, the Viceroy, writing to the Maharaja a letter dated 12 April 1944 expressing his Governments' gratitude.[144]

The Changing Time

The World War and the post world war period was a crucial time in the history of the native states. While the struggle for freedom under Mahatma Gandhi was moving ahead for a logical conclusion of ending the British Empire, the Prajamandal movement in the Princely States was also rising in Intensity and forcefulness demanding an end of the feudal social order of the Feudatory Chiefs. There were as many as six hundred Princely States and Orissa had twenty-six. A new India was to emerge after independence with an uncertain future for the Feudatory Chiefs. Giving expression to his apprehension on the issue, the Maharaja wrote to the Raja of Dungarpur stating[145],

"The cause of monarchy is at discount all over the globe. We are told that the Institution of Kingship has out lived its utility and it is an anachronism and a feudalistic relic.He further wrote,[146]

"Let us consider our present position. It is not enviable." He was unhappy over the increasing interference in day to day administration as well as personal affairs which did not escape the scrutiny of the Resident.

"We are puppets and tools in their hands. Our protest and representation against their interference are ignored. We are powerless to resist because we lost all powers to resist long ago. The yellow patches (Princely States) on the map of India are a mockery[147]."

The Maharaja being a practical man had made a very rational analysis of the political situation of the time. In the context of the Prajamandal movement of the peasants he had observed correctly to say,

"We are nothing but anachronism and feudalistic relics to the vast majority of our political minded countrymen. They have no sympathy for us. They feel that we are the worst type of reactionaries, and had it not been for us, the British rule would have long ago crumbled in India. There is no denying this; we have always taken a doubtful pride in having come to the rescue of the Paramount Power when ever it was in danger[148]." Prophesying the future he correctly predicted,

"I realize that we are at cross roads. If we try to resist the historical forces, we are doomed. The wave of democracy is rolling down on us. Either we step aside and left it roll on, or we stand in its way and get floundered. We cannot trick history and seek compromises and adjustments with the will of the people[149].

He had rightly visualized that the rising tide of democracy would sweep away the Princely order. The dilemma was whether to flight against the people for survival and shed blood or to give up the throne honourably. He was a statesman with great political foresight. He realized the voluntary termination of the Princely rule and was prepared to set an example before others. To many of his friends he had said before that he was not born to succeed to the throne; he got the throne under fortuitous circumstances whose course was set by destiny. Therefore, he took a stoical view of things and decided to quit before it was too late. He wrote to the Nawab of Bhopal, the President of the Chamber of Princes,

"The Rulers may be acclaimed as Heroes, who, by an unprecedented act of self-sacrifice, have made a valuable contribution to a permanent solution of a complicated political order. If on the other hand we cling to our so-called sovereign rights and continue in a career constantly bickering with our people and British India, a renunciation of this character may be forced upon us in far less pleasant circumstances. By postponing the evil day, we may merely be denying ourselves the chances of an honourable exit from the stage, because when it comes about a later date our exit may well have the appearance of an ignominious dismissal[150]."

The noble character of the Maharaja was revealed when he informed the Nawab.

"We may eventually be confronted with an impasse which will compel us to take up arms against our own people. And speaking for myself, it would cause deep anguish to be driven in any circumstances to fight my own people to whose welfare I have devoted most of my life and energy[151].

In the same vein he wrote to the Raja of Dungarpur that;

"I shrink from the contemplation of such a possibility. I would not like to wait till I am actually told to go by my people. It would be a graceless exit and quite out of tune with our tradition of honour and self-respect[152]."

The fait accompli arrived on 15th August 1947 when the British Government transferred powers to Indian leaders making India free. The British Paramountcy which had kept six hundred Princely States bound to them lapsed and the Native Princes were without a Protector. The Empire was a matter of history.

Maharaja Pratap Chandra Bhanjdeo was well prepared for the eventuality. He had a clear vision of the future shape of things to come. So he engaged Radhagovind Das, the Chief Revenue Officer to negotiate with the leaders of Mayurbhanj Prajamandal. Neither he wanted to antagonize his people nor adopt coercive measures like the Rajas of Talcher and Dhenkanal. The Prajamandal agreed to give a list of members from the erstwhile Prajasabha and Kendra Parishad who would take over power from the Maharaja to establish a popular responsible Government as an independent unit of Indian Union. On 9 December 1947 the Maharaja nominated Sarat Chandra Das, Bidyadhar Mohapatra and Maheswar Naik to constitute a three member Cabinet who took over the power of administration over Mayurbhanj. The transfer of power took place on 10 December 1947 and simultaneously a Constituent Assembly was setup to frame a Constitution within the ambit of which the state was to exist as a separate and new unit of the Indian Union[153].

Shortly, thereafter, the Maharaja left for Calcutta where he lived when the Prajamandal Government functioned as a Popular Government and failed ultimately in keeping Mayurbhanj excluded from the mainstream of Indian politics.

The Bhanja rule of Mayurbhanj ended on 10 December 1947 after almost one thousand years of unbroken history.

References

1 Srinath Bhanj was weak, pleasure loving and was misled by the court sychophants. He was issueless and of intriguing nature. The maladministration in Mayurbhanj was a direct outcome of his in capacity to rule. Sarkar SN. Biography of the Maharaja Sriram Chandra Bhanjdeo, Calcutta, 1918, p.20-21.

2 Stokes Eric, *the British Utilitarians of India* (orient longmans) 1959 see introduction.

3 Senapati and Sahu, *Orissa District Gazetteers, Mayurbhanj* (1967) p.76.

4 Ibid, and sarkar SN. P.26.

5 Senapati and Sahu, p.27

6 Ibid, p.28

7 Ibid. p.30.

8 Chanda, R.P. *Notes on the History of Mayurbhanj* 1930 p.26.

9 Sarkar S.N. op.cit. p.30.

10 Ibid. p.31.

11 Ibid pp.31-34.

12 Proceedings A political–1, May 1883, k–w, nos. 6-8, p.1

13 Maharaja Krushna Chandra had two younger brothers–Brundaban Chandra Bhanj and Gokul Chandra Bhanj.

14 Proceedings A political– I, May 1883 K– W nos 6-8, pp.1-3, Also see PB peacock Secretary to Government of Bengal to Secretary to Government of India, Foreign Department No.110, p. dated 12 January 1883.

15 Ibid.

16 S.N.Sarkar, *Biography of the Maharaja Sriram Chandra Bhanjdeo* op.cit. p(1918) pp.18 – 40.

17 Ibid.

18 Ibid p. 48.

19 Ibid p. 49.

20 The regulation of Mayurbhanj State Council Baripada, 1905, p.1 and Interview Harekrushna Dash, leading Advocate and State Pleader.

21 Regulation, op.cit, 1905. pp.3-4. Senapati & Sahu, op.cit. p.78.

22 S.N.Sarkar, Op.cit p.101-104 At first there were three subdivisions. Kaptipada subdivision was created in 1896.

23 Senapati and Sahu, op.cit. p.78 and Sarkar SN. Op.cit. pp.101-04

24 S.N.Sarkar, P.103.

25 The license was first granted to M/S Tata and Sons who in 1907 transferred the lease in favour of Tata Iron and Steel Company Ltd. It was approved by the Maharaja under clause 7 No.1867 P.D., political Branch. EV Levinge ICS officiating Chief Secretary to the Government of Bengal To Hon'ble SH Butler CIE, Secretary to the Government of India Foreign Department, dated 2 July 1910.

26 It is not known whether the law was applied to any body in the time of the Maharaja. But his son Maharaja Purnachandra had

applied it to expel the contractor named Walji who had twisted the moustache in the Court, an offensive act to the Chief. Interview Brajasundar Rath, a leading social worker of Baripada.

27 Interviewed Harekrushna Dash, Also see the State order 5 March 1947 in RAM - 1946-47.

28 Interview Prasanna Kumar Dash, Prajamanda Leader and Minister as well as speaker of the Assembly also see his Autobiography '*Karmir Sadhana*, 1996, pp.8-9. Also Mishra, P.K. *Changing Pattern of political culture*, 2000, p.18.

29 R.C.Mazumdar, *Struggle for freedom vol.XI*, 1978, pp.117-118.

30 Ibid.

31 The regulation of the Mayurbhanj State Council, Calcutta, 1896, pp.3-4 S.N.Sarkar, op.cit. p.100.

32 No 379 P.-D, from CW Bolton, Officiating Chief Secretary of the Government of Bengal to the secretary of the Government of India Foreign Department dated Dargeling, 13 October 1896.

33 Ibid, para - 3 "The letter observes, The Raja of Mayurbhanj now virtually claims entire independence in the administration of the State and if his claim were admitted, the other Garjat Chiefs would be entitled to follow his lead".

34 S.N.Sarkar, op.cit. p.108 and the Mutation Regulation of Mayurbhanj 1910.

35 Ibid, p.109.

36 Ibid. p.109.

37 Report on the *Administration of Mayurbhanj*, 1908-09, p.59.

38 S.N.Sarkar. Op.cit. p.112. Also see Report on the Administration of Mayurbhanj, 1909-10,p.70

39 The Star of Utkal vol.II, Cottack, 26 May 1906.

40 Ibid. 1908-09, p.73.

41 Ibid. p.70

42 Ibid. p.99.

43 Report on the *Administration of Mayurbhanj*, 1905-06, p.65.

44 Das, Suryanarayan, *Utkalmani Gopabandhu* (Oriya), Cuttack, 1975, p.103.

45 Ibid. p.104.

46 From Chief Secretary to the Government of Bengal no.3370, p. dated 29 December 1896. Proceedings no.277-278. Also see no.1223 p. Political Department (Political Branch) Officiating Chief Secretary to the Government of Bengal to the Secretary to the Government of India. Foreign Department dated 23 April 1898.

47 Chief Secretary to the Government of Bengal to the Secretary to the Government of India dated 13 May 1898 (Foreign Department) Also see proceedings of the Foreign. Department, February 1904, Maharaja's letter to the Superintendent, Tributary Mahals, Orissa dated 24 December 1903.

48 S.N.Sarkar, op.cit. p.117 and 119.

49 No. 3171 P from EV Levinge, Chief Secretary, Government of Bengal to Secretary to the Government of India, Foreign Department dated 13 August 1910. Also see scheduled A to no. 2594 P dated Cuttack 14 November 1902 from KG Gupta Superintendent Tributary Mahals to the Maharaja of Mayurbhanj.

50 Senapati and Sahu, op.cit. p.432.

51 It is named as Sriram Chandra Bhanj Medical College.

52 Senapati and Sahu, op.cit. p. 80 See Proceedings of the Foreign Department, September 1908 for Agreement between the Maharaja and the British Westinghouse Company Limited for the Formation of a Joint Stock Company for the purpose of generating and supplying electrical energy from the Borabalang river in the Mayurbhanj state. No. 1989 p. dated Calcutta, the 16th May 1908. It contains the Draft Agreement.

53 Letter from British Embassy in Tokyo dated 1st July 1910.

54 Ibid. Last para written by Clouds M. Mac Donald, the ambassador.

55 Mishra, PK, *Political History of Orissa* 1900-1936,New Delhi, 1979, pp.85-86. Orissa History Congress Souvenir Special Issue (1982) p. 9. The Association was called Association for the advancement of scientific and Industrial Education with its headquarters at Calcutta.

Also see Mahapatra, BP. *Madhusudan Das and His Times* (2004) p. 78

56 Senapati and Sahu, op.cit, p.79.

57 Ibid.

58 Sarkar SN, op.cit. pp.55.56.

59 The Bengals (Daily from Calcutta) 23 February 1912 The Utkal Dipika (Daily from Cuttack) 24 February 1912 Also see Sarkar SN. Op.cit. pp.90-93. On the Shikar expedition the Maharaja was present along with his brother-in-law SC Sen, Mr Godfney and Mr. Miller of the BN Railway. The accident took place at Krushna Chandra Pur near Baripada.

60 Proceedings, A political I, May 1883 KW Nos. 6-8, p.3 and *notes on the History of Mayurbhanj* (1930). P.26.

61 Laeequddin Mohammad, *Census of Mayurbhanj*, 1931, vol.I, Report Calcutta, 1937, p.25.

62 Report on the *Administration of Mayurbhanj* 1916-17, p.78.

63 Senapati and Sahu, op.cit. p.82. Also see Report on the *Administration of Mayurbhanj* 1917-18, p.83

65 Report on *the Administration of Mayurbhanj*, 1917-18, p.61-64

66 Notes on the History of Mayurbhanj, p.26.

67 Playnee Somerset, *Indian States*, 1921-22, p.703. Also Senapati and Sahu, op.cit, p.82.

68 Notes on the *History of Mayurbhanj* (1930) p.26

69 Ibid p.27.

70 *Reports on the Administration of Mayurbhanj* 1917-18.

71 Reports on the Administration fo Mayurbhanj, 1945-46, see the introduction.

72 Lakhraj lands were tax free grants to the Brahmins.

73 Reports on the Administration of Mayurbhanj, 1942, 1942-43, pp.40-41.

74 Ibid, 1937-38, p.19.

75 Mishra, PK. *Archaeology of Mayurbhanj*, 1996, p.5.

76 Ibid pp. 4 - 10.

77 Ibid. pp.15 also p. 20 and 21.

78 Ibid. pp.22-30. Bihar and Orissa Research Society, R.10,000 (RP Chanda, *Notes on the History of Mayurbhanj*, 1930, p.28)

80 *Reports on the Administration* of Mayurbhanj 1945-46 see the introduction.

81 Banerjee RD, *History of Orissa* Vol.I 1930, and Vol.II 1931.

82 Mishra, PK, op.cit. p.29.

83 Pratap Chandra was born on 18 February 1901 and was educated at Mayo's College, Ajmere, and Muir Central College, Allahabad. He visited Europe twice with his brother in 1924 and 1926. See Foreign and Political Department, 1930 File no.179.R .30 See Notes dated 9 June 1930.

84 Lauquddin M, op.cit. 1931, Report Vol.I (Calcutta, 1937) p.27.

85 *Report on the Administration of Mayurbhanj*, 1928-29, p.101.

86 *Report on the Administration of Mayurbhanj*, 1928-29, p.102

87 *Report on the Administration of Mayurbhanj*, 1930-31, p.1.

88 Lauquddin M. op.cit. p.27.

89 Report on the *Administration of Mayurbhanj*, 1941-42, p.27.

90 Ibid, 1945-46 p.10.

91 Senapati and Sahu, op.cit. p. 91.

92 Interview with Brajasundar Rath and Durga Charan Mohanty (Former and social worker and latter a retired Judge)

93 *Report on the Administration* of Mayurbhanj, 1934-35, p.4. see the report.

94 Mahatab, H.K., *Autobiography* (Oriya) 1971, p.349.

95 Mayurbhanj State Gazette, Krodapatra (Oriya, Part-V) 22 August 1940.

96 Senapati and Sahu, op.cit. p.91.

97 Ibid p.83.

98 *Report on the administration of Mayurbhanj,* 1945-46, p.11.

99 Ibid, 1934-35, p.85 and Ibid 1935-36, p.4.

100 Ibid 1935-36, p.4.

101 Ibid, pp.4-5.

102 Ibid. 1936-37, p.4.

103 Ibid., p.i.

104 Interview with Durga Prasad Mohanty, Retired Judge

105 *Report on the Administration of Mayurbhanj* 1938-39, pp.15-16.

106 Interview with Bibhas Chandra Bhanjdeo, Member, Royal Family.

107 Interview Arvind Dash, Secretary Mayurbhanj Athletic Association; Kaminikanta Patnaik, a noted Advocate and former Secretary, Mayurbhanj Athletic Association and A.P.Mohapatra, Vice-President, Baripada Club.

108 Interview with Purna Chandra Bindhani, an octogenarian photographer who often attended the Maharaja on call.

109 Report on the administration of Mayurbhanj, 1937-38, p.6.

110 Ibid 1944-45 p.10 and Extraordinary Mayurbhanj State Gazette 23 April, 1945 the Kendra Parisad Order 1945.

111 Ibid.

112 Report on the Administration of Mayurbhanj, 1938-39, pp.3-5.

113 Mishra, P K, *Archaeology of Mayurbhanj* (New Delhi, 1997) chapter-III, pp35-81

114 Mayurbhanj information Bulletin, 7 May, 1947.

115 *Report on the administration of Mayurbhanj,* 1934-35, p.VI. Annual report of the Dewan to the Maharaja.

116 Ibid.

117 Ibid.

118 Silver Jublee Souvenir of MPC College, 1948-73, p.1

119 Interview Bimal Mukherjee, leftist advocate of Baripada.

120 Report of the administration of Mayurbhanj, 1941-42, p.29, interview with Durga Charan Mohanty, retired Judge.

121 Ibid.

122 Senapati and Sahu, op.cit p.426.
123 Interview with Durga Chanran Mohanty, Retired judge, Baripada and Dr. Binod Shankar Das, Rotarian, Baripada.
124 Interview Durga Chanran Mohanty and Sri Bharati Das, Rotarian
125 Senapati and Sahu, op.cit p.380, Interview Durgacharan Mohanty, Retired Judge and Purna Chandra Mohanta, Senior Advocate.
126 Mayurbhanj State Gazette Krodapatra (Oriya0 22 February 1941.
127 *Report on the Administration of Mayurbhanj*, 1934-35, p.IV.
128 Ibid. pp.14-15.
129 Mayurbhanj information bulletin 7 December 1944.
130 *Report on the Administration of Mayurbhanj*, 1941-42, pp.10-11.
131 *Report of Administration of Mayurbhanj*, 1941-42, p.22
132 Ibid. 1936-37, p.ii
133 Ibid 1938-39, pp.5 and ii
134 Ibid 1944-45, p.ii
135 Ibid.
136 Interview with Kaminikanta Patnaik, former secretary.
137 Mishra, P.K., *Mayurbhanj Itihas Sanskruti* (2000), p.123-ft. Mahapatra, S. *Chhau Dance of Mayurbhanj*, (Oriya)
138 Interview Turi Babu, Research Scholar on Chhau, Baripada.
139 Report on *Administration of Mayurbahnj*, 1943-44, p.15.
140 Mayurbhanj information bulletin 22 December 1944. & Report on *the Administration of Mayurbhanj*, 1938-39, p.16.
141 Report on *the Administration of Mayurbhanj*, 1943-44, p.159.
142 Mayurbhanj Information Bulletin, 7 December, 1944.
143 Report on *the Administration of Mayurbhanj*, 1943-45, p,i.
144 Ibid, p, 196.
145 Mahtab H.K. *Beginning of the End, Cuttack*, 1972, p.,51. letter dated 9 May 1946.
146 Loc. Cit.
147 Loc. Cit.
148 Mahtab H.K., Op.cit. p.52.
149 Ibid. pp.54-55.
150 Ibid p.46 letter dated 19 September 1946 from His Highness the Maharaja to the Nawab of Bhopal.
151 Ibid. p.47.
152 Ibid p. 54.
153 Extraordinary Mayurbhanj State Gazette, 13 December 1947.

3 Prajamandal Movement or the Peasants Movement 1939-48

The British Government had tactfully excluded the Feudatory States of Orissa and several hundred Princely States elsewhere in India on account of their inaccessibility and relative backwardness. Consequently the people living in the States experienced the disadvantages concomitant to feudal order of society and oligarchical Government. Though there were exceptions like Baroda and Mysore outside Orissa and Mayurbhanj in Orissa, the overall atmosphere was one of simmering discontent. The Feudatory States being well protected by the British armour could afford to impose mal-administration on the illiterate and backward people of their states. Therefore, there were possibilities for the bubble of discontent to burst. While the whole country was highly surcharged with the spirit of nationalism and challenged the Colonial Government in a nonviolent confrontation of Non-Cooperation in 1920 and afterwards, forcing many political activitists to take shelter in the Feudatory States to escape the brutalities of police action, the passive people in the states could not remain indifferent to the national struggle for freedom. The miracle of Gandhian leadership had touched the rural folks as never before though in a slow motion. In the states of Baroda, Mysore, Kathiawar and other states having an elite mass, the impact of Gandhian mass movement was not only lightening, but also momentous. The resultant effect was the formation of the Prajamandals demanding two major things – (i) Civil liberties for the people and (ii) the Rule of Law. The formation of the Prajamandals paved the way for convening the All India States Peoples Conference (AISPC) in December 1927 to coordinate the activities of the political units of the States. At first, the Conference acted as a moderate body of the elites limiting its activities to Prayer and Petition like the Indian National Congress during 1885-1915[1].

A change in the political situation in India was ushered in 1935 when the Government of India Act, 1935 was implemented providing the country the scheme of a Federation in which the Princely States were given the opportunity to send nominees to the federal legislature. Since the states had no democratic machinery to elect representatives of the people it was anticipated that as the nominees of the Rajas they would be mere supporters of the colonial government without any desire to serve the well being of the people they represented. They would rather be impediments to political progress as a reactionary group at the back and call of the British Government.

The Government of India Act 1935 was merely an imperial device to keep the Indian people divided in the federal framework of the constitution. A desire, therefore began taking shape in the AISPC (All India States Peoples' Conference) that their representatives should be elected by the people and not nominated by the Rajas. This idea took firm roots after 1935 elections in which the Congress Party was voted to power in many states giving clear indication to things about to happen. The peoples' expectation to share power in the administration to give a popular colour to the Government motivated vigorous political activities. It was difficult to contain the political aspiration of the States' people when revolutionary changes in the British administered provinces were in the offing. There was a spontaneous growth of Prajamandals in several Princely states which were watching the changing situation from close proximity as adjacent to the Provinces where the Congress formed the Government[2].

Instinctively the Congress workers in the Provinces and political activities in the Princely States came closer to each other exchanging ideas about their ensuing programme. At first, the Indian National Congress as an All India body was averse to participate in states politics. The Congress leaders in their attitude of aloofness wished the states people to fend for themselves, and not under the banner of the Congress. The resolution adopted at the Haripur Session in 1938 clearly stated that they would give moral support to the States peoples movement[3]. But in 1939 there was a radical and sudden change in the attitude of the Congress when Pandit Nehru was elected President of the Ludhiana Session of the AISPC facilitating the fusion of the Prajamandal agitation in the States with the Congress movement in the British ruled provinces. In 1939 Subhas Chandra Bose at the Tripuri Session of the National Congress admired the unprecedented awakening in the States and urged upon the Congress leaders to adopt a new attitude to their people's agitation. He was of the opinion that the Congress Policy of non-intervention should be abandoned and Congress should come closer to the people of the Princely states. The Tripuri Session established a bridge linking the Congress and the AISPC leading finally to the identification of their goals. In 1942 the Quit India Movement was not a clarion call for the people of the British ruled provinces alone; it was also a call for the people of the Princely States to fight for Independence. The Congress and the AISPC decided to fight against the Imperial Government shoulder to shoulder[4].

That the Feudatory States of Orissa was ailing due to mal-administration and feudalistic attitude of the Chiefs soon became evident in 1928 when the people of Nilgiri State protested against forced labour (*bethi*) and *Magan* which was an illegal imposition. Similar protest movements were launched in Talcher State in 1932. The people of Dhenkanal resisted the arbitrary decision of the Raja who imposed forest rules and enhanced land revenue. But the movements were abortive due to the help the Imperial Government gave to the Rajas[5]. There were sporadic incidents, which may be viewed as people's protests in the light of subsequent events of the 1930s.

Prajamandal in Orissa

The Prajamandal movement started in Orissa states in the later part of 1930s. The Chiefs had successfully kept their people excluded from the national main stream by disallowing the Congress leaders to visit their states and proscribing newspapers and publicity literature carrying the news of Gandhian struggle of non-cooperation and civil disobedience for fear of their adverse impact. However, the first meeting of the Orissa States People Conference was convened at Cuttack in 1931 by Radhanath Rath, Balunkeswar Acharya, Madhusudan Patnaik and Govind Chandra Mishra. The Conference was presided over by Bhubanananda Das, a member of the Imperial Assembly. The Conference voiced their demand for improved administration. Thereafter nothing happened. Simultaneously, another small organisation called the Garjat Praja Sammilani had come in to existence under the leadership of Balukeswar Acharya, of Hindol State, Radhanath Rath of Athgarh State and Sarangdhar Das of Dhenkanal State[6]. But it was considered to be a paper organization[7].

Serious effort was made in 1936-37 to revive and reinforce the Orissa States People Conference (OSPC) at the second session held at Cuttack on 23 June 1937 under the Chairmanship of Dr. B. Pattabhi Sitaramiyya, the Congress leader. It was declared at the Conference that they would demand for the establishment of responsible Governments by the people of the states. They also insisted for the enforcement of the Rule of Law in place of arbitrary Government, protection of peasants' rights on their holding and to grant basic rights to the residents. The conference expressed in clear terms, its dissatisfaction over the collection of illegal impositions like–*rasad, bethi, magan* and other arbitrary cesses[8]. To assess the condition of the people of the states an Enquiry Committee called the Orissa states Enquiry Committee was set up with Satis Chandra Bose, Balwantrai Mehta, Brajasundar Das and Sarangdhar Das. Harekrushna Mahatab was appointed as Chairman of the Committee. Subsequently, the constitution was modified with Harekrushna Mahtab, Chairman and Lalmohan Patnaik and Balwantrai Mehta as the members[9].

The OSPC of 1937 opened a new phase in the peasants movement in Orissa throwing light on their agrarian problems and demanding change in the operational aspect of the Feudalistic Government of the Rajas. This was possible on account of the formation of a Congress Government in British Orissa who lent moral support to the aggrieved peasants. Consequently, Prajamandals cropped up in several states like-Nilgiri, Ranpur, Nayagarh, Dhenakanl, Talcher, Athgarh, and Hindol etc. Those who organized the Prajamandals were residents of the same states having a honourable status and respectful image in the society. They were - Sarangdhar Das and Maheswar Subahu Singh of Dhenakanl, Radhanath Rath of Athgarh, Kailas Chandra Mohanty of Nilagiri, Balukeswar Acharya of Hindol, Pabitramohan Pradhan of Talcher, Nirmal Munda of Gangpur,Apudu Sahu and Sanghapriya Devi of Kalahandi, Satyananda Mishra and Dibakar Bohidar of Bolangir, Damodar Danduasi of Baud and Sarat Chandra Das of Mayurbhanj[10].

How the Ministry of Biswanath Das in Orissa extended its support to the states people is discussed below. Although in accordance with the provisions of the Government of India Act 1935 neither the provincial Government nor the Central Legislature had any right to interfere with or to speak about the affairs of the Feudatory states, Biswanath Das appealed to the Rajas of Orissa States on 12 November 1938 to restore peace and tranquility in their domains by making compromises with their subjects[11]. There was an exodus of people from the states to the adjacent districts for fear of oppression. A number of Prajamandal leaders had taken shelter in the districts to avoid arrest. This situation was not only embarrassing for the Congress Government but also very sensitive. When the Rajas demanded the extradition of the Prajamandal leaders so that they would be dealt with properly, the Congress Government took it as a moral duty to provide protection. Nehru as the President of the National Congress emphatically said,

"No Congress ministry could agree to loosing honours and betraying our comrades in the States and being false to our principles[12]."

Lord Linlithgow, the Viceroy during his visit to Orissa discussed the states problem with the Congress Ministry and in an address admitted that there was no geographical boundary separating Orissa Province and the Orissa States. Such view of the viceroy had an impact on the peasants and the people of Orissa who decided to forge close contact with each other by a common programme based on nationalism[13].

But just then the Second World War broke out and the Congress Government in the provinces tendered their resignation on a question of International magnitude. During the war the Colonial Government strengthened the grip of the Rajas to preserve the Empire. The Defence of India Rule and the Princes Protection Act were strictly enforced leading to the arrest of the Prajamandal leaders. The Prajamandals in the states were declared unlawful public meetings and presentation of Petitions were banned. Civil liberties were totally absent. Fearing arrest and police torture many leaders went underground and conducted their agrarian movement secretly with support of adventurous youths. Notwithstanding the oppressive policies of the Government the States people were caught in a nationalist frenzy. With unprecedented zeal and enthusiasm they agitated against the feudal Chiefs and their oligarchy[14].

Prajamandal in Mayurbhanj

The proximity of Mayurbhanj with Bengal and Balasore had a salutary effect on her people who could not escape the fire of nationalism. They came to know about Mahatma Gandhi, Harekrushna Mahtab and the Salt Satyagraha of Inchudi where thousands of Congress volunteers had courted arrest for breaking the salt law and the prohibition order of the Police[15].

Mayurbhanj, even after being administered by a series of benevolent rulers, experienced peasants uprising. Most of her people were tribals who lived on agriculture and forest products. Most of them were marginal farmers who lived from hand to mouth unless supplemented by wages earned as daily labourer. They were treated reasonably well by the state where stringent exploitation was absent. The general people except on the borders of Midnapore and Balasore and Tatanager did not have much knowledge with the outside world, nor had the political awareness about main stream events. Yet the news about the Gandhian movements of non-cooperation and civil disobedience created mild ripples in their mind. The events of Balasore had their impact on Mayurbhanj due to percolation of Satyagraha news via Nilgiri[16].

Other Factors

There was discontent among the people which paved the way for Prajamandal movement. A circular order No.3 dated 25 April 1925 had prohibited public meetings without prior permission. This circular had stifled the freedom of expression and though it was withdrawn on 25 November 1935 an adverse opinion had been created against the state administration. This was opposed to the formation of political association and holding of public meetings. The feudal practice of *begari*, *magan*, *bethi* and *rasad* being prevalent had caused resentment as evil practices. These feudal levies had been officially abolished as early as 25 July 1893. The revocation of the evil practices was repeated under the provisions of the Mayurbhanj Tenancy Regulation of 1904. Yet, the Sardars had not fully given up the practices for which another order was issued on 15 November 1938. Although, the state laws stipulated adequate money compensation for illegal practices, surreptitiously the Revenue officials were practicing the method for their gratification[17].

The Sardari system of revenue collection was prone to extortion. The Sardars were outsiders temporarily settled in Mayurbhanj. They not only amassed huge landed property of high quality paddy yielding category well irrigated or close to the rivers and canals, they proved to be occasionally oppressive to the innocent rural folks. If an area was distantly located from the capital, the chances and degree of exploitation was more[18]. The sardars forced the rural labourers to work free for them. They were also engaged as coolies on various occasions to serve the Sardars or to curry favour from the touring officers. In the Panchpir Subdivision *bethi* system was prevalent which the unscrupulous officers took advantage of during the excavation of irrigation projects like Pradeep Sagar of Karanjia[19].

Another irritating factor was caused by the hunting expedition and *Kheda*[20] operation of the Chief and his guests when the tribal drummers and village folks were engaged to chase the wild animals towards the Hunter's *Machan*[21]. During such chase many beaters got injured or mauled by wild animals for which there was no adequate compensation from the state. Sometimes these operations continued for a week or more when the beater was not engaged in any work to earn his bread as he was away from home.

The practice of collecting gifts or nazrana during the marriage or coronation ceremony was also an abominable practice causing annoyance. In the Jashipur area, the people had to pay Payaka pancha in kind during special occasions. The tribals had to pay tax for using various forest products like lak, mahua flower, Sal leaves and Sal seeds, and honey etc. They sold these forest products in the local market to Agents of merchants coming from either Calcutta or Ranchi[22].

Taking advantage of the illiteracy and poor economic condition, the moneylenders had a heyday in money lending business. They collected the principal and interests in the harvesting season for loans they advance during social obligations like marriage, funerals and famine conditions. There were no Banks to help the people at reasonable rate of interest. The state had some cooperative societies which could not cope with the requirements of the people[23].

The money lending business was in the hands of the Bihari Muslims who had their roots in Chaibasa, Ranchi, Tata and other places outside Mayurbhanj not under the control of the State Government. They had penetrated to the Tribal villages to take advantage of their simplicity. They would give loan in rainy reason to facilitate cultivation and collected double the amount after the harvesting of crops. The Muslims being non residents had no sympathy and they suck the life blood of the peasants to their satisfaction[24].

According to the Regulation II of 1908 the state had the power to expel any undesirable person from Mayurbhanj within twenty four hours. This was a provision of state law which scared the people[25].

The States Enquiring committee under the leadership of Mahtab went round several Feudatory States collecting data and information by meeting the people. In August 1939 the committee submitted a report to the Viceroy during his visit to Orissa. The report contained a brief picture of the tribals of Mayurbhanj and their grievances. The essential features which the report highlighted related to their grievances. The grievances were;

(i) They paid annas four per month per family as fuel fee,

(ii) They paid two annas per head of cattle for grazing in the village ground.

(iii) They paid a fee of four annas per head of cow

(iv) They paid rasad[26] to the officers during shikar[27]

(v) They served bethi for repair of roads, building of schools and state bungalows.

(vi) They were not allowed to take their carts on the main roads.

(vii) They paid fees for obtaining Sal wood to make agricultural tools @ four annas per yoke

(viii) They paid chowkidari Tax

(ix) They paid marriage tax ranging from annas four to annas Eight.

(x) They paid cess for Tussar cultivation[28].

The tribals who deposed before the committee complained of non-availability of medical aid during epidemics and inadequacy of schools. There were other humanitarian problems and deficiencies which the Committee listed in the Report[29].

Though the Maharaja took pains to tour his state to meet the people to know their problems and grievances, probably the visits were not frequent or failed to cover the border villages. But whenever any malpractice was reported to him, action was taken against the erring officer or Sardar. One such example was the confiscation of the property of a Lakhrajdar[30] of Rajaloka. The tribals were not very vocal to place their view points before the Maharaja; they are even now quite reticent and incapable in articulating their views.

In 1939 the situation in the states of Orissa was heading towards a crescendo. Dhenkanal, Talcher, Ranpur and

Sarat Chandra Das

Prasanna Kumar Das

Gangpur were very much in the news for police lathicharge and firing Compelling the Chiefs to declare the Prajamandals as illegal. On 5 January 1939 Major Bazelgette, the Political Agent was brutally killed by the mob which had surrounded the Raja's palace in Ranpur state. This ghastly incident shocked the entire Orissa province besides Mahatma Gandhi and the Congress leaders who could not approve of such violence. But, the political temperature was so high that the Prajamandal leaders of Mayurbhanj could not remain as mere spectators[31].

The Prajamandal of Mayurbhanj was the brain child of Sarat Chandra Das[32] who as President had given it a strong foundation and he was assisted by Prasanna Kumar Dash (1919-2005), the General Secretary[33]. Both were dedicated workers whose personal life was free from blemish as they followed the path of Gandhian austerity. While expressing the accumulated grievances of the people of Mayurbhanj Prasanna Kumar Das stated,

> "Instances of forced labour and illegal exactions and realization of exorbitant rate of interest are to be met even at this advance stage of the world and under the very nose of the government. The people being ignorant and timid, this state of theirs was taken advantage of and for a paltry

amount of loan, they had to pay double, triple and four folds and at last have lad in many cases to part with their ancestral lands with tears in their eyes[34]."

Launching of the Movement

The nationalists of Mayurbhanj who participated at the salt satyagraha of Inchudi were Gourmohan Pradhan, Panchanan Rai Singh, Manmohan Dwivedy, Santan Pradhan and Surya Mohan Das. After returning to their respective villages they plunged in to the Prajamandal movement Bansidhar Parida of Dhadangir was a leading figure in the movement. He arranged the first Prajamandal meeting at Simla defying the Prohibition order of the State since no prior permission had been obtained. Though Behera was taken to Police custody on the previous night, the meeting was held as per schedule. Soon thereafter another meeting was held by Gourmohan Pradhan of Bellanpur. A young group of activitists gave him support in holding the meeting. Since public pressure was mounting to hold peaceful meetings the state discreetly withdrew the Prohibition order on 25 November 1938[35].

On 25 November 1938 the Maharaja took a bold step to involve his people in the state administration by notifying the Mayurbhanj State Praja Sabha Order, 1938 proclaiming the establishment of Five Prajasabhas, are each for four subdivisions – Sadar, Bamanghaty, Kaptipada, Panchpir and the fifth one at Baripada, the Capital headquarters[36]. These representative bodies were intended to ventilate public opinion on all matters relating to the well-being of the people and also to serve as an useful platform to project public opinion for the guidance of the state administration. The Preamble of the Mayurbhanj Praja Sabha Order read,

> "Whereas it is the intention of the Maharaja to bring the people of Mayurbhanj in to closer touch with the state administration, and whereas it is expedient, as a step in that direction, to constitute regular representative institutions in

order to enable them to formulate local opinion in all matters concerning the well being of the people in general, and serve as a media of communication of such opinion to the state authorities[37]."

Formation of the Praja Sabhas

According to the Prajasabha Order, 23 November 1938, the composition of each would be as under[38]:

(i) Such number of members as may be prescribed by notification in the State Gazette to be elected by the adult male population of the Subdivision concerned; and

(ii) Such number of members to be nominated by the Dewan as may amount to not more than fifty percent of the elected members under preceding sub clause.

The Land Revenue Officer, Sadar and the sub-divisional officers of Bamanghaty, Panchpir, and Kaptipada shall be Chairman of the Praja Sabhas of the respective Subdivisions and Sadar subdivisional officer shall be the Chairman of the Baripada Praja Sabha[39]. The tenure of the Praja Sabha would be three years from the day of its first meeting, after which it would be automatically dissolved. The Dewan was vested with the power to dissolve any Praja Sabha sooner than its full term and to extend its term by a period not exceeding two years[40]. The Praja Sabha shall meet at least twice a year at such time and place as may be notified by its Chairman. A Praja Sabha was empowered to consider all questions affecting the well being of the people on matters relating to; (i) Education, (ii) Public health and Medical relief, (iii) Water supply, (iv) Agriculture, (v) Communication and (vi) Grievances of a general character deserving consideration of the state authorities[41].

The Chairman of the Praja Sabha was given the responsibility of maintaining a record of the proceedings of every meeting a copy of which was to be forwarded to the Secretary, General Department[42].

As per the Rules promulgated under clause (a) of section 9 of the Mayurbhanj Praja Sabha Order 1938, the constituencies and number of members to be elected to represent the constituency were fixed. The rules specified the number of member to be elected to different Praja Sabhas was as under[43].

(i)	Baripada Town	14
(ii)	Sadar	80
(iii)	Bamanghaty	65
iv)	Panchpir	54
v)	Kaptipada	35

The Praja Sabha Order laid down the rules and qualifications or eligibility of a person seeking election as a member. It said[44]

(i) He shall be an adult male person

(ii) He shall be the resident of the constituencies

(iii) He shall not be a whole time servant of the state or has not been dismissed from service of the state.

(iv) He has not undergone a sentence of imprisonment upon conviction in a criminal case involving moral turpitude,

(v) He is not an undischarged insolvent

(vi) He is not of unsound mind.

It is significant to note that Praja Sabha election was based on male adult franchise and polling was not by secret ballot, but by raising of hands. The Election Officer would ask the voters to assemble at the polling station forming separate groups as they support candidates. The total number of the voters would then be counted to find out the majority. A case of disputed election could be filed before the Dewan within seven days[45]. On 29 May 1939 the Rules of business was promulgated empowering the member of the Praja Sabhas to address questions to the Chairman of the sabha seeking information on any specific issue of public interest relating to their own local area or the state as a whole.

Members could move resolution in the form of recommendations to the state authorities on any matter of public interest[46].

After first general election to the Praja Sabha were over by 20 April 1939, the Maharaja sent a message-giving vent to his sense of satisfaction. The message read[47],

> "I have watched with interest the first election under the Mayurbhanj Praja Sabha Order 1938 which has just been concluded. Representative bodies like the Praja Sabhas are altogether an innovation in Mayurbhanj and the first elections naturally caused some amount of bewilderment among the people inspite of the effort made to explain the object with which I desired the creation of these Sabhas. I hope that the political education of my people. Which has thus begun, will in the fullness of times enable all sections of them to take an intelligent interest in the administration of the state[48]."

The Maharaja gave some hints about the future course of his political reforms. His aim was to establish a Central legislature for the people of Mayurbhanj and some of the members to the Central legislature would be selected among the Praja Sabha members. Thereby he assured his people that more reforms were coming to give the people an opportunity to elect their own legislature. He was aware that for the success of reforms and popular Government what was needed was honesty of purpose, integrity and true spirit of dedicated service. He wanted the process of change to be peaceful. He urged his people to have patience and genuine pride in being citizens of Mayurbhanj. For holding meetings of the Praja Sabha of Baripada, he took steps for the construction of a hall near the Purnachandra Industrial Institute in 1941-42[49].

The Sadar Praja Sabha consisted of 80 elected and 40 nominated members. It was presided over by Bholanath Panda. The Baripada Praja Sabha consisted of 14 elected and 7 nominated members with its activities limited to Baripada Municipal Town. The Bamanghati Praja Sabha consisted of 65 elected and 32 nominated members and was presided over by Siris Chandra Ghose. The Panchpir Praja Sabha consisted of 54 elected and 27 nominated numbers. It was presided over by Gopinath Dhal. The Kaptipada Praja Sabha had 35 elected and 17 nominated members with Prafulla Kumar Das as the President[50].

The above Praja Sabhas were to deal with;

(i) Education of the Poor,

(ii) Extension of Adult education,

(iii) Night Schools,

(iv) Providing Poor Peasants with wood from the Forest for making agricultural implements,

(v) construction of Tanks, wells, bridges and roads,

(vi) State Hamars and grain golas;

(vii) Reconstruction of Irrigation Projects etc.

The scheme of having the Praja Sabha as a political machine to accommodate people and give them a forum for expressing their problems as well as to recommend remedial measures to the state authorities was a good idea based on innovative spirit. The absence of secret ballot system and the ineffectiveness of the recommendation were two major defects in the scheme. The scheme was not aimed at transferring power to the people, but just a camouflage of democratic practice. However, the elections to the Praja Sabhas went on smoothly proving thereby that there was no resentment. The general public realized that the scheme was well intentioned to involve the people in administration and to discuss matters of common concern. The Chief was not coming to the picture directly. The office of the Diwan was the shock absorber. By all means, the Praja Sabha marked a positive step in creating a state legislature and a representative Government. The innovation of the Maharaja was really commendable.

Achievements

The Praja Sabhas gave on opportunity to vocal persons to discuss various policies and rules of the State

Government. They gained confidence in facing the officials from the lower level to the Diwan. They criticized the state policy to supply timber to Railway and Government either at nominal cost or free of cost. They were unhappy at the destruction of the forest wealth. Those members like Lalmohan Pati of Baripada pleaded for withdrawal of all restrictions on the tribals in collecting forest products. The Praja Sabha of Bamanghaty wanted to know how the enemy war planes would be recognized. The Sabha demanded for appointment of adequate number of teachers in the schools. They expressed their anxiety for the reconstruction of damaged irrigation projects[51].

The Panchpir Praja Sabha resolved to undertake irrigation projects on priority basis and digging of tanks for lift irrigation. The members were worried over the rising cost of essential goods like clothes, kerosene and sugar. There was a consensus for the establishment of price control committee and fair price shops where essential consumers articles would be made available to card holders. As in 1942 there was a famine in Bengal which had a peripheral impact on the bordering villages, the Government was urged upon to provide food for work scheme. This helped the rural labourers in the distressed area. Under pressure, the government took measures to stop the export of paddy outside the state. The food grain merchants were asked to declare their stock by 8 August 1942 and export was totally banned. This got people's appreciation in clear terms[52].

In a special session of the Praja Sabha, the Diwan announced the establishment of two representative bodies-Mayurbhanj Flood Relief Committee and the Food Advisory Committee. Members for the committees were carefully chosen from cross section of the people. An amount of rupees twenty thousand was provisionally sanctioned for the purchase and distribution of seeds for extensive Rabi sowing in the state[53].

The measures were adopted by the Maharaja to give an opportunity to associate the people with the Government. He thereby thought of neutralizing their hostile attitude. But except giving them the opportunity to discuss problems, there was no other benefit for them. There was no transfer of power in true sense of the term. The election of members to the Praja Sabhas was by direct voting through raising of hands[54]. The length of the queue decided the majority choice. The elections were open and conducted in public places like weekly on daily markets. Though this was a weak point, the intention of the Maharja was good. The criticism of the Prajamandal leaders to the above experiment was scathing. They were not satisfied with the reforms as was revealed by the statement of Prasanna Kumar Das. He said,

> These Praja Sabhas are so many shame institutions quite independent of each other and with no central body of a coordinating character. They have got no real power in them to carry any binding effect of their decisions on the Executive Head of the state.

In fact the recommendation of the Praja Sabhas had no binding force on them as the Chief was not bound to accept them. This was a severe weak point of the whole experiment[55].

Prajamandal of Mayurbhanj: Its Operation and Achievements

The rising tide of Indian nationalism was sweeping the whole country with the mass sentiment reaching an all time high in 1939. Inside Orissa, the people of Nilgiri, Ranpur and Dhenkanal were surging ahead under their respective Prajamandals having an unprecedented impact on the people of other Feudatory States. The people of Mayurbhanj could not afford to remain passive onlookers. They realized that like the British Empire counting its days in India, the monarchical order in the Princely states was also due to crumble to prices giving way to a new socio-political order. The path was shown by Bansidhar Behera, the Congress activist of Kuliana. Behera became a household name due to his anti-Darbar stance and boldness. The people were not unaware of the developments of Nilgiri. Gradually, the Prajamandal began to draw more attention and public support. The failure of the Praja Sabha experiment was a shot in the arm for the Prajamandal. Youngmen like Prasanna Kumar Das responded to the call of Saratchandra Das of Ambajora. Many other like minded people, viz. Krushnachandra Mrugaraj of Jashipur, Kantharam Das of Karanjia, and Shyam Singh Tipiria of Raruan joined the band wagon of Saratchandra. A new wave of political awareness swept through Panchpir and Sadar subdivisions[56].

Saratchandra Das had adequate training in nationalist activities as a Congress Party worker in Balasore. He was the Vice President of the Balasore Congress Committee for long five years, 1920-25. Earlier, he was a Pleader having independent profession and a supporter of Utkal Union Conference[57]. As a dedicated social worker he was popularly known as "Sarat Gandhi". He was an inhabitant of Ambajora village near Betnati. At his farmhouse he convened a meeting of young nationalists on 24 March 1939. This was a significant milestone in the history of Prajamandal movement in Mayurbhanj. The meeting was attended by a large number of likeminded persons, viz. Jagannath Kamila, Girischandra Roy, Gourmohan Pradhan, Gajendra Nath Patnaik, Hrudanand Das, Hadibandhu Rout, Govindchandra Naik, Laxmidhar Tripathy, Sakila Soren, Ramchandra Patnaik, Laxman Charan Parida, Dhruva Charan Rout, Krushnachandra Swain, Ramchandra Mohapatra, Adityanath Lal, Laxmidhar Pradhan, Madan Mohan Panda, Madan Mohan Mishra, Aparti Biswal, Ramnath Patra, Biswambhar Maharana, Kailas Chandra Naik and the Convener Saratchandra Das[58]. They took a pledge, in the name of God, to work as faithful and devoted soldiers of the nonviolent freedom struggle and would gladly accept the sufferings and privations that may came on their way. This gave birth to

Mayurbhanj Prajamandal organization, though it was not formally announced and no member was formally enrolled. The members promised to work for creating a consciousness among the villagers on public health and hygiene. They setup the Pragana Samiti to undertake village level social works like village cleaning, construction and repair of roads and bridges, to create a village fund by collecting donations, removal of illiteracy, untouchability, establishment of Night Schools and non-government cooperative societies[59]. Soon afterwards Pragana Samitis were formed at Sathilo, Banahari, Rahanda, Barpera, Barsahi, Kudadiha, Manitri, Akhuadeulia, Morada and in Kaptipada Sub-division at Khunta, Dukura, Kainsari, Sainkola, Aarpata, Taldiha, and Chilima[60]. To provide consistent leadership to the Pargana Samitis, Sarat Chandra Das gave up his legal practice assuming full time Presidentship. Since then Ambajoda became the nerve center of Prajamandal movement whose initial objective was village reconstruction with a new look to the rural life. The social reconstruction programme also included in its objective emancipation of women from the Purdah system. So the movement had to enlist women activists. For the women a meeting was held at village Madhunanda where the wifes of Gourmohan Pradhan, Adaityanath Lala, Madan Mohan Panda and a few others assembled wearing long veils. The next meting of the women was held at Pratinadezpur where twenty two women were present. Thereafter special meetings of the women succeeded in drawing together ladies of programme minded families. In the village of Kundapada the meeting was presided over by Katika Mani Mahapatra. That was gradually ice of Purdah system began to melt and more and more women were attracted to the vortex of Pargana Samiti with enthusiasm for village transformation. Gradually, they gave up their shyness and had no problem in joining meetings together with men folk. This was a great achievement for Sarat Chandra Das and his young compatriots as the end of Purdah system ushered in a process of social change. Sarat Chandra

Das' leadership was acknowledged by all and sundry and he emerged as the undisputed leader[61] of Mayurbhanj.

In 1940 the Prajamandal movement gathered momentum in all the four sub-divisions. In May a three day session was held at Tental with Sarangdhar Das, the General Secretary of AIPSC as the President. There was a heavy attendance of more than ten thousand workers from the whole state. In course of his speech, the President commended upon the good works done by Mayurbhanj Prajamandal. He attended a community lunch arranged by the Dalits and Tribals. The Prajamandal's village reconstruction programme and Gandhian programme against untouchability, and illiteracy impressed him profoundly. Even Pandit Nehru made eloquent appreciation of the leadership of Sarat Chandra Das. On 23 May 1940 in a letter he wrote[62].

> "I have learnt of the work that is being done among the people of Mayurbhanj State, more than especially the Santals, Kols, Bhumija and Kurmis. I am glad to hear of this and I wish it all success. To those who are working among them to raise them I send my cordial good wishes."

The success of the Tental session gave wide recognition to the able leadership and organising capacity of Sarat Chandra Das inside and outside Orissa. It was then decided to change the Pargana Samiti's name as "Mayurbanj State Prajamandal"[63]. Since then it assumed a political colour demanding the introduction of responsible Government with the Maharaja as the Constitutional head. The Prajamndal resorted to nonviolent method of peaceful agitation to achieve the goal. A working committee of the Party was constituted[64] with Sarat Chandra Das as the President, Gajendra Nath Patnaik as the Vice-President, Prasanna Kumar Das as General Secretary, Laxmidhar Tripathy as Treasurer and twenty one other members. A permanent party office was set up at the farm house of Sarat Chandra at Ambajoda. The Mayurbhanj Prajamandal was affiliated to All India States

Peoples Conference and it was made a point to submit fortnightly reports to Pandit Nehru who was the President of the All India Organization. At the Gwalior Session of the AISPC in 1941, Sarat Chandra Das was given opportunity to elaborately focus upon the works his party did in Mayurbhanj. That gave Mayurbhanj the scope to find a place at the national level of the Prajamandal agitation[65].

Reaction

The steady growth in the popularity of the Prajamandal organisation became a source of concern for the State administration. Not only some vested interest groups tried to poison the ears of the Maharaja, the Sardars and officials made an effort to malign the names of the leaders of the Prajamandal by adverse publicity. Under the Presidentship of Harish Chandra Dash, the State sponsored a party named as "Prajamangal". It may be interesting to note that Harish Chandra Dash was the younger brother of Ram Chandra Dash, the Superintendent of police of Mayurbhanj. Among the Sardars who actively supported this malicious propaganda against Prajamandal, mention may be made of Ratikanta Patnaik, Umakanta Patnaik, Pitamber Choudhary, Rashbihari Das and Braja Sundar Das[66].

Apart from forming the Prajamangal Party to counter the popularity of the Prajamandal, the state authorities resorted to threat and intimidation. They even kept some of the leaders under surveillance[67]. Bhaktabandhu Mohanta, teacher of an ME school in Karanjia was kept under close watch. He found it difficult to organize public meetings. To put him at a disadvantage he was transferred to Nalgaja, far away from Karanjia[68].

The formation of the Prajamangal was the most sinister move against Sarat Chandra Das and his associates. The aims of the Prajamangal were;[69]

(i) To mobilize public opinion against the Prajamandal

(ii) To Create disturbances in the public meetings organized by the Prajamandal

(iii) To oppose and frustrate all constructive works of the Prajamandal

Sometimes the Prajamangal engaged hired Goondas[70] brought from outside Mayurbhanj to disrupt the Prajamandal meetings. They created disturbances by various methods like beating drums and giving catcalls. Not that they could be neutralized at times, but it created unpleasant situations. The Prajamandal tried to counter them by nonviolent means and thereby could win more public support. Though the Prajamangal leaders made efforts to pretend their innocence, the actual facts were not unknown to the people[71].

The people were aware that the Prajamangal activities were sponsored by the Superintendent of Police and the Dewan. The Dewan was financing all the anti-Prajamandal activities which had indirect blessings of the Maharaja. Yet, the relation between Sarat Chandra Das and the Maharaja remained as cordial as ever. The Maharaja was held in high respect. However, neither Prajamandal nor the Prajamangal succeeded in disrupting the political stability in the state because of the high public image of the Maharaja[72].

There were examples when some of the Prajamandal leaders were falsely implicated in criminal cases by the Police. One such case was against Jagannath Kamila for outraging the modesty of a lady of doubtful character. In the trial Kamila was acquitted as the Police could not prove the allegation[73]. Other examples were cases initiated against Bhagwan Das and Huding Singh of Balidiha for the alleged offence of preventing Revenue collectors to collect revenue[74]. Similar case was instituted against Harihar Sahu of Itamundia. A case of alleged stealing of a cock was instituted against Purna Choudhury of Badakhunta[75]. Giris Chandra Ray was also arrested in a false case. From Ambajoda village alone eighteen persons were to face prosecution for alleged land grabbing[76]. But they were acquitted.

Sarat Chandra Das in a booklet "Gadjat Sasan' had referred to these cases and incidents. He has vividly described how the Sub-Inspector of Khunta Police Station with a group of armed Constables and hooligans tried to disrupt the meeting of the Prajamandal on 15 November 1943. They attempted to present public from entering the meeting place and created enough disturbances by beating empty tins. But as the workers of Prajamandal restrained themselves from being provoked there was no escalation of the crisis[77].

Another strategy, which the State Government adopted against the Prajamandal was to create division in the Party by encouraging black sheep either through bribe or through intimidation. There were spies engaged by the police to give them prior information about meetings and movements of the leaders[78].

Why the Prajamandal was Popular?

There were several factors responsible for making the Prajamandal organization popular in Mayurbhanj. The tide of the time was flowing against the Princely order and the feudalistic society. Though the people of Mayurbhanj had not envisioned liberation from monarchy, they very much wanted the Sardars to be cut to size as they were the bulwarks of the illegal taxation, torture and harassment. For them the Prajamandal provided the forum to demand changes besides motivating them to agitate against injustice and accumulated grievances. The Prajamandal warned at the grass root level to derive public support. By working for village reconstruction and social reforms, cleaning tanks to make them usable for drinking purpose, drive against illiteracy and untouchability they touched the emotional chord of the common man and succeeded in consolidating the party organization. With people's cooperation the Prajamandal could complete the

Silaghati bundh[79] facing the hazards of the Government action. The Sub-divisional Officer of Kaptipada declared 144 in the area with strict instruction not to proceed further with the work as reserved forest was being destroyed. The police arrested Giris Chandra Ray, Ram Chandra Mohapatra, Purna Chandra Choudhury and Purna Chandra Parichha and tried them. Finally, they were sentenced to various terms of imprisonment. After a brief delay, however, the construction work could be completed[80].

With the initiative of the Prajamandal many Grain Golas were established in villages to give paddy loan to farmers to save them from unscrupulous money lenders. On 26 January 1943 the Prajamandal started the construction of a dam over Budhi river, a Tributary of Gangahar. This was a preventive measure against flood, which often caused great damage to crop in the lower areas of Mayurbhanj. Even Balasore district was also affected at times. The dam was named as Sarat bundh[81].

The popularity of the Prajamandal in the Panchpir Subdivision was on account of the hard work of Bhaktabandhu Mohanta, Siba Prasad Mohanta, Baidyanath Mohanta, Daitari Singh and Bhairav Chandra Mohanta. The Panchpir Branch was led by President Umesh Chandra Panigrahi and Siba Prasad Mohanta as the Secretary. To devote himself to organizational work on full time basis Bhaktabandhu Mohanta gave up his Government job[82].

The agitation programme of Panchpir unit began in 1943 and it was commonly called the *Payeka* Agitation. 'Payeka' signified an illegal tax collected by the Sardars and Sarbarakars. The monastery or Matha at Joshipur had been enjoying the endowment of land which it gave to the peasants for cultivation. They paid rent for the land they cultivated. The rent was collected either in cash or equivalent amount of rice by the Mahant (Head) named Balram Das.The matha was a center of Hindu worship. There were some people following either Islam or Christianity who were obliged to pay Payeka to the Matha[83].

The Prajamandal leaders, viz, Ramchandra Mohapatra, Dakhin Majhi, Krushna Chandra Swain and Harekrushna Sahu along with Prasanna Kuamr Das encouraged the peasants to intensify the agitation. But the Mahant was not willing to concede the demand of the Non-Hindus. The Government had to resort to oppression and prosecuted the offenders under criminal charges. It was Biswanath Sahu, the Advocate of Karanjia who valiantly fought for the accused persons free of charges. The news spread to Bamanghaty, the adjacent Subdivision. But finally, the prosecution withdrew the case as Payeka was abolished[84].

The Prajamandal unit of Bamanghaty Subdivision had its headquarters at Rairangpur. The President of the unit was Jit Mohan Mohanta. Under the leadership of Purna Chandra Pani, another unit was set up at Bangiriposi. More such units were set up at Rasgovindpur, Khunta and Amarda. At Baripada the unit was opened by Braja Sundar Rath in a Private rented house. At this stage some young members joined the organization. They were Harihar Mohanty, Purna Chandra Mohanta, Gour Mohan Mohapatra, Anant Rath, Bidyadhar Mohapatra, a reitred Sub-divisional Officer and Maheswar Nayak, the retired Registrar of Co-operative Societies[85].

In the context of the refusal of the National Congress to accept the August offer of 1940, the Colonial Government resorted to drastic police action against the nationalists under the provisions of the Defence of India Act[86]. The situation was so tense that Prajamandal leaders like Jagannath kamila and Bansidhar Raj were arrested and imprisioned for more than a year. Though the Hard Core officials were keen to arrest more activists to thwart the Prajamandal movement, the Maharaja did not agree. Only two persons were arrested. It is not known how the British Government looked at the decision of the Maharaja[87].

The Prajamandal participated at the Bombay Session of the AISPC where Sarat chandra Das unequivocally supported the Quit India Resolution of the National Congress. On their return Das and Ram Chandra Mohapatra organized a large public meeting of at least 50,000 persons and resolved to go on a procession to Baripada shouting 'Quit India' slogan[88].

The above procession was led by Prajamandal stalwarts like Prasanna Kumar Das, Girish Chandra Ray. Baikuntha Nath Sadual, Ram Chandra Mohapatra, Gour Mohan Pradhan and when they proceeded towards Baripada, the Maharaja sent an emissary requesting them to remain peaceful and nonviolent. About fifteen kms short of Baripada at Ragdha the Police had imposed section 144 of cr. P.C. and conveyed the request of the Maharaja. Since the relation of the Maharaja with Sarat Chandra Das was quite cordial the latter decided not to proceed further. It was a moment of great significance which showed the maturity of Das; though some other leaders were unwilling to return to Betnati his decision was respected[89].

Paik Rebellion

After the World War ended in September 1945 the Prajamandal movement of Mayurbhanj took the shape of a Paik rebellion led by Baikuntha Nath Sadual. The Paiks were from Sainkula, Kauamara, Chilima, Mangovindpur, Aarpata, Kathpal and Kalma. They were mercenaries who were given land in lieu of salary. Their job was to fight for the State under the banner of the Maharaja. The tradition of enjoying rent-free land was an age-old practice. But after the British Paramountcy was established there was no need to utilize the services of the Paiks for war. However, the Paiks continued to enjoy the jagir lands and rendered the service of watch and ward in the palace for a month every year. But it was a light duty not comparable with war service of the by gone days.

The Institution had become obsolete. In course of time the Paiks adopted corrupt practices like engaging hired substitutes to perform palace Guard duties. But their joining the Prajamandal movement was like last hair on the camel's back which the state was not prepared to tolerate. So the state insisted upon rendering Guard duties by real Paiks and did not accept any substitute. Wherever a default was detected his jagir land was confiscated. This gave birth to the Paik rebellion of 1946 under the leadership of Baikuntha Nath Sadual of Deulia. Other leaders who instigated the Paiks were Ramchandra Mohapatra, of Sainkula, Chakradhar Mohapatra of Mangovindpur and Baisnab Charan Naik of Chilima. They organized a meeting of the Paiks to protest against the decision of the state. The step taken by the state to disallow proxy duty and to confiscate the jagir land when malpractice was detected was probably quite justified. But in the context of the Prajamandal leaders' action to politicize the issue the disturbance was precipitated[90].

Baikuntha Nath Sadual was a Paik himself. He had inherited jagir land and acted as Pradhan to collect land revenue for his Sardar. In 1939 he joined the Prajamandal to become a staunch follower of Sarat Chandra Das. When he led the Paik rebellion he became the President with Ram Chandra Mohapatra as the Secretary of the Paik organization. In December 1946 he led a procession of the Paiks in front of the Palace at Baripada shouting slogans against the state order to confiscate Paik land and demanding conversion of Paik jagir land to Hasilat[91] land. The procession had included both men and women from the neighbouring villages. The Paiks shouted 'Down Down Maharaja' while carrying black umbrellas as a token of protest. Baikuntha Nath Sadual claimed to marry the only daughter of the Maharaja to provoke action against him. But the Maharaja did not react. Thereafter, the processionists quietly dispersed to their respective villages[92].

On 5 March 1947 the Maharaja as per the provisions of Regulation II of 1908 issued an order asking Baikuntha Nath Sadual to leave Mayurbhanj within twenty four hours. Sadual was charged with criminal conspiracy spreading disaffection among the Paiks and was declared a persona non grata. His stay in Mayurbhanj was considered undesirable due to the illegal movement he was leading. As Sadual did not comply with the order he was arrested and kept in the Baripada Central Jail from 14 March 1947 to 26 June 1947 as an undertrial prisoner. Thereafter, the Maharaja ordered for his release[93].

A legal query is generally raised on the issue of Sadual. In comparison he was less important than Sarat Chandra Das who was spared by the Maharaja. The expulsion order accused Sadual for leading disaffection among the Paiks and for demanding the Paikali land to Hasilat giving permanent ownership to the Paiks. Though this charge was officially labeled against him, Sadual's public demand to marry the Princess was not only a direct affront against the Maharaja, but was in bad taste. However, the provisions of Regulation II of 1908 were applied for the first time against Sadual and he was taken to custody for having defied the royal order.

The Prajamandal took up the issue by lodging protest against the royal decree through public meetings arranged at different places. On 30 March 1947 a huge public procession marched through the main streets of Baripada giving slogans for his immediate release. The meetings condemned Sadual's arrest as undemocratic and arbitrary[94].

On 17 March 1947 Sarat Chandra Das moved a resolution in the Kendra Parishad to vacate the order under Regulation II of 1908 in respect of Baikuntha Nath Sadual and to abolish the Regulation itself. Though Lalmohan Pati, the President of Kendra Parishad disallowed the resolution the pulse of the people was tested by the State administration[95].

The Prajamandal continued its effort to widen the base by organizing regular meetings and rallies. In May 1946, the conference of the Volunteer Corps was held at Pratappur with the efforts of Giris Chandra Roy, a firebrand activist. At the meeting Sarat Chandra Das and Prasanna Kumar Dash were again elected as the President and General Secretary respectively of Mayurbhanj Prajamandal. The Conference was addressed by renowned Socialist leaders of Orissa viz. Biswanath Pandit and Baikuntha Mohanty. They inculcated the principle and ideology of Socialism in the minds of the volunteer corps giving a new dimension to the Prajamandal programme. The Pratappur session was significant because there it was decided to have a conference of the, The Eastern States viz. Madhyapradesh, Orissa and Assam at Cuttack. The Pratappur session elected by secret ballots eight members to represent the Mayurbhanj Prajamandal at the proposed All Eastern States People Conference. They were Sarat Chandra Das, Prasanna Kumar Das, Harihar Mohanty, Jagannath Kamila, Giris Chandra Roy, Sakila Soren, Purna Chandra Parichha and Baikuntha Nath Sadual[96].

State Sponsored Democracy

During the preceding five years (1941-46) the Prajamandal of Mayurbhanj continued with its agitation demanding a responsible Government in the State. The organisation had several meetings in which resolutions to that effect were passed. Though it was an echo of the nation's demand for freedom from British rule and Transfer of power to a responsible Government constituted by the National Congress, the struggle remained, by and large, nonviolent and peaceful. The Maharaja also exhibited great maturity and restraint, unlike Talcher and Dhenkanal, not resorting to violent action against the people's movement.

But with the failure of the Prajamangal of Haris Chandra Das to counter the popularity of Prajamandal, the Maharaja had to think of other plans to pacify the people. On the occasion of his 44th birth day on 23 April 1945 a royal proclamation declared his intention to establish a Mayurbhanj Kendra Parishad or a Central Legislature with 27 members including the President, among whom 15 would be nominated representing various interests like Industry, Trade, Tribal population and the remaining 12 would be elected. The Kendra Parishad would make laws for the whole state. The Preamble of the Mayurbhanj Kendra Parishad order declared[97].

Whereas it is the declared intention of the Maharaja to bring the people of Mayurbhanj in touch with the State Administration.

And whereas it is the desire of the Maharaja as conveyed in his message issued on the 20 May 1939, in connection with the constitution of the Praja Sabhas, that the next important step in the direction of administrative development shall be the establishment of a Central Legislature for Mayurbhanj[98].

Kendra Parishad

The Kendra Parishad was to function for three years from the date of its first meeting after which it would stand dissolved. The Maharaja had the power to extend it for a year. It would be convened by the Maharaja and must meet once a year. The members would take an oath expressing loyalty to the Maharaja. He would nominate the President and the Vice President from among its members. All questions discussed at the Parishad would be decided by majority votes and the attendance of 14 members in a meeting would constitute the quorum. For seeking election a candidate shall be minimum 25 years of age and that he must not be disqualified by law. In the Parishad the members would enjoy the freedom of speech and no member would be liable to any proceeding in the court for his opinion or views expressed in the Parishad or any vote given by him in the Parishad or in 'Committee'[99].

Its Constitution

The Constitution also stipulated that the Parishad shall have the right to make laws for all persons, all courts, all places and things in Mayurbhanj State and for the subjects of the Maharaja wherever they may be. But no bill or amendment shall be introduced or moved in the Parishad affecting or relating to;

(i) The Maharaja and his family

(ii) Relating to the Maharaja with the Paramount power or any British Indian Government or any State or its ruler,

(iii) Matters governing treaties, Sanads, convention of Agreements now in force.

A bill passed in the Parishad may become act after it had received the assent of the Maharaja[100].

The order further said that members to the Mayurbhanj Kendra Parishad would be elected by the elected members of the Prajasabhas in the following order[101].

Constituency wise distribution-Sadar Praja Sabha would elect 3 members, Bamanghaty Praja Sabha would elect 3 members; Panchupir Praja Sabha would elect 3 members, Baripada Praja Sabha would elect 1 member and Kaptipada Praja Sabha would elect 2 members. Accordingly, the first election took place in July–August and was completed by 7 August 1945. The list of 14 nominated members was also finalized by then.[102]

The inaugural session of the Kendra Parishad was held on 10 January 1946. On that occasion, the Maharaja said[103],

> "To day is indeed a good day for us as it marks an important stage in the course of development of the Constitution promised by me so long."

It may be pertinent to mention here that the Mayurbhanj Prajamandal had no demand earlier to 1944 for a Central Legislature. Even at Madhuban Session which was held in 1945, the Prajamandal did not raise the question of a Kendra Parishad and nothing was thought of its membership. Thus, the Kendra Parishad was purely a brain child of the Maharaja who proposed this reform measure to preempt the move by Prajamandal. The Praja Sabha of 1938 were purely an Advisory body. Hence, the next constitutional reform was logically the royal order on a Central Legislature or Kendra Parishad. The Kendra Parishad delegated the power of law making to the people through their elected and nominated members.

The Maharaja further clarified to state;

> "I am particularly happy today that I have been able to add a further link in the chain that has been forged in the last three generations. It gives me great pleasure that I have today the opportunity of addressing the accredited representatives of my people sitting side by side with the state officials and dignitaries with the common purpose of serving the state[104]."

Reaction

The establishment of a Kendra Parishad was a bold step taken by the Maharaja, probably with a genuine desire to share power with the people through elected representatives. Even the Prajamandal welcomed the step. But to nominate as many as 14 members to the Parishad, which was more than the elected members, was a retrograde step not in consonance with the principle of democracy. But no Prajamandal leader expressed any criticism. Sarat Chandra Das was a member of the Parishad himself. In his booklet 'Garjat Sasan' or 'administration in the Native states' printed by Giris Chandra Roy at Cuttack[105]. Sarat Chandra Das made some sweeping comments on the administration of Mayurbhanj and other Native States. The Dewan of Mayurbhanj in a letter dated 20 February 1944 addressed to the Orissa Government wanted the booklet to be proscribed. In reply the Under Secretary to Orissa Government informed that the booklet was not having wide circulation in British Orissa and the State should take any action against Sarat Chandra Das as it would deem proper[106]. The matter was not pursued further.

In the above mentioned booklet Das had written[107]; In our State our Prajamandal is a living peaceful organization with national hopes and aspiration (freedom from British Rule). Though this organization is not affiliated to the Indian National Congress, its aim is to make the bigger movement in greater India successful by training our people to establish responsible Government under our Highness, the Maharaja as a unit of the Independent Federation of India, that means to crown the movement for the independence of entire India with success, while we the people of Native States achieve our Independence.

Here it is evident that Das wanted to have a responsible Government with the Maharaja as the constitutional head. He had no desire to abolish the Princely order. Secondly, he had thought of keeping Mayurbhanj a separate unit in the Indian Federation. He was a true Gandhian who espoused the ideal of nonviolence. But the reform scheme declared by the Maharaja fell far short of his expectations. So the Executive Committee of the Prajamandal met at Ambajoda on 30 July 1947 to form a War Council to exert pressure on the Maharaja to establish a Government responsible to the Legislature. The Council consisted of seasoned leaders, viz., Sarat Chandra Das, Harihar Mohanty, Gour Mohan Pradhan, Bhakta Bandhu Mohanta, Ananta Rath and Prasanna Kuamr Dash. This was the first time when the Prajamandal of Mayurbhanj placed its demand for a responsible Government accountable to the Legislature[108].

That Sarat Das was not prepared for a responsible Government when the Kendra Parishad was established on 10 January 1946 would be clear from an excerpt from his maiden speech at the Kendra Parishad. He said[109].

The ideas of responsible Government is certainly to be welcomed, but must not be forgotten that a double edged sword can cut both ways if improperly handled. Hence, patience, care and attention should be exercised at the time while one is learning its use.

But other changes were in the offing. Despite the unpreparedness of Sarat Chandra Das, the Maharaja was having a tromp card in his pocket as the subsequent events would show.

British withdrawal and Independence

The British Government made it public on 28 February 1947 that they would transfer power to responsible Indian hands not later than June 1948. With the arrival of Lord Mountbatten as the new Viceroy in March 1947 the process was fast expedited. This situation suddenly electrified the political parties in British India as well as in the native states. The Prajamandal of Mayurbhanj urged upon the Maharaja to introduce democratic form of responsible Government on or before 30 June 1947.

Since Prajamangal organisation of Haris Chandra Das had become defunct, a new party called Praja Parishad came in to existence. Its President was Loknath Patnaik who spread a malicious propaganda against the Prajamandal of Mayurbhanj saying that it was a destructive force aimed at exploiting the good name of the Indian National Congress[110]. Taking this as a sly political move of the Maharaja, the Prajamandal leaders of the Kendra Parishad tendered their resignation from membership.

The vacancies created by their resignations were promptly filled up by members of Praja Parishad party which embittered the relation between the Raj Durbar and the people. The irate Prajamandal constituted an Action Committee on 3 July 1947 with Sarat Chandra Das, Prasanna Kumar Das, Harihar Mohanty, Gour Mohan Pradhan,

Bhaktabandhu Mohanta and Ananta Rath to pressurize the Maharaja to accept the charter of demand dated 30 June 1947 for the prompts establishment of a Responsible Government[111].

Under the circumstance a disillusioned Maharaja dissolved the Kendra Parishad on 5 July 1947 which he had established to satisfy the people. The Prajamandal leaders threatened the Maharaja with mounting pressure of hartal and hunger strike and issued an ultimatum to concede to their demand by 16 September 1947. The Maharaja opened negotiation through Radha Govind Das, the Chief Revenue Officer for an amicable settlement. Being a liberal monarch he did not wish to alienate his people[112].

On the day India gained her freedom the state made a programme in which it was mentioned that the state Flag of Mayurbhanj would be hoisted at the Police Parade ground and the Salute would be given with the Maharaja on the dais, and then the national tri-colour would be unfurled by the Maharaja followed by a police march past. Though 15 August 1947 was a day of national jubilation, the Prajamandal of Mayurbhanj boycotted the State function and held their separate meeting at Madhuban. The students also joined the Madhuban function in large number. After the meeting at Madhuban a huge procession went round the street of Baripada town shouting slogans of 'Jaihind' and 'Bandemataram'[113].

On 15 August 1947 the British Paramountcy over the Indian states lapsed and the states were free to join the Indian Federation. With the withdrawal of the British Government the Prajamandal activities became more vigorous. In the adjacent state of Nilgiri, the people set up a parallel Government of the local unit of Prajamandal. As the situation was quite explosive there, the government of India authorized the Collector of Balasore to take over the administration on 14 November 1947 without any trouble. This was the first incident of integration of a Princely State with the province of Orissa[114]. This was a direct morale booster for the Mayurbhanj Prajamandal which encouraged them to save an ultimatum upon the Maharaja.

In the negotiation with the Prajamandal it emerged that they would furnish a list of members from the Praja Sabha and the defunct Kendra Parishad to function as the members of an Interim Government. That interim Government would receive power of administration from the Maharaja who in the meantime conceded their demand to establish a responsible Government in the state as an Independent unit of the Indian Union. He also agreed to discharge the function of a constitutional head with abjure authority[115].

The events developed so fast that tomorrow appeared uncertain. While the Prajamandal gave a list of members to constitute the Interim Government, the Maharaja prepared to Transfer power to that body till new Praja Sabhas and Kendra Parishad were elected.

Accordingly on 9 December, 1947 the Maharaja nominated Sarat Chandra Das, Bidyadhar Mohapatra and Maheswar Naik to Constitute the three member Interim Cabinet with following Portfolios[116].

Sarat Chandra Das designated as Premier was given Home, Finance, Audit, Planning and Reconstruction; Bidyadhar Mohapatra was allotted Revenue, Law, Health and Local Government Portfolio, and Maheswar Naik was to handle the Portfolio of Development, Education, Supply, Transport, Public works, Commerce and Labour.

Thus, Mayurbhanj was the first Princely State in India to have a popular Government soon after the Independence of India was achieved. The understanding and cordiality with which such a milestone in political development was peacefully reached appears to be quite significant an achievement for the Prajamandal leadership. The establishment of Prajamandal Government got wide publicity outside Mayurbhanj and Orissa. It was also intimated to the government of India. Both Prime Minister Jawaharlal Nehru and Dr. Rajendra Prasad sent their best wishes to Sarat Chandra Das the Premier[117].

The Maharaja of Mayurbhanj handed over all Executive powers to the Das Ministry and simultaneous steps were taken to set up a Constituent Assembly in order to draft a constitution within the ambit of which the State of Mayurbhanj was to function as a new unit of the Indian Union[118].

Prajamandal in Power

The Prajamandal enjoyed power for a short period only 9 December 1947 to 16 October 1948. It was a period of regrettable experience in administration. While in power, the last conference of the party was held in May 1948 at Simla, the same place where ten years ago, Bansidhar Behera of Dhadangir launched the first peasant movement in the form of a public meeting defying the order of the state. While in 1938 the Party was sober and docile, a decade later in 1948 it was inflated pride derived from power and influence that made the meeting vibrant. Though it was the same water of river Balanga flowing by the temple premises, the attitudinal difference of a decade had brought about remarkable changes.

The meeting place in 1948 was under the sword of Damocles which in the form of Orissa Government very much desired the independent existence of Mayurbhanj to end soon so that the oriya speaking states would be wholly integrated together. While enjoying power as Ministers and Members of the Vyavastha Parishad, the Prajamandal leaders forgot the objective of bringing the oriya states together in one province and developed centrifugal ideas against oriya irredentism.

At the Simla Conference, the Party changed its name to Mayurbhanj State Congress[119]. But Sarat Chandra Das declined to hold the posts of Premier and Party President. So Harihar Mohanty was unanimously elected as the President and Prasanna Kumar Das as the Vice President of the State Congress. Gourmohan Pradhan was elected as the General Secretary. The working Committee consisted of the three Ministers besides a few others. On 16 September 1948 the State Congress merged with the All India Congress as an affiliated Unit of the Utkal Pradesh Congress Committee Subsequently, the working committee agreed to merge Mayurbhanj with Orissa Province[120].

Once the Prajamandal assumed the identity of the Utkal Pradesh Congress many unscrupulous persons who were once opposed to Prajamandal got entry in to the Party. The Sardars, the Landed aristocrats, Haris Chandra Das etc became Congress Members behaving as Big Brother of the ex-Prajamandal members and they had the support of the Provincial Congress Party. The former leaders of Prajamandal including Sarat Chandra Das felt very small and humiliating. The situation led to the resignation of all former Prajamandal members from the Congress Party and circulated a booklet among the Members of the Legislative Assembly giving reasons as to why they left the Congress[121].

Failure of Prajamandal Government

The Prajamandal Government of Sarat Chandra Das could not manage the State of affairs due to their lack of administrative experience. When Sardar Patel visited Orissa on 13 December 1947 to persuade the Feudatory Chiefs to voluntarily integrate their states with the Province of Orissa by signing the Merger document all except the Maharaja of Mayurbhanj signed and a larger Orissa could be formed on the basis of linguistic and cultural homogeneity. The Maharaja explained that he had already granted responsible Government in his state where a popular Government was functioning headed by Sarat Chandra Das, the Prajamandal leader; hence he was unable to sign the Instrument of Accession without consulting his Ministers. Therefore, Mayurbhanj remained excluded from the process of integration and enjoyed briefly a separate status for which the people had to pay heavily as the events would show[122].

It may be briefly mentioned here that the Popular Government of Sarat Chandra Das could not manage the State finances and internal administration properly. There was a serious Tribal uprising threatening the law and order situation. Finally, the Government of Orissa province headed by H.K.Mahatab in his eagerness to complete the unification of the Oriya Feudatory states with the Province mobilized political and social pressure for the integration of Mayurbhanj. The Prajamandal Government found itself between the Scylla and Charibdis and finally signed the Instrument of Accession in New Delhi with the States Ministry of Sardar Patel along with the Maharaja. The State Administration was taken over by the Government of India from 16 October 1948 and administered by a Commissioner (D.V.Rege, ICS) till 1 January 1949 when the State merged with the Province of Orissa[123].

An Assessment of the Prajamandal

Notwithstanding the ultimate success of the Prajamandal of Mayurbhanj in forming a Government to take over power from the Maharaja and the pathetic end result of nonperformance, the whole episode of ten years require an assessment and analysis. The formation of the Mayurbhanj Prajamandal came much later than the Prajamandal elsewhere like Nilgiri, Dhenkanal, Talcher and Athgarh. The political impact of the Congress programme in Mayurbhanj was slow and hesitant on account of the progressive and benevolent monarchy of Mayurbhanj; the prospect of emergence of a leader was quite remote. Sarat Chandra Das had his political training and experience in nationalism in the civil disobedience movement at Balasore. His message for village reconstruction at Ambajoda, a remote village of Mayurbhanj failed to inspire the tribal population whose poor status in literacy and political consciousness was not the congenial ground for the ideas of Sarat Chandra Das to spread. He spoke to a people who were both dumb and deaf. The high principles of freedom, liberty, and equality were meaningless jargons for them.

The Prajamandal of Mayurbhanj considered feudal social structure as the most vulnerable point in State administration and the Sardars, Zamindars with their Pradhans and Piadas symbolized the exploitation method on which the agrarian attack was launched. That was why the Prajamandal drew up a series of agrarian grievances to draw the attention of the people seeking their redressal by the Maharaja. To draw more supporters, the Prajamandal also took up the construction of irrigation projects which would facilitate cultivation. That method succeeded in getting the support of marginal farmers and agricultural labourers. But the support of the non-tribals was not adequate to make the movement result-oriented.

As the agrarian movement was limited in area and, public support, the state administration did not adopt any policy of drastic repression. The attitude of the Maharaja was to a great extent tolerant and progressive. He not only followed a policy of compromise but also strategy to neutralize the Prajamandals through the Prajamangal's counter move. The constitutional reforms which he proposed aimed at taking away the wind from the sail of the Prajamandals. His actions were more of preventive type and neither there was large scale arrest nor police action of Talcher type. His good relationship with Sarat Chandra Das paid dividend by de-escalating a crisis.

As long as the Prajamandal organisation centred round Sarat Chandra Das at Ambajoda there was no punch in the movement. A rural based organisation did not have the capacity to make a dent on the state administration. After its headquarters was shifted to Baripada and when a young, generation consisting of Harihar Mohanty, Purna Chandra Mohanty, Gour Mohan Mohapatra, Anant Rath and Braja Rath added strength to the organization, the effectiveness of the Prajamandal movement was felt by the state administration.

The reasons explained above made the Prajamandal movement of Mayurbhanj less vigorous than Nilgiri, Dhenkanal, Talcher and Athgarh. The leadership of Sarat Chandra Das by concentrating more on socio-agrarian changes undermined the political aims of the Prajamandal. His leadership was neither militant nor assertive. The aggressive nature was exhibited by Baikuntha Nath Sadual's Paik rebellion in 1946. Sarat Chandra Das' vision of a responsible Government was a borrowed idea having no indepth urge. It was mooted in the pattern of national event when the British Government searched for a Responsible Agency to whom power was to be transferred after the Attlee declaration.

Prajamandal Activists

Appendix-I

Sadar sub-Division	Bamanghati Sub-Division
Sarat Chandra Bhanjdeo	Harekrushna Patnaik
Bidyadhar Mohapatra	Sunaram Majhi
Lalmohan Pati	Mahendra Majhi
Trilochan Das	Aswni Kabi
Suresh Chandra Das	Govind Agrawal
Madhusudan Parida	Shyam Charan Majhi
Umakanta Patnaik	Ghasiram Sandil
Ratikanta Patnaik	Jitendra Mohanta
Hariram Mohanty	Jagat Charan Majhi
Purna Chandra Mohanta	Gopinath Naik
Sarat Chandra Das	

Baikuntha Nath Sadual
Gour Mohan Pradhan
Harihar Mohanty
Gour Mohan Mohapatra
Sokila Soren
Jadabananda Murmu
Prasanna Kumar Das
Amarendra Das
Purna Chandra Pani
Laxmidhar Dhal
Dhyan Chandra Tudu
Brajagopal Ghosal
Damodar Mohanty

Panchpir sub-Division

Sirish Chandra Das

Charu Chandra Das Adhikari
Biswanath Sahu
Harihar Mohanta
Maheswar Naik
Karunakar Majhi
Bhaktabandhu Mohanta
Shiba Prasad Mohanta

Kaptipada Sub-Division

Biadhar Majhi
Biadhar
Rasananda Bhol
Giris Chandra Ray
Radhagovind Naik

New Constitution

Appendix-II

The Provisions of the New Constitution were as follows:

1. **Definitions** - In this proclamation unless there is anything in the context to the contrary :

   (a) 'Maharaja' means His Highness the Maharaja of Mayurbhanj, his heirs and successors in the sovereignty of the Mayurbhanj State.

   (b) "Mayurbhanj State' means the territories governed by His Highness Maharaja of Mayurbhanj.

   (c) 'High Court' means the High Court of Judicature established under the provisions of the Mayurbhanj High Court Order, 1938.

2. **His Highness** - The territories vested in His Highness the Maharaja governed by and in the name of His Highness.

3. The revenue of Mayurbhanj State shall be received for and in the name of His Highness Maharaja.

4. **Legislature and Executive** - Without prejudice to the rights, privileges and immunities exercised by His Highness as the Sovereign ruler of Mayurbhanj State, His Highness may entrust administrative functions to a Council of Ministers.

5. The Legislature of Mayurbhanj State shall consist of His Highness the Maharaja and one chamber to be named and styled as the 'Mayurbhanj Vyavashtha Parishad, here-after called the Parishad.

6. The Mayurbhanj Vyavastha Parishad shall consist of 51 representatives of the people of Mayurbhanj at present froming the Mayurbhanj Constituent Assembly with power to co-operate additional members as occasions may arise.

7. The Parishad shall elect a President and a Vice-President from amongst its members.

8. Subject to the provision to this proclamation, His Highness many from time to time -

   (a) Summon the Parishad to meet at such time and place as he thinks fit.

   (b) Prorogue the Parishad.

9. The Parishad may make rules for regulating, subject to the provisions of this proclamation, its procedure and the conduct of its business.

10. The Parishad shall have the power to act notwithstanding any vacancy in the membership thereof, and any proceedings in the Parishad shall be valid notwithstanding that it is discovered subsequently that some person, who was not entitled to do so, sat or voted or otherwise took part in the proceedings.

11. The Parishad shall have full powers to frame laws for the governance of Mayurbhanj State.

12. All laws and resolutions passed by the Parishad shall be submitted to His Highness the Maharaja for his assent subject to the rules made on his behalf.

13. Every member of the Parishad shall before taking his seat make and subscribe on oath before His Highness the Maharaja or the President of the Parishad or any person acting as President, in the form prescribed for the Mayurbhanj Constituent Assembly.

14. The Executive Government of the State shall be carried on by and with the advice of the Council of Ministers.

15. The Ministers shall be chosen from among the members of the Parishad and summoned by His Highness the Maharaja, shall be sworn in as the membei of the Council and shall be removed from

office by His Highness when they resign or when a vote of no confidence is passed against them by the Parishad.

16. The Ministers shall be jointly responsible for all acts of administration to His Highness the Maharaja and the Mayurbhanj Vyavastha Parishad.

17. His Highness the Maharaja in his discretion may preside at meeting of the Council of Ministers.

18. Orders and other instruments made and executed in the name of His Highness the Maharaja or the Government of His Highness the Maharaja of Mayurbhanj shall be authenticated by a Secretary to the Government of His Highness the Maharaja and the validity of such an order or instrument which is so authenticated shall not be called in question on the ground that it is not an order or instrument made or executed by His Highness or the Government.

19. High Court-The High Court shall be Supreme Court for the administration of justice. The Judges of the High Court will be appointed by His Highness the Maharaja in consultation with the Council of Ministers and hold office during his pleasure.

(Extraordinary State Gazette, 10 December 1947).

References

1 Bipan Chandra, *India's Struggle for Independence*, New Delhi 1989, p.357 and Sarkar, Sumit, Modern India, 1885-1947, Orient Longman, 1983, p.341.

2 Sarkar S. Ibid., and Bipan Chandra, op.cit., p.359.

3 Sarkar S. op.cit., p.366.

4 Urmila Phadnis, *Towards the Integration of Indian States*, 1919-1947, APH, 1968, Pp.127-128.

5 Rath, Radhanath, *The Story of Freedom Movement in Orissa State*, Cuttck, 1964, pp.16-17.

Patra, K.M. *Orissa State Legislature and Freedom Struggle*, Delhi, 1979, p.270.

6 De S.C.(ed) *Whos Who of Freedom Movement* in Orissa,Dhenkanal.

7 Nehru Memorial Museum and Library (NMML) AISPC File No.127, pp.365-368.

8 Patnaik, L.M. *Resurrected Orissa*, p.329.

Patra, K.M. op.cit., p.272

Mahatba, H.K., Autobiography,Sadhanar Pathe (Oriya), 1971,pp.184-185.

9 Pradhan, A.C. *A Study of the History of Orissa,* 1988, p.383.

10 Patra, S.C. *Formation of the Province of Orissa,* 1979, pp.230-231. and Also Pradhan, Sadasiba, *Agrarian and Political Movements,* New Delhi, 1986, pp.81-100. alo, p.143.

11 The Samaj, 16 November, 1938.

12 The Statesman, 17 February, 1939.

13 Interview Gour Mohan Pradhan, Senior Advocate and Congress Leader of Mayurbhnaj.

14 Ibid.,

15 Inchudi is a small village in the Coast of Balasore District, a distance of 60 kilometres from Mayurbhanj. The civil disobedience movement under the leadership of H.K.Mahatab had created a sensation in Orissa and elsewhere. Mahatab, H.K., Sadhanar Pathe, 1972, pp.128-129; Mahatab (ed.) *History of Freedom Movement in Orissa,* Vol.III(1955), p.89. Choudhury, *S. Economic History of Colonialism,* 1979, p.194.Mohanta, B. Panchpir *Prajamandal Andalan* (Oriya), 1974, p.4.

16 Mahanta, B. op.cit., p.4.

17 Report on the *Administration of Mayurbhanj,* 1938-39, p.6.

18 Interview Gour Mohan Mohapatra and Braja Sundar Rath

19 The name of the Crown Prince was Pradeep Chandra to the Irrigation dam was named after him.Mohanta, B. op.cit., p.1.

20 Operation to Catch Wild Elephants by trapping them in Trenches.

21 A temporary platform on tree for the hunter's safety

22 Mahanta, B. op.cit., p.2.

23 Ibid.

24 Ibid.

25 Interview Kamini Kanta Patnaik, Younger brother of Sardar Ratikanta Patnaik and an Advocate.

26 Ration/Provisions for grocery and food

27 Hunting

28 An anna was 1/16 of a Rupee which will be equivalent to 6 paise of the present value of exchange.

29 Report of the Enquiry Committee, OrissaStates pp.218-220.

30 Rent free land given to a person for his services.

31 Rath, Radhanath, op.cit., p.24.Mahtab, H.K., Autobiography, op.cit., p.201.Das, Prasanna Kumar, *Mayurbhanj Mukti Samgram ra Samkshipta Itihas* (Oriya) 1997, pp.7-8.

32 See Appendix for biodata

33 See Appendix for biodata

34 AISPC (NMML) File No.128, p.115.
35 Das, Prasanna Kumar, op.cit., p.16
RAM, 1938-39, p.6.
36 Ibid., p.5
Also Orissa History Congress Special Issue on Mayurbhanj, 1982, p.2.
37 Extraordinary State Gazette, 23 November, 1938.
38 The Praja Sabha Order 1938, Clause 3(i) p.2.
39 Ibid., Clause 4, p.2.
40 Ibid., Clause 5, p.3.
41 Ibid., Clause 7, pp.3-4
42 Ibid., Clause 8, p.4.
43 Ibid., Constitution for the Praja Sabhas, pp.5-8.
44 Ibid., Praja Sabha Electoral Rules, 1939, Rule 3, p.9.
45 RAM 1941-42, p.125.
46 Ibid.
47 Mayurbhanj State Gazette, 7 March, 1939
48 Ibid, 22 May 1939 Massage of the Maharaja.
49 RAM, 1941-42, p.124.
50 Ibid., pp.124-128.
51 Mayurbhanj State Gazette, 7 February, 1942.
52 Ibid, 7 May and 7 June, 1942.
53 Ibid., 22 August, 1942.
54 Interview, Prasanna Kumar Das
55 AISPC (NMML) File No.128, p.111.
56 Interview Prasanna Kumar Das
57 B.Mahanta, op.cit., pp.4-5 and Interview Gour Mohan Mahapatra and Prsanna Kumar Das
58 Prasanna Kuamr Das, op.cit., pp.16-17.
59 Ibid.,
60 Souvenir, Orissa History Congress, 1982, p.3.
61 Ibid., and Also Prasanna Kumar Das, op.cit., pp.21-22.
62 Who's who, Mayurbhanj, p.4.
63 Prasanna Kumar Das, op.cit., p.18. Also see his Autobiograpy KarmiraSadhana, 1997, op.cit.
64 Ibid., p.19.
65 Prasanna kumar Das, op.cit., p.28.
66 Interview Gour Mohan Mahapatra, Purna Chandr Bindhani and

Purna Chandra Mohanta.

67 Mohanta B. op.cit., p.12.

68 Confidential letter No.1301, dated 15 October, 1940 from the Superintendent of Education to B.Mahanta, and letter No.1339 dated 3 November, 1940.Also see Panchpir Prajamandal Andlolan (Oriya), p.13, No year, no place of publication.

69 Das, Prasanna Kumar, op.cit., p.28.

70 Hooligans or Bullies or Goons

71 Government Orissa, 1944 (Special Section, Confidential) No.141, O.S. Archives, Account No.2865 (Conf.) p.12.

72 Interview Purna Chandra Mohanta

73 Das, Prasanna Kumar, op.cit., p.32.

74 Ibid., pp.32-33.

75 Ibid.

76 Das, Prasanna Kumar, *Autobiography, Karmir Sadhana*, op.cit., p.15.

77 File No.141, Account 2865 (Conf.), p.12.(OSA)

78 Das, Prasanna Kumar, op.cit., p.41.

79 An embankment or a reservoir.

80 Das, Prasanna Kuamr, op.cit., p.41.

81 Das, Prasanna Kuamr, *Autobiography* (Oriya), p.32.

82 Das, Prasanna Kumar, op.cit., p.43.

83 OSA, File No.141, Account no.2865 (Conf. Op.cit., p.21.

84 Das, Prasanna Kumar, op.cit., pp.43-44.

85 Das, Prasanna Kuamr, *Autobiography* (Oriya), p.35.

86 Majumdar, RC. *Struggle for Freedom*, Vol.XI (1928), pp.624-631.

87 Das, Prasanna Kuamr, *Autobiography* (Oriya), p.28.

88 Das, Prasanna kumar, *Mayurbhanjara* MuktiSangram, op.cit., p.46.

89 Das, Prasanna Kumar, *Autobiography* (Oriya) op.cit., p.30. Das was opposed to the decision.

90 Das, Prasanna Kumar, *Autobiography* (Oriya), p.36 and *Mayurbhanj Mukti Sangramar Itihas*, op.cit., pp.48-52. Also Interview with Kamalakanta Sadual, son of Baikuntha Nath Sadual.

91 Revenue Paying land with permanent Proprietorship through granting of Patta (Deed)

92 Interview with Kamalakanta Sadual

93 Order of Maharaja Pratap Chandra Bhanj Deo dated 5 March 1947 and the Certificate of Superintendent of Baripada Central Jail dated 26 June 1947.

94 *Who's who Mayurbhanj*, op.cit., p.7.

95 Mayurbhanj State Gazettee, 7April, 1947.

96 Das, Prasanna Kumar, *Autobiography*, Oriya, op.cit., pp.37-38.

97 Extraordinary Mayurbhanj State Gazette, 23 April 1945

98 Ibid., Also See RAM 1945-46, Introduction.

99 Ibid.

100 Ibid.

101 Ibid.

102 The elected members were–from BaripadaLalmohan Pati, from Sadar–Umakanta Patnaik, Sarat Chandra Das, and Ratikanta Patnaik, from Bamanghaty,Chaturbhuja Moharana, Jitendra Nath mahanta, and Fagu Charan Majhi, from Panchpir, Biswanath Sahu, Padmalochan Sahoo, and Siba Prasad Mohanty, from Kaptipada–Gangadhar Jena and Giris Chandra Roy the nominated members were–Lal Saheb Sarat Chanddra Bhanj Deo, Rajat Chandra Parakrama, D. Chand (Law Officer Tata Company) Ayodhyanath Mohanta, Major B.P.Pande (Dewan), T.S.Rajgopalan (Secretry), K.R Browankar (Secretary, Law) A.Das (IFS) R.G. Das (Chief Revenue Officer), R.C.Das (Superintendent of Police), S.A.Kikkeri (Chief Engineer), C.M.Sinha (Chief Medical Officer), S.D.Bahuguna (Director, Education), Maheswar Naik (Dirctor,Industries) (Mayurbhanj State Bulletin, 22 July 1945).

103 Mayurbhanj State Bulletin, 22 January, 1946.

104 Mayurbhanj State Bulletin, 22 January, 1946.

105 OSA, file No.141, Acc No.2865 (Conf.), p.1.

106 Ibid, letter dated 28 February 1944.

107 English Translation of a passage of the booklet.

108 Who's who of freedom workers – Mayurbhanj, p.8.

109 Mayurbhanj Information Bulletin, 22 January 1946.

110 NMML, AISPC File No.112, p.1.

111 Interview Durga Charan Mohanty

112 Extraordinary Mayurbhanj Stae Gazette, 14 July 1947

113 Interview Prafulla Kumar Choudhary, Student leader who led the procession of students.

114 Patra, K.M., op.cit., p.283, Pradhan, S. Agrarian and Political Movement (1986), pp.101-03.

115 Mayurbhanj State Gazette, 7 October 1947.

116 Extraordinary Mayurbhanj State Gazette, 10 December 1947.

117 Both the letters were published in the State Gazette dated 22 January 1948.

118 The members of the constituent Assembly or Vyavastha Parishad were at Appendix - I to this Chapter.

119 Das, Prasanna Kumar, *Mayurbhanj Mukti Sangram*, p.56.

120 Who's who – Mayurbhanj, p.10.

121 Das, Prasanna Kumar *Autobiography*, Oriya, pp.48-49.

122 For details see Infra Chapter-IV.

123 For details see Infra Chapter-V.

4

Prajamandal in Power:
Its Failure and Merger with Orissa

The Feudatory of State of Mayurbhanj was unlike other Feudatory States of Orissa. In many ways it was different. Since the time of Sreeram Chandra Bhanj Deo there was an effort to train the people in the art of self Government. That the rulers believed in devolution of power was evident on 1 August 1892 when the Mayurbhanj State Council order was promulgated exhibiting a new facet of kingship. In 1905, the establishment of Baripada Municipality further widened the process of democratic experiment. Though the measures fell far short of universal adult franchise, elected legislature and responsible Government of today, a modest beginning had been made to experiment with democracy under the benevolent Chief. Mayurbhanj being a tribal populated state with rampant illiteracy and wide spread poverty, relatively it was much better than other states in administration. The Maharaja experimented with the State Council with two non official members having power over Legislation, annual budget, and taxation. He followed the pattern introduced by the Indian Council Act of 1892, but did not live long enough to continue with his experiments further as he died in an accident in 1912[1].

On account of the minority of the heir apparent Purna Chandra Bhanjadeo the State came under the administration of Court of Wards till 1920. Purna Chandra's rule was too short as he also died accidentally in 1928 and then the State was ruled by the younger son of Maharaja Sreeram Chandra Bhanjdeo who enjoyed a long and eventful reign from 1928 to 1947. He had facilitated the growth of democratic experiment expressed through the Praja Sabha order of 1938[2] and formation of the Kendra Parishad in 1945[3]. Though the weightage then given to the nominated members was more than the elected members, the fact that the rulers were not despotic or autocratic can not be denied. That way Mayurbhanj benefited by the liberal attitude of the enlightened rulers notwithstanding the limitations.

Transfer of Power

Though the working of the Kendra Parishad was above criticism the people's expectations were not fulfilled. After the formation of an Interim Government in New Delhi, the Prajamandal aspiring for similar political change in Mayurbhanj to take over the administrative powers of the Chief demanded in the Kendra Parishad in a resolution passed on 11 October 1947, that

This Kendra Parishad recommends to the Government of the Maharaja of Mayurbhanj to set up at an early date a Constituent Assembly of 51 chosen representatives of the people of Mayurbhanj here in below named with power to co-opt, for the purpose of framing a Constitution for the establishment of a responsible Government in this state.

The list contained 24 members from Sadar Subdivision, 10 from Bamanghaty, 8 from Panchpir and 9 from Kaptipada subdivision. Most of the empanelled persons were avowed supporters of the Chief. The Resolution further stated that the following powers will be reserved for the Ruler; viz.

(i) Succession to the throne; Rulers prerogative, his civil list, his staff and other expenses, educational allowance of the Heir

Apparent, Personal allowances of the members of the Raj family;

(ii) Summoning and dissolving of Legislature,

(iii) Control of expenditure from the Reserve Fund

(iv) Residuary Powers and emergency power in case of breakdown of the Constitution[4].

The response of the Maharaja for the above Resolution was in the affirmative. He replied to the Kendra Parishad saying;[5]

> "I greatly appreciate the desire of my people as expressed in the Resolution adopted by the Mayurbhanj Kendra Parishad on 11 October 1947 to take the initiative in framing a constitution for the establishment of responsible Government in the State. I heartily welcome the spirit underlying the Resolution and I hereby direct that a Constituent Assembly in the manner recommended by the Mayurbhanj Kendra Parishad be constituted."

Thus, the Constituent Assembly was set up to draft and approve a democratic constitution, which would prepare a responsible Government to be established in the State. The prompt response of the Maharaja was evident enough that he was not averse to any proposal for the Constitutional development of Mayurbhanj in a democratic manner.

The inaugural session of the Constituent Assembly was summoned to meet on 10 November 1947 in the Kendra Parishad Hall which is now known as the Council Hall. Sarat Chandra Bhanjdeo[6], the cousin of the Maharaja was to act as the President of the Assembly till its own President was elected. As the Maharaja was to remain away from the capital, he appointed a Committee of three to help the Assembly during his absence[7].

On 8 December 1947 the second session of the Constituent Assembly was held under the Presidentship of its permanent President, Bidyadhar Mohapatra. In this session a very important Resolution was moved by Sarat Chandra Das, the Prajamandal Supremo of Mayurbhanj[8].

(i) The Assembly should elect one member from among them whom the Maharaja should accept as Prime Minister and invite him to form an Interim Government.

(ii) The Kendra Parishad should be dissolved and till the formation of a new Legislative Assembly, this Constituent Assembly should perform the function of the Legislature and it be declared that the Ministry so formed shall be responsible to the Legislature.

The Resolution was passed after discussion and Sarat Chandra Das was elected unanimously as the Premier. He had no contestant[9]. The Resolution was accepted by the Maharaja and a Proclamation for the formation of Interim Government was issued. The Interim Government would function till the new Constitution would come in to force. The proclamation further added that the Interim Government would be set up immediately. A Council of Ministers responsible to the Legislature was set up. The Legislature to be known as Mayurbhanj Vyavastha Parishad would have 51 members. They were the same as members of the Constituent Assembly[10]. The Legislature with the Maharaja's assent would make laws for the State. It was endowed with full Legislative powers. The members of the Council of Ministers would be chosen from among the members. The Council of Ministers would be responsible for all acts of the administration to the Maharaja and the Vyavastha Parishad.

The High Court was to act as the Highest Court for the administration of justice and the Judges were to be appointed by the Maharaja in Consultation with the Council of Ministers[11]. With these implementation, the Mayurbhanj Kendra Parishad Order 1945 was cancelled.

As per the provisions of the Interim Constitution, declared on 9 December 1947, the names of the Ministers were announced on 10 December. The list of names included

Bidyadhar Mohapatra

Maheswar Naik

Sarat Chandra Das appointed the Premier, and two Ministers were Bidyadhar Mohapatra and Maheswar Naik[12]. Same day the Maharaja handed over power to the Ministry of Das. The Maharaja retained the following powers himself:

(i) To nominate the Ministers

(ii) To summon and prorogue the Vyavastha Parishad and to give his assent to laws passed by it

(iii) To administer oath of office to the Minister of the Council and members of the Vyavastha Parishad,

(iv) To preside at his discretion, in the meetings of the Council of Ministers,

(v) To appoint Judges of the High Court in Consultation with the Council of Ministers[13].

The Maharaja also distributed portfolios among the Ministers with real executive power vested on the Premier, the powers and functions of the Maharaja were considerably reduced. He retained only nominal powers, identical to those of a Governor under the present day Indian constitution.

The life of the Interim Government lasted only eleven months and before the new Constitution could operate, Mayurbhanj merged with the Indian Union in November 1948. So what would have been the attitude of the Maharaja vis-à-vis the responsible Government of the Prajamandal could not be tested. But during the eleven months of its existence there was no occasion of Constitutional crisis or deadlock as the Maharaja all throughout remained away in Calcutta and did not either evince any interest in the administration or interfered with the Prajamandal Government's day to day affairs. His role was that of a passive observer.

After the formalities of Transfer of Power were completed, the Prajamandal Ministry extended its humble gratitude to the Maharaja for his great sacrifice and service to the people. On 10 December 1947 the State declared a Public holiday of celebration by observing public meetings and speeches befitting the occasion. Maheswar Naik, the Minister stated that it was a Red letter day when the Sovereign Power could come to the people without bloodshed or revolution[14]. Mayurbhanj was clearly different from Talcher or Dhenkanal where hundreds of people were mercilessly shot dead by the State Police. That difference was enough for the expression of gratitude by the government of Prajamandal. The Transfer of Power was completed just in two days. The process of forming the Constituent Assembly, Interim Government and relinquishment of Sovereign Power took only forty-eight hours.

The Council of Ministers was sworn in on 10 December 1947 and the Maharaja ceased to rule. Events moved at an unbelievable speed that the observers remained stunned. It is believed that the man who advised the Maharaja during the above period was Khitis Chandra Neogi who was a Cabinet Minister in the Nehru Government. Neogi had deep personal knowledge about Mayurbhanj as he had served the

Maharaja as his Dewan and subsequently the Chief Justice during 1935-40. Both were very good friends[15].

Neogi had knowledge about the policy of the Government of India which included the integration of States with the Indian Union. The State Ministry under Sardar Patel was then contemplating about the merger of Orissa Feudatory States with the Province of Orissa. Before the liquidation of the States under Patel's drastic policy, the Maharaja might have thought of retaining the good will of his people by transferring power to the Prajamandal. It is further believed that all documents of Transfer of Power in Mayurbhanj were prepared by Neogi. The long absence of the Maharaja at Baripada during this period preceding the Transfer of Power authenticates the speculation[16].

However, the political changes coupled with the analogous Constitutional changes brought an end to one thousand years of Bhanja rule. It may be unfair to suggest that the Maharaja's haste in transferring power to the Prajamandal was a strategic move to preempt Patel's strong arm tactics to force the Rajas of Feudatory States of Orissa to sign the Instrument of Merger. Because, as early as 1947 the Maharaja in his letter to the Nawab of Bhopal had given vent to his idea saying that the liquidation of the Princely States was the only solution to India's problems. He was advocating voluntary abdication. After the Transfer of Power his attitude of aloofness from the state of affairs was tantamount to abdication. His idea to keep Mayurbhanj as an independent unit was never indicated even when the Maharajas of Balangir and Kalahandi wanted him to join the Eastern States Union. But, the State could escape the scalpel of Sardar Patel for almost a year because; the Maharaja having transferred power to the Popular Government on 9 December 1947 could not sign the Document of merger on 14 December at Cuttack when all other Oriya Chiefs yielded to the pressure of the States Ministry[17].

Prelude to Merger

The Princely States were a bulwark of British Imperialism. Integration of these states with independent India was a significant event in the post 1947 period and the main architect of this process was Sardar Patel. As long as the British Empire lasted, the Feudatory Chiefs did not care to ensure the welfare of their people and any popular uprising could be crushed with the help of the British Government. In most of the States the people were groaning under autocracy. This climate facilitated the growth of popular movements and the birth of the Prajamandal was the direct outcome of feudal autocracy. Therefore, when the National Congress waged a long struggle to end the British rule for India's liberalism, the Prajamandal started a relentless movement to end the princely order. The Indian Independence Act of 1947 released the states from all their obligations to the empire and a political vacuum of several independent units was created between the Union Government and the Feudatory States[18].

In 1935 the first step taken to define and setup the Constitutional relationship between the Indian States and British India by proposing the federal scheme[19]. The accession of the States to the Federation was to be effected by the Instrument of Accession. Of course the accession of the states was voluntary, but the accession of the provinces was compulsory[20].

The Orissa States being 26 in number covered a huge area having abundant natural resources making it politically and culturally imperative for their integration with Orissa Province to ensure a holistic economic development of the Oriya speaking people. But its accomplishment was easier said than done. On 27 June 1947 Lord Mountbatten closed down the Political Department which was dealing with the Indian States and created the States Department headed by Sardar Patel with VP Menon as his Secretary[21]. On 5 July

1947 Sardar Patel issued a statement saying that apart from Defence, External Affairs, and Communications, the States would have an autonomous existence in the new union. The future relationship would be governed by an Instrument of Accession details of which would be prepared in the line of 1935 Act[22]. Accordingly, on 25 July 1947 Lord Mountbatten called a special meeting of the Chamber of Princes and advised the rulers to accede to the Indian Union on matters relating to Defence, External Affairs and Communications and assured them they would have no financial liability and there would be no encroachment on their internal sovereignty[23]. The States Department then began negotiation with all states to accede to the Dominion of India on three subjects – Defence, External Affairs and Communication as defined in the Government of India Act 1935[24]. By conceding the three subjects, the Princes virtually accepted the substitution of British Government by the Indian Government. India had become one Federation with the Provinces and the States as integral parts. This prompted Lord Mountbatten to declare in the Constituent Assembly on 15 August 1947[25].

'With the accession of the states a unified political structure was established in India.'

The process then just began for the gradual integration of hundreds of states including twenty-six of Orissa. With the advent of independence the popular upsurge in the states for attaining the same measure of freedom as was enjoyed by the people in the provinces gained momentum and unleashed strong forces for the transfer of power from the Rulers to the People. The movement became severe and violent in Nilgiri, Talcher and Dhenkanal. Though in Mayurbhanj there was peaceful Transfer of Power from the Ruler to the People, the story had not come to an end.

As early as 1930, the Sub-committee headed by C R Attlee appointed by Simon Commission to consider the problems of the Oriya speaking people had expressed the view that[26],

> "The Orissa Feudatory States, which are not part of British India should be brought in to relationship with any administration set up in Orissa."

In the second session of All Orissa States People Conference an Enquiry Committee had been set up to go in to the details of the problem of the people and the Committee Report on 18July 1939 revealed about the prevalence of feudal practices like *Bethi*, *Beggari*, *Magan* and *Rasad* etc. and unanimously recommended the granting of the right of self Government and self determination for the states' people. The Report said,[27]

> "The acceptance of the recommendation will bring these states under the jurisdiction of autonomous provinces and the people concerned will be enabled to join hands with their brethren in the Province of Orissa in their attempt to solve the problems common to them all."

The Cabinet Mission visited India after 19 February 1946 to facilitate smooth transfer of Power[28]. It was appointed by the Labour Government of CR Attlee. Harekrushna Mahtab, the Prospective Premier of Orissa Province and a stalwart of the Congress Party met the members of the Cabinet Mission on 6 April 1946 in Delhi to plead for the amalgamation of the Feudatory States with Orissa on geographical, political, economic, historical and linguistic grounds. He explained how the same river systems serve both; same literature encourages them awakening common ideals and aspirations. He left no stones unturned to convince the Mission for amalgamating the states with the Province. The Mission, however, left it to the negotiation between the states and British India or its successor Government[29].

Mahtab became the Premier of Orissa on 23 April 1946. Soon thereafter, he accelerated the process of integration of the states with the Province. He appealed to the Chiefs to cooperate and agree for amalgamation. As independence approached the aspirations of the states people and the apprehensions of the Chiefs began to grow. The rulers of the states having formed the Orissa and Chhatisgarh States Union in July 1946[30] were trying hard to consolidate the Union to maintain the status quo while the people were pressing their respective rulers to agree for representative and responsible Governments. The Governor of Orissa in his letter to Prime Minister Nehru informed[31],

> "Everyday Orissa Press carries stories of repression in one or other of the petty states. The Federation (Eastern States Union of the rulers of Orissa and Chhatisgarh) has employed a Police force of 700 recruited from Pakistani Muslims and others and so on. The Prajamandals in some states are carrying on vigorous propaganda and we get the familiar account of Lathi charge, arrests and detentions without trial. I think these states should be definitely told that they can not be permitted to swagger about with notions of independent Kingship and sovereignty. Many of them are not even as big as the Zamindaries of United Provinces. The Orissa Press, Dailies, Weeklies, Conveying the mass opinion strongly advocate the establishment of genuine Governments in the states. Having regard to the slender resources of the Province and of these states acting in isolation, it is imperative in the interest of further development that there should be the closest cooperation between them."

But the Premier and his Congress party colleagues held different views. They advocated amalgamation as the states were small in size and had limited resources. They would not be able to sustain independent Government[32]. Though Mahtab met the rulers at Sambalpur on 16 October 1946, his persuasion failed to bring an understanding. The rulers remained rigid and stubborn to remain independent. They met at Raipur on 21-22 December 1946 to Chalkout their future course of action. The Conference was attended by 23 rulers and the Resident of Eastern States Agency and the Political

Agents of Orissa and Chhatisgarh states. The Eastern States Union started functioning from 1 August 1947[33] with an elaborate Constitution and funded by the Constituent States. The Union maintained an Eastern States Joint Police Force.

The Post-Independence period witnessed two processes going on simultaneously – the process of integration by the Congress Government of Orissa province led by Mahtab and the frantic efforts of some rulers to remain out of the Province as a separate entity. The second effort was one of Balkanisation and its leaders were the Chiefs of Balangir, Kalahandi and Sareikela.

However, the strong action of Sardar Patel did not allow the cessationist move of the Rulers to succeed. The States ministry was determined to impede the move of Balkanisation. Mahtab had submitted a memorandum to Sardar Patel mentioning the difficulties created by the Orissa States. He highlighted the problem of law and order, smuggling across the borders, food supply, communication and the river valley projects[34]. At this juncture the Prajamandal agitation in Nilgiri took a violent turn in October – November 1947. It turned out to be a bloody conflict between the tribals and the non-tribals. To ward off the crisis escalating in to mass massacre, the States Ministry authorized the Government of Orissa by telegram dated 8 November 1947 to depute the Collector of Balasore with adequate armed forces to take over the administration of Nilgiri. On 14 November, the District Magistrate of Balasore authorized by the Government of Orissa took over the state administration. The Raja voluntarily handed over the administration without any protest[35].

Sardar Patel in Orissa

To discuss the memorandum of Mahtab to Sardar Patel a meeting was arranged by V P Menon on 20 November 1947 at New Delhi to discuss the issue of merger of Orissa States with the province. The meeting was attended by Col B D S

Bedi, the Regional Commissioner at Sambalpur. At the meeting three conclusions were drawn;

(i) the Eastern States Union should not be recognized by the Government of India;

(ii) the 'B' and 'C' class states should be asked to agree to common administration of certain subjects and

(iii) a meeting should be called by the States Ministry of 'B' and 'C' class states at Cuttack in December. The discussion was briefly intimated to Sardar Patel next day[36].

V P Menon convinced Sardar Patel that under the circumstance of increasing lawlessness in the states and the non coperative attitude of some Rulers, there were two options open:

(i) either to bring about a sort of administrative cooperation between the Province and the states or

(ii) to merge the Orissa States with Orissa province and the Chhatisgarh group of states with Chhatisgarh[37].

Sardar Patel decided to go all out to secure the merger of all three classes of Orissa States with the Province of Orissa and told Menon to invite all the Rulers of Orissa States to Cuttack for discussion in the second week of December. Accordingly, 13 December 1947 was fixed as the date of visit and meeting. On arrival Sardar Patel witnessed a huge demonstration from Bhubaneswar Airport to Cuttack demanding the merger of the states[38]. Patel first met the Ministers and the Governor. VP Menon prepared a memorandum on the merger of all states for circulation among Rulers next day[39].

Mayurbhanj and Merger

The Maharaja of Mayurbhanj was under no illusion about the future status of the Ruling Princes in independent India. He had a realistic approach to the issue. In a letter to the Raja of Dungarpur (Madhya Pradesh) he had raised some pertinent points regarding their sensitive positions. To him, the rulers had no authority, and they were anachronisms and feudalistic relics. In his letter to the Nawab of Bhopal he wrote on 19 September 1947[40],

"One result of the British policy towards Indian States whether deliberately intended or not, has been to undermine the authority of the Rulers over the people. Our people have thus been alienated from us. British India again, while befriending the cause of our people has painted us as mischievous relics of an archaic system which is propped up by the British authorities merely for their own purpose."

Since the Maharaja was painfully aware of his own delicate predicament he did not wish to alienate his people and transferred power to the popular Government on 10 December 1947[41].

The Conference at Cuttack convened by the State Ministry with the Rulers of Orissa began at 10 AM on 14 December 1947 in which Mahtab, Sardar Patel, KVK Sundaram ICS, V Shankar ICS, the Revenue Commissioner, the Chief Secretary of Orissa and VP Menon were present. At first the meeting at 10 AM was for the 'B' and 'C' class states. The 'A' class states met at 2 PM. In both meetings the Sardar made an identical speech persuading them to join Orissa Province. He emphatically said[42],

> "The safety of the Rulers as well as the people was in danger in Orissa and he had come to Cuttack to render friendly advice to the rulers."

He suggested that the Rulers should unhesitatingly merge with Orissa. When he sought their views, the Maharaja of Patna, an avowed champion of the Eastern States Union raised several issues and each issue was tackled by the Sardar and his staff. All the 'A' class states except Mayurbhanj were involved in talks with Patel. Sardar Patel was extremely persuasive and told them that he had come to Cuttack not as a representative of the British Paramountcy or any foreign power, but as a member of the family trying to solve a family problem. He told them that the growing discontent of the people of their states would not allow them to continue in power for long and if they did not listen to his advice then the Rulers may find themselves in a position in which no help could be given. During their first meeting the Rulers were unwilling to merge, and the Sardar was very much disappointed with their attitude. The Government of India did not want to adopt coercive measure, they wanted peace. Patel also agreed that the need of the hour was peace, merger could wait, but peace could not be sacrificed. If any body wanted to keep out of the merger agreement them it was the Ruler's choice. He had not come with an aim to chastise. All 'A' 'B' and 'C' class signed the merger document one after the other[43]. On the next day the Maharaja of Mayurbhanj was invited to a lunch where both Patel and Menon were present. When Patel asked for his views, the Maharaja replied[44],

> "I have no right to say anything about my state. I have given my state to the people. If any body has any right to say anything in this mater it is the people of Mayurbhanj. A popular Ministry has been formed in my state whose Premier is present at Cuttack and if you want to ask anything, you may ask him."

Sardar replied that let the administration of Mayurbhanj be carried by the Ministry as at present. In case of necessity of law and order, Mayurbhanj would get military assistance from the Government of India, the Sardar assured. Though Patel appreciated the position of the Maharaja he frankly uttered note of warning to the effect that the position of Mayurbhanj would take such a bad step in future that the Maharaja would have to regret for staying away from the merger scheme. Patel had high respect for the Maharaja whom he considered to be "an intelligent and clever person"[45]. In fact the Maharaja had probably no prejudice or ill feeling against the responsible Government of Das as was quite evident from his reluctance to sign the merger document without the Premier. Thus, while all the Feudatory States of Orissa merged with the province with effect from 1 January 1948 See Appendix-I Mayurbhanj alone remained outside. The Maharaja with the Premier returned home to enjoy the consequences of remaining independent.

Das' Ministry at work

Since the Popular Ministry of Mayurbhanj headed by Sarat Chandra Das had its roots in the peasant's grievances, it had to take up agrarian legislation on priority basis and the first work was the conversion of Paikali jagir (rent free land given to the Paiks on hereditary basis) to hasilat (permanent ownership) to give the aggrieved Paiks the full proprietorship over the land. The Paiks had existed for centuries though their burden in the recent years had become lighter. The state had the right to resume the land for non-performance of service or non-availability of an heir to inherit the service and land.

The Prajamandal movement had included many Paiks in its vanguard and the institution of the Paik had been politicized. The movement initiated by Baikuntha Nath Sadual under the banner of the Prajamandal had not achieved success because in the time of Maharaj Pratap chandra the demand to convert Paikali Jagir to hasilat was not conceded[46].

Sarat Chandra Das was sympathetic to the cause of the Paiks as he was well supported by the Paik members of the Prajamandal. By a notification dated 9 January 1948 the state abolished the Paik force with immediate effect. But it also ordered that the Paik jagirs would be settled with them as hasilat free of salami, but assessed to full standard rent as per the prevailing rates. The rent shall be payable from 1 April 1947. The notification benefited about 300 Paik families who got the right to full ownership with right to sell, mortgage or transfer at their will. The state derived a revenue receipt of about Rs.30,000/- per year[47].

Another significant work of the Prajamandal Government was the abolition of the much hated Sardari system. For revenue collection Mayurbhanj was divided in to subdivisions and each Sub-division in to several Parganas. For each Pir there was a Sardar to collect land revenue through Pradhans. Each Pargana had several Pir & each Pir had several Villages. The amount of tax one had to pay was mentioned in the Patta and it was collected in cash. The peasant was to get a Money Receipt for the payment he made to the Pradhan. It was then deposited with the Sardar who deposited the same in the State Treasury. The Sardars were mostly outsiders and Karan by caste they had some knowledge on accounting and documentation. They were literate and intelligent[48].

The Sardar system was loathsome to the common men for the atrocious manner they adopted in revenue collection. Not only they were rigid during revenue collection, they also exploited the peasantry for bethi, magan and rasad etc. They represented the obnoxious feudal practices, a standing grievance of the people. The Sardars were painted as Devils by the Prajamandal Party[49]. A legislation dated 20 march 1948 abolished the Sardar system with effect from 1 June 1948. This naturally aggrieved the Sardars who lost their long enjoyed privileges. Naturally they were opposed to the Prajamandal Ministry of Das and to counter the growing influence of the Prajamandal demanded merger with Orissa Province. The abolition of Sardari system did not carry any compensation of any kind. They had no other go but to join politics and spread canard against the Ministry. They were welcomed by the Prajamangal Party which subsequently merged with the Congress organisation[50].

The progressive nature of Das' Government was evident in some welfare works it undertook. It helped the poor people by distributing kerosene, cloth and sugar etc. Essential commodities were controlled by the Civil Supply Department and distributed in fair price shops. But when the supply position improved the restriction on distribution were withdrawn from 22 December 1947[51].

The Makar Sankranti being a great annual festival of the Adivasis, the Government distributed clothes liberally to all classes of the poor people. At several distribution centres the Ministers were personally present to endear themselves to the people. Those who could afford to purchase got the material at a reasonable rate. As many as 1, 67, 584 peices of Dhoti and Sari were sold to such people[52].

To please the Government employees the rate of Dearness Allowance in the range of salaried persons receiving a salary of Rupees Three to one hundred was raised with effect from 1 January 1948. This benefited all those who were getting salary of above Rupees 39 per month. An additional relief in the form of one month's pay was also given to those receiving a salary of Rupees 7 to Rupees 19 and half a month's pay to those receiving salary of Rs. 20/- to one hundred per month. These were populist measures.

There was a long standing demand of the people to have a College at Baripada. This was fulfilled by establishing the Maharaja Purna Chandra College with Arts and Science. The Dowager Queen of Maharaja Purna Chandra donated adequate land for the college at Takatpur. Initially, the High school building at Baripada was used to hold College Classes. The first Principal was Sardar Gurdial Singh, a highly learned man of Punjab. The Hostel of the College was started in a rented building at the Station Bazaar with 46 rooms[53].

Simultaneously, the Maharani Premkumari Girls School at Baripada was upgraded from ME standard to High School. This gave an opportunity for aspiring girl students to go far secondary education[54].

Sometime ago the Prajamandal activists had started building the Silaghati reservoir in Kaptipada Sub-division. The first batch of volunteers was led by Sarat Chandra Das and

Prasanna Kumar Das in 1942. But it could not make much progress due to many untoward impediments. While in power, the Prajamandal naturally wanted to complete the unfinished project. Its construction was completed by 26 January 1948. In this construction works the sons of the Maharaja took active part as labourers[55]. This gesture of the ruling family was highly appreciated by Sarat Chandra who expressed his gratitude to the Maharaja and promised more such irrigation projects in the State.

Another populist measure of Sarat Chandra was his visit to Baripada Hat on 25 December 1947 along with the Civil Supplies Officer to check the weights and measures and to hear the problems of the traders. The Civil Supplies Officer was asked to ensure that cloth was sold as per the printed price and to take strong action in case of fraud. Das personally verified the stock and Account Books of the cloth merchants to find out if black market practice had prevailed[56].

The Government notified the establishment of a Maternity Training Center for giving opportunity to girls to get employment. The state banned some political parties like the Rastriya Swayam Sevak Sangha, Muslim National Guard and Khaksar Party[57].

The Popular Government tried to improve the Local self Government by bringing changes in the Baripada Municipality. The prevalent practice of electing the Ward Commissioners and nominating the Chairman was modified. According to the new system the chairman was also to be elected. This amendment was brought about by the Mayurbhanj Vyavastha Parishad Bill no. 4 of 1948 which provided that in the meeting of the Commissioners of the Municipality one of the members would be elected as Chairman[58].

As growth of Primary and Secondary Education was a great concern, the State Government decided to take over many aided Schools. In the Schools of Simlipal Hilly area the teachers were granted a special allowance called Area Allowance. The Budget made an allocation of Rupees 6500/ - for the Night Schools. If any Middle English School was started by Private Agency, the State committed to give financial aid[59].

The assassination of Mahatma Gandhi on 30 January 1948 was a tremendous shock to the people. At it's meeting on 16 February 1948 the Constituent Assembly passed a condolence resolution on the sad demise of the Mahatma.

This time there was a growing pressure for the merger of Mayurbhanj with Orissa. The Socialist lobby under Surendra Nath Dwibedy was working assiduously for that. Under the persuasion of Dwibedy, Girish Chandra Ray, an avowed champion of the Prajamandal and member of the Vyavastha Parishad resigned from the membership. The vacancy created by his resignation was filled up by Rajat Chandra Parakrama Bahu Mandhata, the Sarbarkar of Kaptipada. He was elected uncontested[60].

On 18 February 1948 the Assembly adopted a very significant resolution along with the amendment proposed by Sunaram Majhi, a prominent tribal leader of Bamanghaty Sub-division. The resolution read[61],

> "The Mayurbhanj Constituent Assembly formally declares that Mayurbhanj is an independent State with in the Indian Union and is now going to draft a Constitution for the administration of the State and also for the establishment of full responsible Government under the aegis of the Ruler".
>
> "Whereas certain powers have been conferred, and some duties have been imposed by the Indian Union, and excluding those powers and duties, the State Government of Mayurbhanj can use all other powers and do all other things".
>
> "Whereas all powers and authority shall be vested in the people and they shall be entitled to get social, economic and political justice, equality, before the law and shall enjoy the

> right to freedom of expression, freedom of religion, and the right to carry on any trade or business, and right to form association and unions and whereas the rights of the minority and the undeveloped sections of the society will be reserved and protected" and
>
> "Whereas Mayurbhanj will be able to maintain its independence and sovereignty and shall work independently within the Indian Union and shall achieve its rightful place within the Indian Union."

The above Resolution resembles the Preamble of the Indian Constitution and contains some noble ideas and sentiments of the people of Mayurbhanj. The Drafting Committee of the Constitution consisted of three Ministers and (i) Braja Gopal Ghosal, (ii) Harihar Mohanty and (iii) Prasanna Kumar Das, (iv) Sakila Soren, (v) Dhyan Chand Tudu, (vi) Gourmohan Pradhan, and few others as members[62].

Another achievement of the Popular Government was the Mayurbhanj Temple Entry and Worship Act of 1948 which provided that all public temples of Mayurbhanj shall be open for worship to all classes of the Hindu community including those sections who were hitherto debarred from such entry and worship. Any violation of the provision of the Act became punishable offence, punishable with a fine up to Rs 200. The fine would increase @ Rs. 20 per day if the offender consistently commits the violation[63]. Untouchability also became a punishable offence in the state. These steps were taken because Sarat Chandra Das was a true disciple of Mahatma Gandhi and his ideals.

The last notable achievement of the Vyavastha Parishad was the establishment of Village Panchayats. Each villager got an opportunity to serve his village[64]. It was decided on 2 April 1948 that the Maharaja would be entitled to a Privy Purse of Rs. 3,82,380 per annum. The amount was fixed as per the instruction of the Government of India. Though some members proposed a larger amount, the Maharaja declined to accept that[65].

Hostile Campaign against the Ministry

During the brief period it held office, the Prajamandal Government of Sarat Chandra Das despite its total inexperience in the art of Government made sincere effort to meet some of the aims and aspirations of the people. The Premier was a simple and honest man imbued with the Gandhian ideology of village economy and cottage industries. His colleagues were equally an inspired lot who worked as honestly as their leader. Their aim was to have social equality, political freedom and economic progress. But they had great impediments to overcome. The formation of a popular non-congress Government in a State of Orissa was irksome to the Congress leaders of the Province. Soon a hostile and malicious propaganda started through the Oriya Press to sabotage the stability of the Prajamandal Government. They even had their Agents and supporters who as Pro-merger group caused enough irritation for the Das Ministry. Inside as well as outside Mayurbhanj pressure against independent existence of the state mounted day after day assuming a dangerous magnitude.

The Socialist Party under the leadership of Surendra Nath Dwivedy assiduously tried to create a public opinion and political forum pleading for merger. He wrote regularly in the Samaj for merger and asked embarrassing question like "what is the desire of the People of Mayurbhanj". He did not hesitate to lodge false allegations against the Maharaja and the Ministers. To him the Popular Government of Mayurbhanj appeared to be autocratic and the Maharaja's Transfer of Power was a camouflage of political strategy to remain independent. Though the allegations were refuted by counter and rejoinder, the situation appeared to be utterly misleading and confusing[66].

While serious Press campaign was going on centring round the political status of Mayurbhanj, Mahtab wrote a strong letter to Dr. Rajendra Prasad, the Congress President disapproving his congratulatory letter to Sarat Chandra Das.

Even Pandit Nehru had congratulated Sarat Chandra Das when the Prajamandal formed a Popular Government in Mayurbhanj. Pandit Nehru's letter sent by his Chief Private Secretary HV Iyangar dated 7 January 1948 said[67],

> "I am happy to learn that His Highness the Maharaja of Mayurbhanj had agreed to vest all powers in the hands of a Ministry which is headed by the President of the Prajamandal as the Prime Minister. I hope this new administrative arrangement will be fully fruitful and bring peace and prosperity to the people."

A similar letter dated 31 December 1947 had been sent by Dr. Rajendra Prasad to Das. It read[68],

> "I am happy to learn that an Interim responsible Government has been established with full powers in the State and a Constitution is being prepared which will come in to force by April 1948. I thank you and the Ruler of the state for the wise step and it is my hope that your state will fully play its role in the new Constitutional set up that we are going to establish."

The above two letters annoyed Mahtab who felt that the two central leaders were blessing the independent status of Mayurbhanj which would impede his move to amalgamate the Feudatory State with Orissa. He could not tolerate a Prajamandal Government functioning close to his Province. To him the Prajamandal leaders appeared as puppets in the political game plan of the Maharaja. Expressing these, he wrote to the Congress President Dr. Prasad[69],

> "Now after 15 August when this question (merger) was taken up by the Dominion Government and when it was fairly clear that the states should be called upon to merge in the Province, some of the rulers very cleverly set up some popular leaders or purchased some of them to oppose amalgamation of the states with the Province. For this purpose nominal responsible Government was given. In this, all have failed expect Mayurbhanj. This type leader of the Prajamandal, Sri Sarat Das, has been appointed as the Prime

> Minister by the Ruler and nominal responsible Government has been granted but feeling in Mayurbhanj is very much against him. But you will please excuse me if I say that in this circumstance it is not fair either to the people or to us, that, you as the Congress President, should write to Sri Sarat Chandra Das, Premier of Mayurbhanj congratulating him on his manoeuvre and on the manoeuve of the ruler."

Dr. Rajendra Prasad apologized for having written to Das as he was not aware of the consequences or fallout of his letter[70]. He wrote,

> "I have not been associated with the Prajamandal works anywhere and I had no means of knowing that anything injurious is going on in that state by the body under that name."

The above correspondence show the attitude of Mahtab and the Congress Party in Orissa who considered the experiment in Mayurbhanj was a fake one, not having people's support. His attempt to defame the Ministry of Das and the action of the Maharaja was a calculated move to force Mayurbhanj to merge with Orissa by denying it any moral or material support from any quarter. Subsequent events proved this. He made use of the Socialist leaders like Surendra Nath Dwivedy, Rabi Ray and Gour Das to lobby[71] for the merger of Mayurbhanj. But their persuasion to Das failed to yield favourable results.

A group of Socialist leaders from Cuttack visited Mayurbhanj from 23 to 26 January 1948 with the purpose of motivating the leaders and the people to merge with Orissa. The group consisted of SN Dwibedy, Goura Das, Baikuntha Mohanty, and Nilakantha Sahu. There was apprehension that more people would come to Mayurbhanj sponsored by the Congress Party. To prevent such entry which might lead to internal law and order problem, the Government sealed all the entry points besides requesting the Mahtab Government to dissuade Dwibedy from doing so[72]. There was rumour that the unwanted people would come with arms for a forceful merger. Mahtab did not respond to the request. True to the rumour, Dwibedy with some of his friends stealthily entered Kaptipada through Nilgiri and tried to hold public meetings. But they were greeted with hostile demonstration of the local people showing black flags. The demonstrators shouted slogans "Dwibedy go back, we will take care of ourselves"[73].

Giris Chandra Roy of Kaptipada was a friend of Dwibedy. Together they tried to hold a public meeting at Bhimda the next day. Their next attempt was to hold meeting at Baripada. But at both places, the attempt was unsuccessful. Dwibedy's stubborn effort to hold a meeting at Madhuban near Baripada was foiled by angry mob. Dwibedy returned to Cuttack unsuccessful in creating a favourable public opinion for merger. As a face saving device he informed the Press that his visit to Mayurbhanj was to preach socialism since Mayurbhanj was under feudal social order[74]. It became evident in the course of events that the coastal people (called mughalbandi) were neither liked nor trusted by the people of the Garjats (states). Hence the rising tide of hostility against merger was quite natural and spontaneous.

Orissa Press on the Merger Issue

The Contemporary Oriya newspapers invariably made the prospect of Mayurbhanj's merger their headline and all editorials were on the same issue. This campaign being against the people's will, many noted public of Mayurbhanj viz, Prasanna Kumar Das, Sunaram Soren, Satis Chadnra Das Patnaik opposed tooth and nail the sinister move of the Leading Dailies - The Samaj and The Prajatantra[75]. The atmosphere gradually became tense and antagonistic. Premier Sarat Chandra Das and Lalmohan Pati, member of the Constituent Assembly of India met Mahtab at Balasore to request him to restrain the press to maintain good relationship between the State and the Province. Mahtab pretended ignorance and was rejoicing at the development[76].

On 28 December 1947 the Samaj published a news item stating that the Government of Orissa was contemplating to appoint Sarat Chandra Das as a Cabinet Minister. This news was baseless and misleading. The reaction of Das was predictable as he vehemently denied having been approached for the purpose[77]. The anti-merger group in Mayurbhanj always suspected Mahtab for such publications and rumour.

Mahtab was openly critical of the Maharaja and Sarat Chandra Das for keeping themselves away from the merger and his dream of unifying the Oriya speaking tracts in a Greater Orissa was not being realized. He clandestinely engineered the formation of a party named 'Bhanjabasi Sabha' in the Vyavastha Parishad. The leaders were Haris Chadnra Das of Prajamangal Party, Sribatsa Mishra of Betnoti and Ram Chandra Sahu, Advocate. They were getting financial support from Mahtab to act as an opposition to Sarat Chandra Das' Government[78].

In July 1948 the Union Government gave Sareikela and Kharswan to Bihar. This made it more urgent for the Mahtab Government to see that Mayurbhanj was not lost the same way. There was a move to form Jharkhand State for the tribals of Bihar, Bengal and Orissa. In Mayurbhanj the tribal population was 70% and there was every possibility that they would join Jharkahnd as a part of it. The dangerous prospect of a Tribal State close to Orissa would precipitate the loss of Mayurbhanj. Mahtab was worried. To secure the merger of Mayurbhanj became an issue of 'do or die' for him. His apprehension was justified.

To strengthen Mahtab's strategic move many items of news under the following captions were published in his own paper the Prajatantra and in the Samaj edited by Radhanath Rath. These captions were "Dissatisfaction against the Ministry"[79], "Scenes of Oppression in Mayurbhanj"[80], "Protest against Government budget in Mayurbhanj"[81].

Demand for Representative Government in Mayurbhanj"[82] and "An Appeal to Mayurbhanj" etc[83].

The Newspapers of Cuttack described the administration of Mayurbhanj as feudalistic, non democratic, non-representative, oppressive, dictatorial, full of internal dissension, extravagant, under selfish leadership etc[84]. The Prajatantra published[85],

> "Autocracy has not ended in Mayurbhanj. While the people in general want to integrate with Orissa, the Ministry is wasting public money to circulate anti merger views. The Ministry is threatening to exterminate any person speaking in favour of merger."

The Prajatantra alleged that the Government of Das was leading the state towards bankruptcy. It said that the Ministers and members of the Vyavashtha Parishad were eating away Rupees One and half lakh. The bureaucracy was divided and the Government acted without cohesion[86].

As if this was not enough, the Orissa legislative Assembly passed a resolution in April 1948 recommending the Orissa Government to move the Central Government to take early steps for the integration of Mayurbhanj with Orissa so that peace and stability would prevail and the people could participate in a democratic Government[87].

The Government of Mayurbhanj lost no time in issuing a counter which expressed the desire of the people in the context of Resolution passed by the legislative Assembly of Orissa province[88]. The counter said,

> "The Government of Mayurbhanj strongly deprecates the insinuation made in the resolution that in the non-merger of Mayurbhanj with Orissa is in any way affecting the peace and security of Orissa Province".
>
> "The Government of Mayurbhanj has been a thoroughly democratic manner and the decision for maintaining a

> separate entity of Mayurbhanj was taken in a full democratic process by the Mayurbhanj Constituent Assembly".
>
> "In the circumstances the Government of Mayurbhanj feel that the Resolution of the Orissa State Assembly is uncalled for and provocative. The Orissa State Assembly has no jurisdiction whatever over Mayurbhanj and as such the resolution has no constitutional propriety in relation to Mayurbhanj. The Government of Mayurbhanj feel that such resolution by outside agencies can only serve to create untoward feelings between neighbouring units as the people of Mayurbhanj are united in their determination to preserve their traditional entity under a popular Government"[89].

The Prajatantra adopted a more aggressive stance to blame Mayurbhanj for the loss of Sareikela and Kharswan. It also said that Mayurbhanj cannot remain as a separate state for long and its integration will take place soon. It appealed to Maharaja to work for the whole Province and not to think of Mayurbhanj alone[90].

Within a week, the Prajatantra called upon the people of Mayurbhanj not to be selfish or be carried away by the maneuver of the Maharaja. They should keep the interest of Orissa above their own interest. While praising Mayurbhanj as the crown jewel of Orissa, its loss would be suicidal to the Oriya nation. A call was given to the Younger generation of Orissa to work ceaselessly for the successful integration of Mayurbhanj with the Province.

Perturbed by the vitriolic campaign of Cuttack Press, Sarat Chandra Das held a Press Conference on 4 June 1948 in the State Secretariat in which the members of all leading newspapers, Government official, public figure, Secretary and Ministers were present. While lamenting for the hostile attitude the Premier made it clear that the state would not like to merge with any Province and forceful integration would lead to unfortunate results and may be bloodshed. He was prepared to invite Mahtab and other leaders to ascertain the desire of the people of Mayurbhanj. He was convinced that merger would not be beneficial to Mayurbhanj[91]. Soon afterwards Surendra Natha Dwibedy, Rabi Ghose, Rabi Das, Gour Das, Gokulananda Behera, Kanduri Charan Mallick visited Mayurbhanj in July 1948 and held public meeting at Madhuban[92]. The meeting was conducted by Anant Rath. The issue of merger was discussed by the leaders explaining its advantage and disadvantages. The Tribals demonstrated with Black Flags shouting slogans "Mayurbhanj will remain separate, we don't want outsiders". The effort of the Socialist leaders failed to convince them[93].

On 4 August 1948, the Maharaja convened a meeting of the Ministers in the Palace where he expressed deep anguish at the malicious campaign accusing him as an impediment to integration. He frankly stated that after the transfer of power, the future course of action was to be determined by the Vyavastha Parishad. He had no role to play in the merger. He did not hold any view in the matter. He gave it in writing and the Ministers put their signature.

But it was quite evident that the Das Ministry and his Government was going through mental suffering caused by the mounting campaign of Cuttack Press as it was difficult to neutralize its impact on the people. It was almost like coercion. In July 1948 Mahtab gave Instruction to the Principal of Ravenshaw College and other colleges not to admit students of Mayurbhanj. It was shocking attitude of vendetta and tantamount to coercion. The career of brilliant students was at stake. In some cases the students were asked to pay donation of Rupees Ten thousand. They were ill-treated and taunted[94]. The liberal donation made by Maharaja Krushna Chandra, Sreeram Chandra, Purna Chandra and Pratap Chandra for the colleges of Cuttack were in vain. The Syndicate, Utkal University did not appreciate the attitude of the Government and resolved that it would disaffiliate the college refusing admission to the students of Mayurbhanj. The situation forced many students to go to Midnapore, Calcutta and Patna which was quite expensive[95].

Inside Mayurbhanj the Pro-merger and Anti-merger groups continued to play their role and their mutual relationship was acrimonious. The Bhanjabasi Sabha was creating public support for its merger with the Provincial Congress, but the Anti- merger group disapproved the move[96]. The move of the Bhanjabasi Sabha was quite vigorous on account of the meetings held by Ramakanta patnaik, Ratikanta Patnaik, Giris Chandra Das and Hariram Mohanty. They sent memorials to the States Ministry of the Government of India urging for integration. They also criticized the composition of the Vyavastha Parishad[97]. An absurd view expressed some irresponsible person saying that Mayurbhanj should merge with Bengal was scoffed at by Dr. Prafulla Chandra Ghose of Calcutta who disapproved of it as ridiculous[98].

Unable to contain the ceaseless Pre-merger campaign rising like a Monsoon storm, the Popular Ministry feeling shaken of its survival prospect thought it may pay dividend to approach the States Ministry in Delhi to neutralize the menacing attitude of the Provincial Government. A high power delegation was selected to proceed to Delhi for the purpose with adequate documents and preparation to convince the Home Ministry that the state was doing well in taking care of the welfare of the people besides evolving a Constitution for stabilizing the democratic process and Institution shortly[99]. The delegation moved by Train to Delhi where they first met Mr. Krishnamurthy, the Liaison Officer. Krishnamurthy told them the bleak prospect of their endeavour because the Sardar would not support the move. After three days of waiting and humble effort the delegation could meet Sardar Patel in a grim atmosphere of apathy and aversion. The emotional presentation and pleadings by Maheswar Naik, the State Minister of Industries cut no ice with Sardar Patel who while leaving the meeting curtly told the delegation to go back and merge or face the consequences. With the bitter taste of the Iron Man whose aim was to achieve national integration in India, the state delegation returned home utterly devastated in their hope of keeping Mayurbhanj an independent unit of India. Probably, the visit of the delegation was ominous and suicidal. The lamb had itself walked in to the den of the lion. They realized that continuance of Mayurbhanj with her separate identity was no more possible.

Inevitability of Merger

The state delegation before leaving Delhi had a meeting with VP Menon, the Secretary of the States Ministry who too showed a cold attitude. Menon advised them to convince the people about the advantages of merger making the stand of the Indian Government very clear. The Delegation returned home with a frustrated attitude. On 20 August 1948 the State Government released a press note on the discussion held at Delhi and the views of the States Ministry. A meeting of the Vyavastha Parishad was convened on 15 September 1948. Before the House, the following statement was made by the Premier[100],

> "We met the Secretary of the State Ministry and the Hon'ble Deputy Prime Minister acquainted them with the affairs of this state and sought their good wishes. We told the States Ministry about the peaceful and tranquil atmosphere here, about our constructive work and about future plans and progress. The State Ministry, however, raised the issue of merger for our better interest and for the bigger interest of India. We were advised to comeback and tell our people about this and to explain to them that there would be trouble if Mayurbhanj did not merge with Orissa and continue to stay as a separate entity."

Explaining the matter further, the Premier said that many national leaders at Delhi whom they met were of the view that small political units would create problems for integration and unity of India and as a small unit the State of Mayurbhanj would neither have stable administration nor viable economy.

Despite her rich natural resources the dependence of Mayurbhanj on the center as well as the Orissa Province was imperative. It was, therefore, advisable to merge with Orissa, the Premier concluded[101].

The Premier was convinced that merger was now inevitable. To convince the members of the Parishad he spoke out,

> "It is for everybody to think of India, to stand united and to fall in line with the policy of the Government of India enunciated by our respected leaders. Sentiment should not carry us away from the right path".
>
> "Utkal with which our education has been linked from time immemorial and whose language we are using in our courts, is welcoming us with open arms. I now appeal to you all to take a long-range view of things, coolly ponder over all the aspects of the question as stated before and shape the destiny of Mayurbhanj on right lines[102]."

The sudden change of the Premier's attitude stunned the House. The members could not believe what they heard the Premier was saying, because all the time he was the protagonist of independent entity of Mayurbhanj, but now he was making an earnest appeal to merge with Orissa. There was disbelief and protest. Sunaram Soren, the Tribal leader resigned his membership in protest and in a statement made his position very clear. He was the proponent of separate status and not a supporter of merger because merger was not going to be beneficial for the people[103].

The State Government decided to hold a session of the Mayurbhanj Constituent Assembly to discuss the proposal of merger with Orissa and if necessary to make it Conditional[104]. The terms and conditions of merger would be drafted by a Committee elected by the Constituent Assembly. After the terms were finalized and approved by the Government of India, the Premier along with the Maharaja would proceed to Delhi to sign the documents of merger[105]. It was aptly considered by the Union Government that in view of the hostile feelings created between the State and the Province, immediate merger of Mayurbhanj with Orissa would create problems of maladjustment. The Union Government, therefore, should keep the state under its control for some time. The Center would appoint a representative to administer the state till a favourable situation emerged to justify the taking over of the States by the Province[106].

The tribal leader Sunaram Soren being opposed to merger held a protest meeting in the premises of the Municipal office at Baripada. In his opinion the merger issue could be decided by the people alone. At this juncture, the Maharaja held long Marathon discussion with the tribal leader and succeeded in convincing him the efficacy of the merger. But the commitment of Sunaram did not appear to have a lasting impact on his political move, because very soon he would go back in his worlds and lead an unprecedented tribal uprising on the issue.

Sarat Chandra Das went to Delhi on 26 September 1948 to discuss the terms and conditions of merger. Sardar Patel told him to sign the merger document along with the Maharaja and leave everything else to the Union Government to take care of. Das wanted certain rights of the tribals to be protected and his leaders should find a place in the Executive Council[107].

The Merger

The news of merger spread like wild fire in the State. As per Sardar Patel's advice, there was no need to convene the meeting of the Constituent Assembly. But Sunaram Soren was not happy. The Union Government was probably correct to lay emphasis on the signature of the Maharaja. He was the rightful Ruler of the State. The Premier, however, proceeded to Delhi with the Maharaja on 8-9 October 1948. On 17 October the merger document was signed by the Maharaja.

The Governor General of India was represented by the Secretary, States Department[108]. The Premier was not a signatory. Sardar Patel was not willing to take his signature as a representative of the people of Mayurbhanj.

There appears to be an enigma as to why the Government of India ignored the Vyavastha Parishad and the Premier. The argument advanced by the Maharaja on 14 December 1947 at Cuttack avoiding the signature on the merger document was forgotten in October 1948 when he signed the document handing over the State to the Union Government. The Government of India took him as the rightful owner of the state, having power to cede the state to the Indian Union. The Treaties and Engagements of 1803 were signed between the Company's representative and the Raja. In 1858 the Company was substituted by the Crown who handed over power to the Governor General of Indian Union. In 1948 the same Governor General took over the state of Mayurbhanj from the Maharaja by virtue of the paramountcy. There was no place either for the Vyavastha Parishad or the Premier in the legal hierarchy having authority to transfer the state.

According to the merger agreement signed between the Maharaja and the Government of India, the former agreed to cede to the Dominion Government full and exclusive authority, jurisdiction and power for the governance of the state and agreed to transfer the administration of the state to the Dominion government on 9 November 1948. There were many other terms and conditions embodied in the merger document[109].

The legal and Constitutional propriety, of the merger agreement is significant because it was signed by the Constitutional head without any supporting endorsement by the legislature or without any verdict of the people. Sardar

Patel insisted upon ignoring or bypassing the Vyavastha Parishad. This was as per the documents signed by other Princely states where no Assembly or popular Government's endorsement was felt essential.

In accordance with the merger agreement Sri Dattatreya Vaman Rege Bar-at-law, ICS, the Chief Commissioner designate arrived at Baripada on 6 November and took over the state administration three days later. All Acts and regulations which were in force in the state were to remain in force until further orders. The Vyavastha Parishad and the Constituent Assembly were dissolved with effect from 9 November 1948[110].

Mayurbhanj acceded to the territory of Indian Union as a centrally administered area.

Mayurbhanj: A Union Territory

The administration of Mayurbhanj as a Union Territory lasted for a short period of less than two months during which the Chief Commissioner studied closely and carefully the situation before finalizing his recommendation about the future of the State[111]. In the mean time the tribal leaders of Mayurbhanj who were opposed to merger with Orissa demanded that the state be merged with Bihar. This complicated the issue forcing the Union Government to appoint D.V. Rege ICS as the Chief Commissioner to study and recommend judiciously the course of action to be taken. Rege considered all aspects of the issue and after a careful study gave report saying that the state must go to Orissa for the best interest of the people[112].

After the state Ministry studied the report of Rege, V.P. Menon visited Baripada on 16 December to announce before the Assembly the momentous decision of the Government of India. In the presence of leading citizens, members of the Constituent Assembly, Party Leaders and the Maharaja, he read out a historic document announcing the decision of the Union Government that Mayurbhanj should go to Orissa. He said,

> "All the representative opinion which the State Ministry had gathered recommended that the State should go to Orissa to which it geographically, culturally and to a large extent ethnologically belongs[113]."

The arguments, which were advanced by the Adivasi Sabha for integration of the State with Bihar were rejected because, according to Menon, these arguments had no seal substance in them. The Tribal leaders were assured that all their vital interests would be safeguarded. Finally, he announced that the State of Mayurbhanj should ingtegrate with Orissa from 2 January 1949. He requested the people to accept such integration and work in the best interest of Mayurbhanj and the Orissa Province[114].

Being aware of the resentment of the Adibasi leaders Menon categorically commented that their memorandum contained arguments, which were highly unreasonable. He said,

> "The real leader is not the man who can address large public meetings but the man who can do something for the betterment of his fellowmen. Tested by that standard the Adibasi leaders have failed in their duties"[115].But he assured,
>
> "The Government of India will see and the Orissa Government will see that the lot of the Adibasis is improved and that every fair chance is given to them[116].His last announcement was,"
>
> "Mayurbhanj would merge with Orissa on 2 January[117] 1949. That brought the issue to an end."

On 01 January 1949 Mayurbhanj merged with Orissa as per Home Department Notification 1 January 1949 published in Extraordinary Orissa Gazette (Annexure IV) with clear mention that the whole Mayurbhanj state shall be formed in to a revenue district to be known as the district of

Mayurbhanj with headquarters at Baripada and Subdivisions as specified below:

Name of Sub-division– Sadar, Kaptipada, Bamanghaty and Panchpir with territorial limits as existing on the 31st December 1948.

Accordingly Mayurbhanj became a district in the Province and Executive Officers designated as District Collector and Magistrate and other officers were appointed to carry on Executive administration of the district.

But instead of jubilation in the public, the merger created a tense situation caused by an unprecedented agitation of the Tribals of Bamanghaty Sub-division who were all the while unwilling to merge with Orissa. How the turn of events shook the district administration giving a jolt to the Provincial administration was a crucial development in the history of Mayurbhanj.

It is worthwhile to analyze the events of six months preceding the merger to know why Mayurbhanj slipped away from the grip of the Prajamandal Ministry of Sarat Chandra Das. The main cause which precipitated the merger was the vigorous campaign of Cuttack Press bringing several allegations against Das and spreading wild hostile rumours not based on truth. These allegations, in a nutshell were–

(i) There was no cohesion in the Government and the Ministers held different views not conducive to united action,

(ii) The administration was chaotic having no popular support

(iii) Gross financial irregularity had depleted the State Treasury

(iv) Premier was misappropriating funds through raising Gandhi Smarak Nidhi, of which he was the President

(v) Maharaja was eager that the state administration be taken over by the Government of India.

The Sardars and the newly formed Bhanjabasi Sabha were instrumental in spreading these rumours created by the

Cuttack Newspapers. Haris Chandra Das, the erstwhile leader of the Prajamangal Party having joined the National Congress was the rallying point of the critics. The resignation of Bidyadhar Mohapatra, Minister of Revenue on 4 November 1948 gave credence to the rumours. In a letter addressed to the Maharaja, Mohapatra alleged that the Premier had increased the powers of the magistrates, increased the salary of the officers and employees, spending money beyond the budgetary allocation, leasing Government land to his favourites, spending money from the reserved fund without the approval of the legislature[118].

It was baseless to allege that Sarat Chandra Das was corrupt and involved in nepotism. He was a simple man living a life of austerity. He was born poor, lived poor and died poor. He died in the hospital without proper care and medicine. The misappropriation of Gandhi Smarak Nidhi was a charge leveled by the Bhanjabasi leaders who were opposed to him from the time of Prajamandal activities. It was politically motivated to malign him. With regard to depletion of State Treasury it may be pointed out that DV Rege, the Chief Commissioner handed over to the Government of Orissa on 1 January 1949 a cash balance of one crore and fifty-six lakhs Rupees in the Baripada Treasury. If the salary of the employees was raised on the eve of merger it was done with good intention to help them.

To sum up, it may be said that the popular Ministry during a short tenure of office tried to build up a welfare State. Mayurbhanj could not retain her separate entity because the steam roller of National integration was so powerful and ruthless that the Princely States had to be liquidated for building a new India. Mayurbhanj fell a prey to that National Policy which worked as a powerful historical force in the whole country.

Merger Notification

Appendix-I

The Home Department Notification dated 1 January 1948 read No.1-A. The following notification of the Government of India is republished for General information.

B.C. Mukherjee

Chief Secretary to Government

Ministry of States

New Delhi, 23 December, 1947

No.111-IB-Where as the Central Government has full and exclusive authority, jurisdiction and powers for, and in relation to the Government of the States specified in the Schedule annexed here to;

Now, therefore, in the exercise of the powers conferred by Sub-Section (2) of Section 3 of the Extra Provincial jurisdiction Act 1947 (No.XLVII of 1947) and of all other powers enabling it in this behalf, the Central Government is pleased to delegate to the provincial Government of Orissa, he power conferred by the Section 4 of the said Act to make orders for, or in selection to, the Government of the said states as respects any of the matters enumerated in list II or list III of the Seventh Schedule of the Government of India Act, 1935.

Provided that

i) the exercise of the power hereby delegated shall be subject to the control of the Central Government; and

ii) the delegation shall not preclude the Central Government form exercising the power hereby delegated.

Schedule

Athgarh	Gangpur	Nilgiri
Athmalik	Hindol	Pallahara
Bamra	Kalahandi	Patna

Baramba	Keonjhar	Rairakhol
Boudh	Khandpara	Ranpur
Bonai	Kharswan	Sareikela
Daspalla	Narsinghpur	Sonepur
Dhenkanal	Nayagarh	Talcher
		Tigiria

References

1 Sarkar SN *Biography of Sreeram Chandra Bhanjdeo* (1917) Senapati and Sahoo, Orissa District Gazetteer– *Mayurbhanj (*1967) p.80.

2 RAM, 1938-39, p.6

3 RAM – 1945-46 p.XXIV.

4 See Supra, Annexure I to Chapter III.

5 Mayurbhanj State Gazette, 15 October 1947, Appendix 'A'.

6 He subsequently became a member of the Orissa Public Service Commission.

7 The committee consisted of Radha Govind Das, NM, Sundaram and R.C. Dash. Extraordinary Mayurbhanj State Gazette 2 November 1947.

8 Mayurbhanj State Gazette Krodapatra, Part V (Oriya) 22 December 1947.

9 Ibid.

10 Extraordinary Mayurbhanj State Gazette, 9 December 1947.

11 Ibid.

12 Ibid, 10 December 1947.

13 Ibid, 9 December 1947.

14 Mayurbhanj State Gazette, Krodapatra (Oriya) Part – V, 22 December 1947.

15 Interview Bharati Kumar Das and Purnachandra Mohanta.

16 Ibid Also See Mahtab, H.K, *Sadhanar Pathe* (Oriya) 1972, P.349.

17 Menon, VP *The Story of the Integration of Indian States,* 1985, pp.152-153.

18 White Paper on Indian States, p.32.

19 Government of India Act, 1935 (Delhi) 1936, Section 5 (2)

20 Ibid Section 6(1).

21 White Paper on Indian States, p.32.

22 V. Patel, *On Indian Problems,* (Delhi, 1949) p.3

23 White Paper on Indian States, p.35.

24 Ibid. p.36

25 Urmila Phadnis, *Towards the Integration of Indian States* 1919-47 (Bombay, 1968) p.197

26 Ibid, p.40 Orissa Legislative Assembly Proceedings Vol.II, No22, 1949, p.864 for details See Mishra, P.K. *Political History of Orissa* (1900-1936) 1979, pp.179-183.

27 Report of the State People Enquiry Committee, p.60.

28 urmila Phadnis, op.cit. p.153.

29 Mahtab, H.K. *Beginning of the End*, 1972, p.17.

30 Mayurbhanj did not join the union.

31 Durga Das (ed) Sardar Patel's correspondence 1945-50, Vol. V, (1973) pp. 494-95.

32 Interview Santos Kumar Sahu, Former MLA, Minister and Member, Rajya Sabha-three terms

33 Mahtab, *Beginning of the End*, p.184.

34 Menon, V. P. op.cit. p.149

35 Mahtab, *Beginning of the End*, op.cit. p.28 Proceedings Orissa Legislative Assembly Vol. II No.22, 1949. p.866.

36 Menon, V P, op.cit. p.149.37 Ibid pp.150-151.

38 Nabeen, 16 December 1947.

39 VP Menon, op.cit. p.15540 Mahtab H.K, *Beginning of the End*. Appendix–I.

41 See Supra p.

42 Menon, VP. Op.cit p.155.

43 Ibid.

44 i) Mayurbhanj State Gazette (Krodapatra) Pt. V 22 December 1947;
ii) Extraordinary Mayurbhanj State Gazette, 7 January 1948;
iii) Sarbeswar Satpathy and Prasanta Kumar Choudhury; *Mayurbhanj Sasan Samstha O Bandobast* (Oriya) Baripada. 1966 p.81.

45 Mahtab, H.K. op.cit. p.13.

46 RAM 1947-48, p.6.

47 Das, Prasanna Kumar, *Mayurbhanj Mukti Samgramra itihas*, op.cit.

48 Ibid.

49 Ibid. Also Extraordinary Mayurbhanj State Gazette, 6 May 1948 Das, Prasanna Kumar, Autobiography, p.41. Interview Kaminikanta Patnaik, Younger brother of Ratikanta Patnaik, Sardar, Morada

50 Mayurbhanj State Gazette Krodpatra Pt. V, 7 January 1948 and Extraordinary Mayurbhanj State Gazette, 19 February 1948.

51 Ibid, 22 January 1948.

52 Mayurbhanj State Gazette, 22 January 1948 and Silver Jubilee Souvenir, MPC College 1948-73, p.7.

53 Ibid.

54 Das, Prasanna Kumar, *Mayurbhanj ra Mukti Samgramra itshas*, 1987, pp.41-42.

55 Mayurbhanj State Gazette, 22 January 1948 also of 7 January 1948.

56 Ibid, 7 March 1948.

57 Extraordinary Mayurbhanj State Gazette, 19 March 1948.

58 Mayurbhanj State Gazette, Krodapatra, Part. V (Oriya) 7 April 1948

59 Ibid.

60 Mayurbhanj StateGazette, 7 March 1948.

61 Ibid.

62 Ibid.

63 Extraordinary Mayurbhanj State Gazette, 4 April 1948.

64 The Samaj, 3 April 1948

65 The counter was signed by 12 leading public men of Mayurbhanj. They were–Sarat Chandra Pal (Advocate) Suresh Chandra Bhanj Deo, Trilochan Das (Advocate), Sures Chandra Das (Advocate), Jogeswar Rana (Merchant) Hariram Mohanty (Advocate) Durga Pd. Mohanty (Advocate) Kshetramohan Das, Naresh Chandra Bhanj Deo, Ramakanta Barik, Padmalochan Sahu, Umakanta Acharya etc.

66 Ibid.

67 Choudhury V(ed) Dr. *Rajendra Prasad Correspondence* and Select Documents, Vol. VIII, 1987, p.9.

68 Ibid. pp. 19-20

69 Letter dt. 19. January 1948.

70 Mayurbhanj State Gazette, 22 January 1948

71 Dwibedy, S.N., *Quest for socialism*, 1984, p.87.

72 The Samaj, 22 January 1948.

73 The Samaj 28 January 1948.

74 Letter to the Editor, The Statesman, 28 January 1948.

75 Letter to the Editor, The Stateman, 28 January, 1948

76 Ibid.

77 Extraordinary Mayurbhanj State Gazette, 29 Decemebr 1947.

78 The Prajatantra, 24 March 1948. The Party was formed on 14 March 1948.

79 The Prajatantra, 20 Feb. 1948.

80 Interview Raghunath Mishra, an Octogenarian

81 Mayurbhanj Jagaran, 12 April 1948.

82 The Prajatantra, 20 February 1948.

83 Ibid, 21 February 1948. The Samaj 4 June 1948. Ibid, 7 July 1948.

85 The Prajatantra, 21 February 1948.

86 Ibid, 10 March 1948.

87 Extraordinary State Gazette, 3 May 1948.

88 Ibid.

89 Extraordinary Mayurbhanj State Gazette, 3 May 1948.

90 The Prajatantra, 20 May 1948.

91 The Prajatantra, 27 May 1948. The Samaj 4 June 1948.

92 Ibid, 22 July 1948.

93 Ibid.

94 Interview Gourmohan Mohapatra, Advocate Durga Charan Mohanty, Retired Judge, Dr. Binode Kumar Das, Rotarian.

95 Ibid.

96 The Samaj, 5 August 1948.

97 The Samaj, 5 August 1948.

98 Ibid.

99 The Delegation consisted of Sarat Chandra Das, Maheswar Naik, Harihar Mohanty, Prasanna Kumar Das, Gourmohan Mohapatra, Sakila Soren, Sures Chandra Das, Ramchandra Das, and Basant Kumar Satpathy. Interview Basant Kumar Satpathy, Public Relation Officer of the State who served in Department of Education after States merger with Orissa.

100 Extraordinary MayurbhanjStateGazette, 16 September 1948.

101 Ibid.

102 Ibid.

103 The Samaj, 18 September 1948.

104 The Samaj, 20 September 1948.

105 Ibid.

106 Ibid.

107 Ibid and Durga Das (ed) *Sardar Patel's Correspondence* 1945-50, Vol. VII, p. 538 Also See his letter to Mahtab H.K, Dated 11 October 1948.

108 The Samaj. 15 October 1948.

109 See Annexure–I to this chapter

110 For details see Annexure–II, And also Governor's Secretariat (GS) Orissa, 1949 File no. 8. Acc no. 364 GS (Subject–Agreement made between the Governor General of Indiaand the Maharaja of Mayurbhanj State.

111 Extraordinary Mayurbhanj State Gazette, 8 November 1948 and 10 Novemebr 1948.

112 Ibid.

113 GS Orissa, 1949 File no. 8, Acc no. 365 GS VP Menon announcement in the Vyavastha Parishad 16 December 1948.

114 Para I of the Speech. Dated 16 December 1948.

115 Ibid. para 5.

116 Ibid.

117 See Annexure -IV

118 The Samaj 8 November, 1948 published the letter of registration.

5 Tribal Uprisings

(i) Pre-Independence, 1917

The twentieth century witnessed two tribal uprisings in Mayurbhanj; (i) Pre-Independence period, 1917 and (ii) Post Independence Period 1948-49 with different reasons. But both times the tribals resorted to violence and were suppressed by similar methods.

During the outbreak of the First World War, Mayurbhanj was under the Court of Wards since their heir Apparent Purna Chandra Bhanjdeo was a minor. The British Government being a party in the War, they used Indian resources for their efforts to win. India was a ground for recruitment of good soldiers as well as labourers for various preparations in the field. For that purpose Mayurbhanj offered an ideal place of recruitment of labour force. Large number of tribals were recruited from the Bamanghaty area and sent to the European theatre of War. In the war efforts of the British Government, the Indian rulers rendered active help in men, money and materials. Purna Chandra Bhanjadeo evinced great interest in recruiting the tribals for the Labour Corps and in other preparations. He even offered his personal service, which the Government accepted and commissioned him as an Honorary Lieutenant of the Royal Artillery. He, thereafter proceeded to France where the war was going on. He even went to England towards the end of the War[1].

The active participation of the Chief-designate encouraged the State administration to recruit more tribals for the Labour Corps. But the tribals after experiencing casualties and loss in the far off War field of Mesopotamia, France and other places felt reluctant to join the Army. This reticence soon took the shape of resistance and rebellion. The immediate cause of the rebellion was the pressure of the State Government during recruitment of Labour force for France[2].

The first tribal uprising was reported from the Sadar Sub-division in May 1917. Subsequently, it spread to the Sub-divisions of Bamanghaty and Panchpir in June[3]. The Santals physically assaulted the officials who were conducting recruitment. They also looted shops in the market of Karanjia. Near Bangriposi they caused damage to Railway property[4]. The Government promptly despatched Armed Police Reserve Force from Orissa Division and one hundred Infantry soldiers from Calcutta. The Santals were not prepared to listen to the soothing treatment of the Government and remained unyielding. They held public meetings to project their other grievances[5].

A fresh rising was reported in the Rairangpur town of the Bamanghaty Sub-division in June. The tribals there not only burnt and looted the Bazar, but also murdered a Police constable in mob fury[6]. The armed force had to be deployed to restore order. There was immediate action to apprehend the offenders and their leaders who were tried and convicted. As many as 1118 persons were prosecuted under various sections of the Cr P.C. and those found guilty were sentenced to various terms of imprisonment and other punishments. Seven hundred and twelve persons were tried for major offences and four hundred and six for minor offences[7].The trial was conducted by LTR Locus, the Special Judge and Haridas Bose, the State Judge[8].

The Government had to incur a total expenditure of Rupees 84,002 in suppressing the rebellion. In suppressing the uprising all categories of officers, civil, Police and Military, took concerted action and ultimately achieved success.

In pacifying the rural people the role of one Siba Jena was quite significant. He was a resident of Khuruntia village in Muruda Police Station and was in active service. After he returned home he spoke to his friends and relations the important role of the army. This began to spread among the tribals having a soothing effect.

The young Maharaja also went on tour to many villages talking to the people directly and pacifying them. His appeal was so effective that 78 persons volunteered to be recruited for the Mesopotamia Labour Corps. C.L. Philip, ICS the Political Agent and Commissioner Orissa Feudatory States personally supervised the recruitment work. It was later on found out that as may as 2452 persons of Mayurbhanj had joined the Armed Forces. During their absence at home, the State administration provided sustenance to their families[9].

The British policy towards the Tribals was one of tact and firmness. Their experience on the basis of series of tribal movement in the preceding century was to move with caution as the tribals were an extremely volatile section of the Indian population. It was a totally illiterate community living in most inaccessible areas and speaking different languages that made the situation so grave and explosive. Mayurbhanj fell to the all Orissa pattern. The tribals of Mayurbhanj, South Bihar (now Jharkhand) and West of West Bengal had much ethnic similarities. They lived in a large territory divided in to four provinces which kept them weak. A time would come when the tribals would pine for political union under the leadership of a Moses who would assure them the possibility of creating a home land for the Tribals. This dream or illusion gave birth to Adivasi Mahasabha under the leadership of Jaipal Singh at a time when India was approaching her goal of freedom from the British rule.

(ii) Tribal Uprising 1948-49

Simultaneously when the Gandhian struggle for India's freedom and Prajamandal movement for the liquidation of feudal social and political orders were going on, the Adibasis or Tribals in south Bihar with Ranchi as the epicenter were dreaming about a state unit of their own to be called Jharkhand. The tribals became politically very active in 1947 as fallout of the struggle for Indian independence. The tribal identity required a political identity in the form of Jharkhand. This movement gained momentum in Bihar in 1947 and in the adjoining areas under the leadership of Jaipal Singh and Julius Tiga etc.[10].

The Jharkhand movement had its influence on the Tribals of Mayurbhanj who were awakened by the new wave of the design to have a separate tribal state. Their population being approximately 75% of the total population, the need of the hour was to organize them to a united group. Since the Prajamandal was largely dominated by the non-tribals called 'Dikus' it was not expected to champion the cause of the Tribals. The Mayurbhanj tribals despite their majority did not have a leader of their own and they were divided in to ethnic groups like the Santhals, the Kols, the Bhumij etc. The vaccum of leadership shot in to fame a young tribal leader of Bamanghaty sub-division named Sunaram Soren (also called Majhi). He was a practicing lawyer at Baripada since 1946 after passing law from Cuttack. He was a natural choice for the Adibasi Mahasabha of Jaipal Singh of Ranchi where the tribal movement was gaining momentum. Jaipal was a Charismatic figure having western education and encouraged by the National Congress was successful in organizing the tribals of south Bihar. He inducted Sunaram to the movement inspiring him to organize the tribals for creating Jharkhand State. Hence, parallel to the Prajamandal of Sarat Chandra Das, Sunaram emerged as the rallying point of the Tribals of Mayurbhanj[11].

Sunaram Soren

Sundar Mohan Hembram

Mayurbhanj Adibasi Mahasabha

In the early part of 1947 the Mayurbhanj Adibasi Mahasabha (hereafter called MAS) was organised as a local unit like the Adibasi Mahasabha of Santal Pargana. As en educated Youngman Sunaram Soren became the natural choice for its Presidentship. His associates were – Mahendra Nath Murmu, the Vice President, Shyam Charan Hansda, General Secretary, Sundar Mohan Hembram, Councillor and Ghasirama Sandyl, the Chief Commander. In each subdivision of Mayurbhanj local units were set up with identical office bearers. They were affiliated to the main unit at Rairangpur[12].

The Membership of Adibasi Mahasabha was open to all categories of persons irrespective of their religion, caste, and sex. Even the Government servants were welcomed to join. The MAS set its objectives in the following:

(i) to arouse political awareness among the people of Mayurbhanj.

(ii) To have all-round development and prosperity of all illiterate, poor, exploited, downtrodden peasants and agricultural labourers, irrespective of caste, religion and language.

(iii) To maintain the integrity and independence of Mayurbhanj state.

(iv) To eradicate communalism.

(v) To follow nonviolence in doing works

(vi) To establish responsible Government in a peaceful manner under the aegis of the Maharaja

(vii) To establish Grampanchayat, Praja Sabha and Vyavastha Parishad for the better administration of the State

(viii) To establish adult franchise in all elections and the right to contest for election would have no restriction like property or education

(ix) To establish Panchayat and Praja Sabha etc by direct election

(x) To recognize Mundari as one of the state languages for administrative and judicial works

(xi) To provide elementary education in mother tongue for the cultural development of the society[13].

The MAS was a political party. It refuted the allegation that it was a party of the Maharaja. Like Prajamandal, MAS was also a political organization. These two were the leading parties of Mayurbhanj. There were a few others too, like, Kurmi Kshatriya Sabha, Bhanjabasi Sabha, Swadhin Dal. But none of the Party had its constitution or rules for membership or specified goals and objectives. Though some members called themselves as Socialists, they did not have an organizational base in the state. The party was formed in January 1948 by Surendra Nath Dwibedy and Giris Chandra Ray was the foremost leader. In a paper called "Mayurbhanj Jagaran" edited by Haris Chandra Das six parties of Mayurbhanj were mentioned viz. Mayurbhanj Adibasi Sabha, Mayurbhanj Prajamandal, Mayurbhanj Socialist party, Bhanjabasi Sabha, Kurmi Kshatriya Sabha and Swadhin Dal[14].

The Adibasi Sabha approved of a green flag and green cap as its logo to be used by all members and office bearers of the Party. But in case of the President's cap there would be a sun and a plough embossed on it. The Commander was to have something more special, is a green American cap with a plough and three strokes on his left and right chest. The Party propaganda was led by Sunaram Soren who moved from village to village in the state with local leaders to swell the Party membership. He was soon emerged as the Messiah of the Adibasi and their saviour drawing large crowds in every public meetings he held. He spoke to the innocent primitive looking tribals creating in them an unprecedented awareness and solidarity pining to achieve the goals set by the leader. The foremost among the goals was to have an identity as united homogeneous ethnic group[15].

The MAS was not a parochial organization as it was liberal enough to admit any person irrespective of caste, colour and religion, but native of Mayurbhanj and interested in the development of all sections of the society as a member. This explains the ideals of MAS. It was not exclusively for the tribals, but for all. Among the nontribals who had joined MAS were Promod Ghose, Nilamani Tripathy and Jainarayan Sing Babu etc.[16]. The aim of the Sabha was to establish peaceful responsible Government in the State and in running the administration, priority was given to the Gram Panchayats, Pargana Panchayat, Praja Sabha and Kendra Parishad etc. The members were to be elected directly[17]. The MAS was aware of the purpose of the Constituent Assembly of Mayurbhanj. It wanted the members of the Constituent Assembly to be elected by universal adult franchise. The Adibasis were quite emotional about their language which they wanted to be used for official purpose and elementary education to be given through mother tongue. Though the members of MAS were to carry the bow and arrow, they did not mean any violence. They carried weapons for self defence[18].

The Adibasi sabha insisted upon discipline. It carried the slogan, 'Bhanj disam heq Abawah, Akay Tuluj Han Bab

Misawa' (Mayurbhanj is ours, we will not merge with anybody)[19].

On 15 August 1947 when India became independent and the British paramountcy was lapsed the political scenario in India changed radically. The Princely states reverted back to their earlier position of independent status. The question of integration of the Princely states emerged as an emotional issue of great significance. It was in this context that the MAS repeatedly declared its intention of not joining any province, but to remain independent. The ego of Sunaram Soren as a tribal leader was identical with his desire to keep Mayurbhanj separate from any existing political unit. He found himself at a crucial juncture. He could not remain untouched by the Jharkhand movement and the Tribal demand for a state of their own.

On 19 September 1947 Sunaram Soren in his capacity as the President of the MAS sent a memorandum from Baripada to "The Advisory Sub Committee of Excluded and Partially Excluded areas" supporting the cause of Jharkhand. He wrote,

> "That the Adibasis of Mayurbhanj State fully realized that the Adibasis as a race would remain hewers of wood and drawers of water in their own land unless a separate province is constituted of them".
>
> "That the Mayurbhanj State is predominantly Adibasi and it is practically same with Chhotanagpur Division and Santal Pargana district, ethnologically, geographically, linguistically, culturally, economically and in fact in every material respect".
>
> "That the Adibasis of Mayurbhanj fully realize that unless they are brought under one political unit with the Adibasis of Chotanagpur and Santal Pargana and other predominantly Adibasi tracts, they can not have any real initiative and inspiration to improve their education, language, culture, economy and all that the Mother India needs today".

> "That the demand for a separate autonomous province is not based on racial hatred but on natural justice and fair play and in keeping with the present national policy of India to redistribute the provinces according to linguistic and cultural basis[20]."

Earlier on 6 September Sunaram Soren had addressed a letter to the Maharaja of Mayurbhanj stating that the Adibasis constituting 75% of the total population would support the formation of a Jharkhand state consisting of Chotanagpur, Santal Pargana district of Bihar and the adjoining Adibasi tracts like Mayurbhanj. His letter stated;[21]

> The Adibasis as a race are passionate lovers of freedom and they do not lack in energy, but they are greatly handicapped to develop their own culture, language, education, economy etc unless they have a separate province of their own. Under the present political arrangement, it is crystal clear that they will very soon be extinct as a race from the mother land – India.

The same letter further stated, That so long the state remained as a unit in the Indian Union and Re-question of amalgamation of the state with Orissa Province does not arise, till then the aim of the Adibasis is to demand for responsible Government under the aegis of His Highness the Maharaja. But the moment the question of liquidation of the state comes and if the state will amalgamate with Orissa Province, then the Adibasis aspire that the state should be amalgamated with Jharkhand, the proposed Adibasi province, if at all such a province is constituted in future[22].

The movement for Jharkhand state has been launched in Bihar for the creation of a separate province.

In response to the desire of the Tribals, the Maharaja took steps to include several Adibasi leaders in the proposed Vyavasthapak Sabha (Constituent Assembly) and the Vyavastha Parishad. This step was appreciated by the Tribal leaders and they felt convinced that the Maharaja would gradually introduce representative Government in the State. The tribals were given 12 seats in the Constituent Assembly having 51 members. Maheswar Naik, a Gonda tribal was included in the list and that made the Tribals very happy[23]. The reforms proposed by the Maharaja added new dimension to the movement reducing the pressure for a separate Jharkhand state. Sunaram Soren also felt largely satisfied and the new slogan which the tribals shouted was "Mayurbhanj is ours and we will not merge with any one"[24].

Mayurbhanj Adibasi Sabha and the Prajamandal Ministry

There was no ill feeling or misunderstanding between the Mayurbhanj Adibasi Sabha and the Prajamandal Government of Sarat Chandra Das. As early as 25 December 1947 in a public meeting of the MAS, the President Sunaram Soren was instrumental in passing a resolution which said,

(i) Keeping in view the population, area and the annual income of the state of Mayurbhanj and the newly instituted responsible Government under the Popular Ministry of the State, which is working for all-round development, peace and prosperity of Mayurbhanj, it is firmly believed that the state will make rapid progress in all directions and therefore, the question of merger of Mayurbhanj with Orissa does not arise.

(ii) This meeting condemns with all its force the false and baseless rumours and meaningless questions which are being propagated in the different newspapers of Cuttack relating to the merger of Mayubhnaj.

(iii) This meeting discussed the statements made by the Premier of Mayurbhanj and whole heartedly supports the sentiments expressed there in, and hereby brings to the notice of the Hon'ble Premier that this organization is ready to take all steps and make all sacrifices for the realisation of the goal enunciated by him[25].

The above resolution testified the amount of support and loyalty the Prajmandal Government received from the Mayurbhanj Adibasi Sabha.

The attempt of some socialist leaders to hold public meetings in Mayurbhanj was disrupted time and again by the Tribals as they were opposed to merger with Orissa. In the meetings organized by the MAS on 16 June 1948 Sunaram Soren vehemently argued against the merger with Orissa. Similar resolutions were taken at Jalghati, Pala, Saraskana, Paktia, Digha, Kuliana, Bhadua, Kundalboni, Dakoi, Dublabeda, Jhaliamara and Betna etc opposing any such move by the Socialists. What the Prajamandal Government could not achieve, the MAS could achieve that and a vigorous public opinion emerged to keep Mayurbhanj as a separate entity.

In an emergency meeting of the Working Committee of the MAS held on 4 July 1948 again it was resolved that the malicious propaganda against the Popular Ministry should stop and if necessary the Central Government should intervene. The Working Committee further suggested that to keep the on going development works in progress, the Central Government may impose a strong administration on Mayurbhanj. They unequivocally pleaded to make Mayurbhanj a Centrally administered unit and not to merge it with any province[26]. The resolution was published in the form of a Pamphlet for wide circulation.

It has been discussed earlier that Sarat Chandra Das' effort to keep Mayurbhanj a separate unit with the approval of the States Ministry failed in August 1948. He returned to Baripada totally frustrated and aware of the fait accompli of his Government. He was categorically told to merge with Orissa or face the consequences.[27]

The fallout of Sarat Chandra Das' failure in Delhi had tremendous impact on the Tribal leaders of Mayurbhanj. Das released the contents of his discussion to the Press and informed the Vyavastha Parishad that merger with Orissa was imperative[28]. Its implications being grave, the Tribals could know which way the wind of change would blow. So on 12 September 1948 they held a mammoth gathering at Khorembeda near Bangriposi ghat and resolved for the first time that Mayurbhanj would merge with Bihar. But on 15 September '1948 Premier Sarat Chandra Das in a long statement made at the floor of Vyavastha Parishad declared that Mayurbhanj must merge with Orissa in the greater interest of all.[29]

Tribal Reaction

On 16 September 1948 the working committee of the MAS held a meeting at Baripada with Sunaram Soren as the Chairman. In the meeting it was resolved that the merger issue should be decided by a plebiscite or by a freshly elected Constituent Assembly and Vyavastha Parishad. The Committee requested the Maharaja to hold fresh elections immediately or to have a plebiscite to decide the issue of merger. In a threatening note the Working Committee also said that if any decision contrary to the wishes of the Adibasis would be taken, the same would not be binding on the MAS[30]. The committee also refuted the charge that the MAS was a communal organization and its policy was hatred and violence. The committee laid emphasis on its policy of peace and nonviolence to remove public apprehension. The decisions were printed for circulation through out the state[31].

In September 1948, the political atmosphere of Mayurbhanj was surcharged with Pro-merger and antimerger campaign conducted by various Agencies. Haris Chandra Das with his Bhanjabasi and Bhanja Vahini (a student's organization) supporters was carrying on ceaseless propaganda for merger with Orissa. Giris Chandra Ray and his Socialist comrades were also doing the same thing. They had invited Surendra Nath Dwivedy to address public meetings as frequently as possible. He was supported by Surendra Nath Satua of the Krushak Party. That Mayurbhanj should remain independent was the demand of the Prajamandal party and the Mayurbhanj Adibasi Sabha[32].

When Sunaram Soren changed his decision on 12 September at Khorembeda meeting, certain definite reasons had influenced his mind. These reasons were explained in a pamphlet and circulated[33]. According to the pamphlet;

(1) Under the state of Orissa there will be no development for the people of Mayurbhanj because annual income of the state which amounted to 45 lakhs will be spent for whole of Orissa and not for the people of Mayurbhanj.

(2) Fuel, wood and construction materials for their houses will become scarce. Fuel wood would be sold at the price not less than rupees fifteen per maund, after merger.

(3) Mayurbhanj will be exploited economically

(4) All the lands of Mayurbhanj will be purchased at a very high price by people from outside the state.

(5) Officers will be appointed as Deputy Collectors in Mayurbhanj, who will behave and act like King and swallow everything as is being done in the districts of Koraput and Anugul.

(6) The dream of Panchayat Raj will never be realized

(7) The people of Mayurbhanj will be deprived of the facility of getting speedy justice with minimum expense

(8) The undeveloped and illiterate subjects of Mayurbhanj due to their ignorance will not be able to compete with others in the political field.

(9) The people of Mayurbhanj will not get adequate representation in the services of the state.

(10) Mayurbhanj will not get justice in the field of education and health

(11) The representatives of Mayurbhanj will not get opportunity to hold the reins of Government. The administrators will be chosen from Cuttack, and their brothers and kinsmen will exploit Mayurbhanj for their own selfish interest.

Concluding the apprehensions the Pamphlet said there would be disaster if merger would be imposed at gun point. The language, literature, and culture of the Adibasi being different from the Oriya people will suffer and languish. The Sabha in the Resolution hoped that the Mundari speaking Adibasis would get justice from the Central Government.[34]

Thus, Sunaram Soren's political vision oscillated between merger with Bihar and creation of a separate state of Jharkhand for the Tribals exclusively. In July 1948 he was thinking of keeping Mayurbhanj a centrally administered unit and not to merge with any of the three provinces – Bengal, Biahr or Orissa. In the last part of August when merger with Orissa became imperative he toyed with the idea of holding a plebiscite to know the minds of the people. At Khorembeda meeting he eschewed all ideas to demand merger with Bihar as final move.

Though Sunaram Soren as a leader was found vascillating in August and September 1948, in October he held the firm view to oppose merger with Orissa. On 18 September all tribal members of the Mayurbhanj Vyavasthapak Sabha and Vyavastha Parishad resigned from membership. It was a journey of no return after that. On 17 October the Maharaja and Sarat Chadnra Das went to Delhi to sign the Instrument of merger. The central Government took over the state administration from 9November 1948. Then the tribals began their agitation demanding merger with Bihar.

Sunaram Soren held a huge public meeting at Rairangpur on 30 October 1948 where it was unanimously resolved that Mayurbhanj with 72% tribal population should merge with Bihar[35]. There it was decided that a delegation of 9 Adibasi leaders would go to Delhi to present their case before the National leaders and Union Government[36]. But in fact the Delegation that visited Delhi in the first week of November consisted of 12 members[37]. They presented a memorandum to Sardar Patel. The Delegation advanced arguments for merger with Bihar explaining geographical, economic and cultural homogeneity and for having nothing in common with Orissa. They were told by Sardar Patel and V.P. Menon that the merger issue was under consideration and an Administrator was being sent to study the matter and report. The meeting was not cordial. It ended with a stern warning from Sardar Patel who said, "Merge or be ready to face bullets". Sundar Mohan Hembram replied, "we are ready to face bullets". The Delegation returned home with sorrow and disappointment. They incited the Tribals to shout the Santali slogan "Misa anang Bihar Tulje, Odisa Tuluje bang Misaba"[38].

Sunaram Soren decided to show his strength of public support to protest against the change in administration. To demonstrate his protest he arranged an unprecedented rally of several thousand Adibasis at Baripada from 2 November to 6 November. The Prajamandal Government was counting its last few days in office. In spite of the preventive measures they took to foil the rally, in spite of the harvesting season, large number of Adibasis gathered at Baripada shouting the slogan "Country first and Harvest next".

Sunaram Soren came from Rairangpur to Baripada on foot with a huge procession of men and women. When the procession entered Baripada town the slogans which they shouted said, Mayurbhanj is ours and we want to merge with Bihar and not Orissa. After parading through the street the procession reached the Circus Ground by evening on 1 November 1948.[39]

The marathon meeting of the Tribals continued days and night amidst tribal Songs and beating of drums and speeches by leaders and instigators. Many tribals who took shelter in the courts and other public building were chased away by the police. While some slept in the meeting place some slipped away to go round the town and the market place.[40]

As per the Government of India Notification published in Extraordinary Mayurbhanj state Gazette 8 November 1948 D.V. Rege ICS, the Chief Commissioner designate arrived at Baripada on 6 November to take over the administration as the representative of the Union Government. The Press Communiqué of the Government of India was notified on 8 November requesting the people of Mayurbhanj to cooperate with the Chief Commissioner in the discharge of his duties[41].

When the Chief Commissioner arrived at the State Guest House, Baripada, Sunaram Soren the president of the MAS and A Pankaj, the President of All State Organisation of Adibasi Sabha had an interview with him. They submitted a memorandum on the desirability of giving Mayurbhanj to Bihar. The leaders returned to their office to continue their meeting till the next morning. In the memorial they had also requested for a plebiscite on the issue of merger. The meeting which went through the night concluded with a resolution that Mayurbhanj should go to Bihar.

There was a rumour afloat that V.P. Menon, the Secretary; States Ministry was to visit Baripada on 20 November. In the meantime, the Popular Ministry came to an end after handing over the administration to the Chief Commissioner. The Tribals under Sunaram Soren again planned to have a mass meeting at Baripada during 19 to 22 November coinciding with Menon's arrival to press their demand for merger with Bihar. Most of the tribals this time came from Singhbhum and their leaders were also from that area. Everyday, Sunaram led public processions through the town and at the end in meetings and speeches he repeated the demand for merger with Bihar on the ground of cultural and linguistic offinity with Singhbhum of Bihar.[42]

Menon delayed his arrival deliberately allowing the dust to settle down. He arrived at Baripada on 16 December and made the historic announcement that Mayurbhanj will be a part of Orissa Province with effect from 1 January 1949. He logically countered all the arguments of the Adibasi Sabha for merger with Bihar. He realized that the Adibasi agitation was not spontaneous; it was tutored by extraneous agencies. In his book 'Integration of the States' he wrote later that the peculiar way the Tribals held their meetings while eating, dancing and sleeping was quite amusing. He tried to convince the Tribal leaders the irrationality of their demand. Culturally and economically the ties of Mayurbhanj with orissa were much stronger. He addressed the meeting of the Tribals and the speech was translated in Tribal language. To him the mass rally of the Tribals appeared artificial and stage managed by some vested interest groups[43].

Tribal Rebellion

The Central Government did not waver from its decision. It showed no sign of reconsidering the decision at all. So the working committee of the Mayurbhanj Adibasi Sabha decided on 8-9 January to launch a civil disobedience and non-cooperation movement in the following manner;[44]

(i) No tax campaign

(ii) Boycott of the court and offices

(iii) Boycotting oriya language as a medium of Instruction and the Introduction of Hindi in Schools instead

(iv) Token strike in the mines and factories

(v) Bringing fire wood from the forest without permit

(vi) Selling rice, paddy and food grains without any restriction of boundaries

The meetings resolved to carry on the agitation on nonviolent ways. But this was easier said than done.

The rebellion was widespread in the Bamanghaty sub-division. Sunaram Soren was highly respected by the people in the area. He was like a Demi God whose feet was washed with milk by the tribal women. The meetings he organized were well attended. The call for meetings was given by beating of drums and the leaflets circulated carried the slogan[45].

> "Come, come brothers, come quickly, this time will never come again."

Sitting together, Seeing the Good and the bad, we will find out the good road. There was complete unity and solidarity Messages of rebellion spread from village to village either orally or through knots. The santals were at the forefront of rebellion. They were supported by the Kols, Bathudi, Kharia, and Mundas. Bamanghati being close to Biahr was most affected. It had mining areas at Badampahar, Gurumohisani and Suleipat with workers who could be easily inflamed. Among the people in the sub-division 80% were tribals, prone to rebellion.

Tribal rebellion in Bamanghaty was not a new thing. In 1830, 1857, 1866 and 1917 they had raised the standard of rebellion against the Government. According to H.K. Mahtab whenever there was no Raja in Mayurbhanj, the tribals got an opportunity to revolt.[46]

Counter Measures

The Government did not like the rebellion either to spread to other parts of the State or to cause worsening of law and order situation. On 4 and 5 February the State forces took repressive measures. In the morning of 5 February many tribal leaders were taken under custody. In all 19 tribal's and 2 nontribals were arrested. Among the famous leaders taken to police custody were–Sunaram Soren, Laxman Marandi, Ram Chandra Majhi, Ghasiram Sandyl, Laxman Singh Purti, Dhyan Chand Tudu, Baidhar Tudu, Ramrai Bari, Karunakar Hembram, Lalmohan Murmu, Karda Pingua, Sundar Mohan Hembram and two nontribal–Nishamani Tripathi and Promod Ghose[47]. They were put in the Baripada Jail as ordinary criminals.

At that time the Collector and District Magistrate was B.Mukherjee. He banned the Adibasi Sabha and declared Section 144 of Cr.P.C. in the whole subdivision of Bamanghati. The arrest of the leaders was a rude shock to the rebels. There was no junior leader to continue the rebellion. The propaganda machinery was also made ineffective by police action. A man of the Marwari community named Janaki Biyani was the conduit of Bihar through whom financial support was being sent to the Tribal leaders. He used to stay at Rairangpur having links with Tata[48]. The police took care of him. The Tribal leaders however, denied having any link with Biyani. They also refuted the information that financial support was coming from Bihar. The Tribal uprising needed no financial support; it was spontaneous, they said. In fact, money was not offered to political activists in those days. The tribals were familiar to lead a life of hardship and since they adored Sunaram Soren, there was no need of financial inducement.

The Tribal leaders had committed to follow the nonviolent path. They promised not to work as manual labourers for the Government as an act of non-cooperation. They even urged the supporters not to sell paddy or food grain to the non-tribals. This could affect the markets of the state as local producers did not come to sell their produce in the Hats. The price of essential consumer goods shot up. In many reserved forests of Bamanghati the tribals blindly cut the trees as an act of defiance of Government laws.[49] The Collector announced some relaxation in the Excise rules allowing the tribals to produce and sale Handia, a local drink made from rice. Some relaxation was also given in forest laws. But the appeasement policy of the government failed to pacify the rebels. The liberal use of Handia, the cherished drink of the tribals was helpful to arrange meetings, as the drink attracted them in large number to drink Handia free of cost.[50]

The Sub-divisional officer of Bamanghaty was Sardar Amar Singh, a veteran in administration and a strong disciplinarian. He was a man of action and a tough officer. His language was often abusive no doubt, but he was capable of delivering results. The Tribals were afraid of him and as he was responsible for firing to quell the rebellion, the rebels had announced a cash prize of Rupees one lakh for his head.[51]

Since 14 January was the occasion of Maker festival, the most enjoyable festival in the tribal community, there was no disturbance of peace in the first half of the month. But towards the end of January instance of sporadic lawlessness were reported. The disturbance was in the form of refusal to pay tax, violation of forest laws, forcible occupation of Government land and large scale smuggling of rice and other controlled commodities across the border. Breaking of Prohibitory 144 Cr P.C. was quite common. To restore law and order, the first police firing was at Gunduria village on 6 February 1949. That day about 4000 tribals had gathered there, despite the prohibitory Cr. P.C. 144 order, to protest against the arrest of their leaders, a day earlier. They were armed with lathis, Tangias, bows and arrows. Since the assembly was illegal, they were asked to disperse. The SDO had two platoons of Gorkhas stand by for protection To disperse the mob, the Superintendent of Police ordered lathi charge. As the tribals retaliated, one constable sustained injury near the eye and another suffered a pistol shot. As the mob did not disperse and became violent, the Collector ordered firing. Twenty eight rounds were fired resulting in the death of 7 persons and injury of fourteen. They were taken to the hospital[52]. The incident created top news in the Province causing anguish in the mind of the Maharaja who was in Calcutta. D.V. Rege, ICS the former Chief Commissioner of Mayurbhanj and presently Advisor to the government of Orissa was rushed to the spot for a report. The Report which he submitted was circulated in the Orissa Legislative Assembly[53]. The Adivasi version of the Gunduria incident was published in a weekly paper of Ranchi called 'Abua Jharkhand' giving more details[54].

The police firing at Gunduria was not the only incident of military action resorted to by the Government of Orissa. There were other such incidents in February, viz Jamda near Rairangpur and Bisoi on 8 February, and 9 February respectively where the casualty figure was much large[55]. There were police firing at Nimdih, Bahalda, Bhanjasra, Jilindar, Ranipahar, Chandikhaman, Dhatkidih, Matkamdih, Baradihi, Junubutu etc where besides causing death to numerous rebels, the Tribal villages were burnt and innocent people were victimized[56].

On 14 February a large number of Adibasis suddenly appeared in Baripada town to stage procession and silent demonstration of protest. The police restrained itself and no action was taken except arresting a few activists while the procession was near the police line[57]. These activists were not from Bamanghati subdivision; they came from Bhumij villages adjacent to Baripada town The Bhumij community did not adopt any militant attitude, they were more or less peaceful and did not provoke any harsh action by the Government.

After 10 February Bamanghaty was in peace for a very brief period, as disturbances were reported at Bijatola, Bisoi and often places beyond the Ghat where large number of Tribals congregated at strategic points with bows and arrows. On 23 February at Tiring village, very close to Bihar border the Tribals attacked the non-tribals of Patra (weaver) caste suspecting them as Police Informers and committed cold blooded murder of two persons – Jagta Patra and Gomha Patra. Since it was a mob violence committed by the Tribals the Police took several rebels to custody and charge sheeted 35 persons for the above murder[58].

The incident of Kuldiha was more serious. At Kuldiha there was a Vanadium ceramic factory. Its location being equidistant from Badampahar and Rairangpur there was the congregation of about 15,000 tribals. Since their aim was to damage the factory, Police firing was essential to disperse the mob. Getting this information, the District Magistrate left Baripada for Rairangpur. At Bangriposi ghat he was confronted with road block. When he reached Rairangpur at night with force he was informed that the non Adivasis were escaping to other places in panic for safety. The superintendent of Police and the DIG were already camping there. They were informed that the tribals had made five human sacrifices of person of Pana (Scavenger) caste for success in their insurrection. The Police rcovered three dead bodies. Such violence had to be controlled by strong action. The entire subdivision of Bamanghaty beyond Bangriposi was in anarchy. Communication had been disrupted. Telephone line had been snapped. From the last week of February, no passenger bus could ply through the Jackson Road, which is now called National Highway no. 5[59]. On 1 March the triblas mercilessly killed a retired Forest Range officer in Bangriposi ghat[60]. There were barricades to prevent the deployment of troops for the safety of the civilians. The Army had to be deployed and firing was ordered to restore law and order by dispersing the rebels. The rebels could spread panic in Bamanghaty area by loot and murder of the non tribal civilians. The movement of passengers came to a halt. Under the command of DIG Mr. Cleriese there was large scale reprisal by the Police. Many villages were torched and many rebels fell to the bullets[61].

The infiltration of some communists to the disturbed area had aggravated the crisis. They incited the tribals for more violence in self-defense. Some communists from Bihar had also joined the rebellion to make the situations grave[62]. Communist involvement in the rebellion became evident when red flag was found in possession of some agitators while being chased by the Police. This was admitted by the chief minister H.K. Mahtab in the floor of the Orissa legislative Assembly[63].

To a query made by Nilamani Routray, the Government placed a press communiqué besides making a statement which said,

> "I think the Communique which is being issued today will give the entire picture. It is not the Adibasi affair, nor the affair between Bihar and Orissa. We have ample evidence to show that prominent communists of Bengal are operating there with that area as the base. It is really a communist problem there"[64].

Nilamani Routray taking part in the discussion said that the Adibasis have opened several camps just on the border, is in Sareikela where from they are occasionally coming with the connivance of the Bihar Police inside the Mayurbhanj district so as to create trouble[65]. Corroborating this statement, the communist leaders also confirmed that after the top Tribal leaders were arrested by the Government on 5 February 1949, the communists infiltrated in to the disturbed area to keep the violent agitation alive, though it was not well received by the Tribals. The participation of the Bengali communists escalated the situation resulting in unnecessary killing of many rebels[66].

A pertinent question in this regard is the role played by the Government of Bihar. The Bihar Government was not a silent observer when Bamanghaty was burning due to the Tribal uprising. They maintained supporting attitude through sympathetic propaganda. The Government of Bihar had submitted a memorandum to the State ministry claiming Mayurbhanj and demanding its merger. A high power delegation was sent to Delhi to discuss the issue. The Government of Bihar was unhappy at the decision taken by the centre to merge Mayurbhanj with Orissa[67]. A group of 14 MLAs from Bihar wanted to enter in to Mayurbhanj to study the situation and assess the nature of disturbance and damages caused to life and property. But the Police did not allow them entry. After enquiring at the border areas they made a statement to the press saying thousands have been killed by Police firing. The Congress men of Bihar demanded a judicial enquiry to the whole incident[68].

On 12 March in a public meeting held at Puri Prime Minister Pandit Jawaharlal Nehru told the gathering that Mayurbhanj was amalgamated with Orissa after proper thought and discussion and the decision was irrevocable. He warned those who were opposing the amalgamation and that the opposition would be dealt with firm action. He blamed the newspapers for giving exaggerated news to mislead the public which created tension[69]. There is no denying the fact that in suppressing the uprising the Government deployed Gorkha soldiers who were famous for their mercilessness and bravery. Since they used light machine guns and sten guns, the number of casualties must have been more than 14 which was the official figure. Referring to the Adibasi rising, the Statesman from Calcutta reported,

> "The police firing on the Adibasi mob are said to have killed ten and wounded others. But though they (tribals) can not be allowed to kill or frighten people, something less calumny than counter terror is needed to pacify these primitive folk. In his report to the Orissa, Government and the States Ministry, Mr. Rege, the Adviser is alleged to have said that a showdown was inevitable. That has an unpleasant sound, and we suggest that the States Ministry, which is taking a proper interest, should make further enquiries, possibly through a different officer"[70].

The contention was that instead of dealing with the situation "clumsily" the Government should have adopted a more humanistic approach. The word 'Show down' denotes confrontation of violence and the result of such confrontation was quite inhuman and sad. However, the rebellion was crushed with an Iron hand causing heavy casualties. The numerical superiority of the Adibasi was neutralized by the use of sophisticated weapons by the police. It resulted in heavy loss of life, no doubt, but the insurrection could be suppressed. The Government, thereafter, imposed a punitive fine of

Rupees one lakh to ensure teaching a lesson to the Tribals. The punitive taxes were collected with utmost rigidity and no leniency was shown. The stern action of the Government made the tribals so panicky that several villages were deserted as the inhabitants fled to the jungles to avoid police action[71].

The Aftermath

The Government initiated judicial proceedings against those rebels and their leaders who had been arrested by the police during the uprising for criminal activities. But in course of time the Government changed their mind considering the long term effect of drastic action that might jeopardize the stability of the administration of the new district. Since the merger had recently been done and on the eve of it the Government of India had committed to look in to the welfare of the Adibasis, the nature of action had to be properly thought of. The first task of Mahtab Government was to reassure the Adibasi their safety and to persuade them to come back to their homes in villages to start life afresh. The Government was to help in their rehabilitation and resumption of traditional profession. Mahatab, as the Prime Minister gave this firm assurance[72].

Mahatab, as the Prime Minister of Orissa province paid a good will visit to Baripada and Rairangpur on 19 April to meet the leaders in Jail and the public in general meetings. He expressed his sincere concern about their welfare and as an example of political expediency withdrew all criminal cases against the leaders. In a mammoth public meeting of the Adibasis organized at Baripada he elaborately discussed their problems and solicited cooperation of all sections of people in ameliorating the major ones urgently. He announced the sanction of Rupees one crore for the welfare and development of the tribals. He promised for an Engineering college in the district and a special allocation of Rupees Twenty lakhs for irrigation and drinking water facilities in the villages[73]. He also promised finalisatiion of all cases against the tribals within 3-4 months[74].

On 18 April the working committee of the Adibasi Sabha decided to formally withdraw the civil disobedience and non-cooperation programme in Mayurbhanj. This was possible due to the efforts of Juliun Tiga, the Prabasi Secretary of the Adibasi Mahasabha who was eager to have a peaceful end to the disturbances[75]. At Rairangpur he met Mahtab to discuss relevant issues in a free and frank atmosphere. One of the major points raised by Tiga was the repatriation of about 30,000 Tribals who had fled from Mayurbhanj and took shelter in the adjacent Singhbhum district. Mahatab declared that all prisoners who had no criminal charges against them would be immediately released. On Tiga's persuasion, the refugees started returning home and those who were absconding surrendered to the courts. As per records 13 absconders surrendered before the SDO Rairangpur on 14 May and subsequently all the rest. Tiga took Mahtab's permission to meet Sunaram Soren in the Jail in order to persuade him to endorse the decision of the working committee[76]. Sunaram Soren was still in the Jail.

At last, the Government of Orissa in a press release[77] declared that about seven hundred Adibasis facing trial for the Mayurbhanj uprising and not connected with major crimes would be released. But those charged with murder, human sacrifice, attack on police etc would have to face trial.

Reconciliation

There was strong public opinion that the Government should make a permanent effort to pacify the tribals through measures of reconciliation. The leaders were brought from Rairangpur to Baripada jail where Mahtab could meet them. Only the Collector, Superintendent of Police and the Jail authorities knew about this. Mahtab being a shrewd politician successfully persuaded Sunaram Soren, Ram Chandra Majhi and other leaders to agree to condemn human sacrifice and to stop all rebellious activities. He got a signed document from them. Mahatab thereafter, met the Tribals to assuage their hurt feelings explaining them the objectives of the Government to develop their economic condition through various projects and schemes. Sunaram Soren and other leaders were released from jail[78].

In the public meeting which followed Mahtab declared that the punitive taxes collected from the Adibasi, would be refunded to them. This good will gesture overwhelmed the Adibasis and their joy knew no bounds when the criminal cases were with drawn by the Government[79]. After normalcy was restored in Bamanghaty the tribals reconciled with the reality of Mayurbhanj's merger with Orissa Province.

The above reconciliation was possible on account of the dynamic initiative of V.S. Mathews, the new Collector of Mayurbhanj. He had past experience in Delhi in dealing with the Post Partition trauma and knew how to tackle the problem of repatriation. He wrote to the Government that by a policy of reconciliation alone, the Tribal problem of Mayurbhanj would be solved. In his letter he wrote that what the tribals needed was not bullet, but books for their children, medicine for their sick and potable water in the villages. The Government gave him the opportunity to negotiate with the Tribals. It was he who pleaded for an attitude of reconsiliation with the rebel leaders so that they may return to the mainstream. He met Sunaram several times to know his mind in an one to one discussion. When he prepared the ground for reconciliation, Mahatab visited Rairangpur to go ahead in the policy of pacification. The change in the treatment made the bond of mutual respect and friendship stronger. They accepted the merger as final and returned to the political play ground forgetting the past[80].

In Mayurbhanj the National Congress opened an unit called 'Adibasi Congress'. The tribals joined the party in large number. Their political aspirations could be properly channelized by the Adibasi Congress in the line similar to the National Congress. The popularity of National Congress among the tribals was vindicated thereby. Most of the Tribal leaders contested in the General Election of 1952 and got elected with overwhelming majority votes. The integration of Mayurbhanj was never questioned by them afterwards[81].

Mayurbhanj State Constituted one of the districts of Orissa province from 2 January 1949.

An Analysis

When all other Princely States of Orissa merged in 1948 leaving Mayurbhanj excluded, there were three possibilities for the Tribal leaders to chalk out; either to remain separate, or join with Orissa or with Bihar. The political awareness of the Tribals was a post 1947 phenomenon and it was very much influenced by the Congress programme of making India free as well as to have a written Constitution for her future governance. Their idea of representative Government was also identical with that of the Congress Party. They had an in born suspicion of the coastal people which made them feel safe to be in isolation. They were right to think that post independence politics of Orissa would be dominated by the coastal people and their leaders.

The idea to have a tribal state with tribal tracts of Bihar, Bengal and Orissa was not an irrational concept. Their ethnographical, cultural and linguistic homogeneity justified such a political unit. In India demand for a separate state on these grounds was not new. It was repeated with success in the Post independent period. Even Jharkhand became a political reality. India is a pluralistic country, where multiplicity of religion, languages, race and culture have been clubbed together to shape the political destiny of the Indian people. But the process of Balkanization could not be prevented in Assam, Bihar and Uttar Pradesh where new states were formed.

When they failed to keep Mayurbhanj separate, their next best alternative was to join with Bihar. So the proposal to be a part of Bihar was dictated by ethnic factor because Bihar had the largest Tribal population and the Bihari leaders welcomed the move. But after the loss of Sareikela and Kharswan in 1948, Orissa was not prepared to loose Mayurbhanj. Mahtab had exerted pressure upon the congress leadership to honour the historical oriya movement by amalgamating Mayurbhanj with Orissa. He succeeded in his effort with the help of local press and cooperation of Central leadership. The demand to merge with Bihar was neither supported by history nor popular will. It was a late realization of the leaders who failed to mobilize adequate public support from the beginning when they were toying with the idea of independent identity of Mayurbhanj.

The last alternative was to merge with Orissa. It was the logical choice if the desire of the educated elite of Mayurbhanj would be taken to consideration. The Maharaja was an Oriya, the bureaucracy and socially upper class people were all Oriyas. They dictated the events in favour of Orissa. In view of the desire of the Maharaja, desire of the politically conscious elite merger with Orissa was the best solution. It was inevitable as per the political development, which look shape in 1948-49.

The tribal uprising was a violent agitation against merger with Orissa. A question arises on to whether the illiterate tribals understood the significance of merger. Or was it on account of the end of monarchy that motivated them to revolt? The path of nonviolence was an unfamiliar path for them. There is no evidence that the Gandhian ideal of nonviolence influenced the common tribal. It was a mere slogan of convenience for persons like Sunaram Soren. He was neither a freedom fighter nor an active member of Prajamandal. His baptism in nonviolence was not deep rooted. If he suggested the path of nonviolence for the Tribal supporters he could not control the movement when it strayed away towards violence.

As far as the principle of non-cooperation was concerned Sunaram Soren followed the Gandhian Text Book merely to capture the tribal mind. Not to pay tax, not to seek a permission for cutting wood, not to have Excise permit etc must have touched the tribal mind; but not boycott of courts or Schools as the tribals were neither litigant or seeker of justice form the courts nor keen to join schools for education. Another draw back of the Tribal uprising was the absence of a leadership substitute. After the preemptive arrest on 5 February 1949 the arrest of the leaders left the tribal movement leaderless. Like a ship without a radar moving helter skelter in an uncharted sea, the tribal movement on Bamanghaty was a sporadic affair. There was no coordination, no control room.

Another significant point should not go unnoticed. By 1 January 1949 the tribal leaders contact with Orissa Government was totally lacking. D.V. Rege as the Chief Commissioner or as Adviser to the Government of Orissa on the affairs of Mayurbhanj had not convened any meeting with the Tribal leaders to explain to them convincingly the efficacy of merger with Orissa. After merges, the Government of orissa also did not take the Tribal leaders in to confidence maintaining a distance which could not be negotiated by the frustrated tribals. They could have used the good offices of the Maharaja to pacify the tribals; which they did not do. The tribal uprising was a confrontation between the primitive tribals and Mahatab, the Prime Minister of Orissa. The publicity aspect of the advantages of merger with Orissa was conspicuously lacking.

The suppression of tribal uprising in 1949 was through brute force of the armed police. It was a confrontation between primitive weaponry and modern sophisticated lethal weapons. It was a show down between two unequals. The sufferings of the Adibasis of Mayurbhanj was unprecedented. However, Mahatab applied the soothing balm of making Ministers, member of Parliament and members of the Legislative Assembly from among the tribal leaders. The tall promises of welfare made by Mahatab remained mere illusions, since even today those have not been fulfilled. The apprehension of the Tribal leaders that Mayurbhanj would remain undeveloped came true.

References

1 MayurbhanjStateGazette, 7 September, 1945.

2 Senapati, N. and Sahu, N.K., *Orissa District Gazetteer, Mayurbhanj* (Hereafter ODG) Cuttack, 1967, p.82.

3 Ibid.

4 RAM 1917-18, p.58.

5 Senapati, N. and Sahu, N.K. op.cit., p.82.

6 Ibid.

7 Ibid.

8 Various types of punishments were imposed upon 977 persons. Report on the Administration of Mayurbhanj (RAM) 1917-18, .59.

9 Playnee Somerset, *Indian States,* Biographical, Historical and Administrative Survey (1921-22), London, p.703.

10 Interview Amarendra Lal bose, Journalist, Baripada.

11 Interview Salkhan Murmu, Former M.P. Lok Sabha, Tata and Dipak Sarangi, Singhbhum.

12 Panphlet issued by Sunaram Soren in Oriya "the Aims and Objectives of MAS"(No Dak) Some records have been collected from the family of Sunaram Soren. There will be refered to "Sunaram Papers" hereafter.

13 *Mayurbhanj Jagaran,* 3 May 1948.

14 Interview - Salkhan Murmu, Ex-M.P. and Sunaram Paprs, Proceedings of the meeting, Undated.

15 Pamphlet "*Mayurbhanj Adibasi Sabha*", October 1947

16 Ibid. Aslo see Supra P.about the MAS' objecties.

17 Pamphlet op. cit.

18 Pamphlt "Mayurbhanj Adibasi Sabha O Mayurbhanj, Mishrana Samasya, op.cit., p.3.

19 Memorandum Submitted on behalf of the Mayurbhanj Adibasi Sabha to the Advisory Sub Committee an Excluded and Partion, Excluded Areas, 19 September, 1947.

20 Memorandum to His Highness the Maharaja, Mayurbhanj State submitted on elaf of the mayurbhanj Adibasi Sabha dated 6 September, 1947

21 Ibid.

22 Mayurbhanj State Gazette, 15 October, 1947. The 12 nominated tribal members were–Sakila Soren, Jadabananda Murmu, Dhyan Chand Tudu, Mohendra Majhi, Sunaram Soren, Shyam Chandra Majhi, Ghasiram Sandyl, Jagat Charan Majhi, Karunakar Majhi, Baidhar Majhi, BholanathMajhi and Ramnath Tudu.

23 Pamphlet entitled "Mayurbhanj Adibasi Sabha O Mishrana Samasya (Oriya) op.cit., p.3.

24 Mayurbhanj State Gazette, 7 January 1948 and the Pamphlet issued by the MAS entitled "Mishra Virodhi Prastab" dated 30 December 1947.

25 Sunaram Papers, Proceedings of the meeting of MAS dated 2 June 1948 and Pamphlet issued by Sunaram Soren "What Mayurbhanj Wants" 5 July 1948.

26 Supra, Chapter IV.

27 Extraordinary Mayurbhanj State Gazette, 16 September, 1948

28 Ibid.

29 Proceedings of the meeting of MAS held on 16 September 1948

30 Ibid.

31 Mayurbhanj Adibasi Sabha O Mishrana Samasya, p.4.

32 Ibid., p.5.

33 Ibid., p.5.

34 Ibid. p.6.

35 Sunaram Paprs, Proceeding sof the meeting of 30 October 1948

36 Ibid.

37 They were–Sunaram Soren, Karunakar Hembram, Mahendranath Murmu, BarhaBesra, Ghasiram Sandyl, Sundar mohan Hembram, Dhyanchand Tudu, Shyan Charan Hansdah, Bhugla Majhi, Bayadhar Tudu, Arthur Pankaj, andRam Chandra Majhi.

38 Trans–"We shall merge with Biharand not with Orissa"

39 Interview–Purna Chandra Bindhani, Free lance Photographer and an Octogenarian.

40 Minutes of the meeting of the Adibasi Satha 2 to 6 November 1948, p.l.

41 Extraordinary Mayurbhanj State Gazette, 8 November, 1948.

42 Page 2 of the Minutes.

43 Sunaram Paprs, Proceedings of the meeting of the Adibasi Sabha. Thosw who addressed the meeting were–Sundarmohan hembram, Karunakar Tiriya, Dhyan Chand Tudu, Tulsinath Tiriya, Ghasiram Sandyl, Laxmidhar Nayak, and Ramdayal Murmu, etc.

44 Development in Mayurbhanj Affairs, op.cit.pp.2-3.

45 Interview Aswini Kumar Kabi, Octogenarian Lawyer of Rairangpur.

46 Mahatab, H.K., *Sadhanar pathe*(Oriya biography) p.350. Also Senapati, N. and Sahu, N.K.(ed) *ODG Mayurbhanj*, p.82.

47 Promod Ghose ws ex-army personnel of Baripada with communist leanings. He hailed from Puri and had links with the leftists of Calcutta. Nishamani Tripathi was also from Puri and was a follower of Ghose.

48 Interview–NilratanSaha, Leading merchant and businessman of Rairangpur/Baripada.

49 The Samj. 7 February 1949

50 Ibid.

51 Interview, Govind Prasad Agrawal, Businessman of Rairangpur.

52 The Samaj, 8 February, 1949

53 Orissa Legilative Assembly Proceedings–Vol.IX No.4, 1949

54 Abua Jharkhand, 27 February, 1949

55 Ibid.

56 Developmento f Mayaurbhanj Affairs, op.cit., p.5.(Sunaram Soren Papers)

57 The Samaj, 14 February, 1949

58 Certified copy of the Judgement of Sessions Judge, Mayurbhanj in Trial No. 3, M of 1950, pp.3-4. Deposition of Aman Singh, the SDO, Judgement in Session Trial No.3, 1950, op.cit. Cutack Law Times, 1953, Besra Majhi and other Vs. The State of Orissa, pp.188-195.

59 The Samaj, 2 March, 1949

60 Prafulla Kumar Siha, a Bengali from Bardhaman district.

61 The Samaj 4 March, 1949. Interview–Bimal Mukherjee, Octogenarian Advocate of Baripada.

62 Ibid.. The Samaj 5 March, 1949

63 Proceedings, Orissa Legislative Assembly, 5 March, 1949, Vol.IX, No.4. He replied to a Question No.48, issued by Laxminarayan Mishra.

64 Ibid.

65 Ibid.

66 See the proceedings and the Appendix.

67 The Samaj 5 March, 1949

68 Ibid., 7 March, 1949

69 Ibid. 13 March 1949 and Mahatab, H.K. *Sadhanar Pathe* (Autobiography in Oriya), 1972, p.351.

70 Quoted in "The Samaj", 7 March, 149.

71 Interview–Aswini kumar Kabi, Octogenarian Lawyer of Rairangpur.

72 Mahatab, opcit., p.352.

73 Purna Chandra Mohanty was appointed as a Special Court Judge to try all cases arising out of the tribal disturbances.

74 The prajatantra, 22 April, 1949, and Sunaram Soren Papers. Letter of Julius Tiga dated 28 May 1948 addressed to H.K.Mahatab, Prime Minister of Orissa.

75 Ibid.

76 The Samaj, 11 august, 1949

77 Sunaram Soren Papers, letter of H.K.Mahatab to M.D.Julius Tiga dated 19 July, 1949

78 The Samaj, 11 August, 1949

79 Ibid.

80 Interview Chaitanya Prasad Majhi, Octogenerian Adibasi Leader of Mayurbhanj.

81 Mahtab, H. K. Sadhanar Pathe, op.cit. p.353. Sunaram Majhi got elected to the Assembly from Bahalda Constituency and became a Cabinet Minister. Ram Chandra Majhi got elected as a member of Lok Sabha in 1952.

6 Conclusion

A brief summary of the preceding chapters is being attempted here along with some concluding observations. The erstwhile Princely State of Mayurbhanj having territorial contiguity with West Bengal and Jharkhand Provinces in the East and North is predominately a tribal district. It had been a geopolitical unit of Orissa Province since time immemorial. At present it forms the largest district of Orissa with four sub-divisions – Sadar, Kaptipada, Bamanghaty and Panchpir. The important rivers which flow with the names of Balanga, Kharkai, Son and Gangahar emerge from the Simlipal Hill which is a National Park and also a Biosphere having rich Flora and Fauna. As a tribal district the important tribes who dwell here are the Santals, Kols, Ho, Bhumijs, and Kharias etc. whose socio-economic status is below the poverty line. The district was rich in iron ore a century ago and the present state of its forest wealth is much depleted by reckless deforestation. The tribals' life style is still primitive as they have remained away from the mainstream of socio-economic growth. The non-tribals are more in number in the Sadar Sub-division who are called '*Dikus*' and their high literacy rate has given birth to an elite community whose culture is more modern and progressive. Christianity and Islam are not very popular, though each community has its identity in the form of Church and Mosque. Neither represents a major social force. The tribals keep themselves aloof from the Dikus. Intermarriage between the tribals and non-tribals in strictly forbidden. Yet in religious festivals like Rath Yatra, Dusshara, and Makar Sankranti both join together to celebrate and enjoy. The tribal system of faith and worship is animistic and hey do not shy away from Hinduism, particularly in worshipping mother Goddess. Their languages are different from Oriya, but in the schools and offices oriya is the common language for all. Notwithstanding the differences the social life of Mayurbahnj is one of cohesion, and coexistence showing no sign of tension any time.

The ancient name of Mayrubahnj was Khijjinga-mandala which became a small tribal Kingdom in the 10th Century A.D. under the Bhanja dynasty. As per the family tradition, the Bhanjas were Feudatories of the Bhaumakaras and the Somavamsis in the tenth- eleventh centuries and their capital Khijjingokatta (modern Khiching) was a center of Jainism, Buddhim and Brahmanical religion. This is borne by the fact that the archaeological remains and monuments of Khiching are related to all these religious faiths. After Khijjingakotta was destroyed by Sultan Feroze Shah Tughluq in 1361, the Bhanjas transferred their capital to Hariharpur in 1400 A.D., but on account of frequent incursions of the Muslim Nawabs of Bengal and the Marathas of Nagpur were forced to abandon it in 1803 when Baripada developed as their new capital. In course of these developments, the Bhanjas had become avowed champions of Vaisnavism having developed close links with Gaudiya Vaisnavism of Bengal and Jagannatha Cult of Puri. Since the construction of the Jagannatha Temple at Baripada in 1575 and the Mini (Banthia) Jagannatha Temple in 1863 Baripada, the capital town of Myurbhanj nourished a cultural synthesis between the tribal and non-tribal tradition of the state. This is evident in the Chhau dance, Jhumar Songs, Makar and Bandana (Diwali) festivals which are commonly enjoyed by both groups of people in Mayurbhanj.

The present study has traced the relationship of Raja Damodar Bhanj and his wife Rani Sumitra Devi with the East India Company after 1764 when Bengal suba was ceded to the British who were given the right to collect revenue. Raja Damodar Bhanja was in great predicament because he was sandwitched between the Marathas in the South and west and the Company in the East and North. Mayurbhanj was reduced to a buffer position as it witnessed the rivalry between the Marathas and the British for supremacy. Raja Damodar Bhanja was wise enough to maintain the territorial integrity of his Kingdom by combining diplomacy with force of arms. His wife and successor Rani Sumitra Bhanj also adopted the same strategy with more emphasis on cordial relation.

But as the British interest for the possession of Orissa grew, the strategic importance of Mayurbhanj was increasingly realized. The occupation of Orissa was essential to link up Bengal with Madras for easy troop movement. At first Lord Wellesley tried to get Orissa province from the Bhonsle of Nagpur through diplomatic pressure and offer of due compensation. But when that failed, the Governor General prepared for a military expedition. For the success of the expedition the support and cooperation of Rani Sumitra was most essential. Therefore, the East India Company had to formulate such a policy towards Mayurbhanj which would ensure Rani's friendship and not hostility.

Finally when Orissa was occupied in 1803, the East India Company entered in to Treaty and engagements with the Rajas allowing them to enjoy their Kingdom on payment of nominal amount as annual tribute. The Company did not annex the territories of the Rajas and granted them internal autonomy as well as the benefit of 'non-intervention'. To the new system of Paramountcy, the hill States of Orissa fitted themselves very well after signing the Treaty engagements. The Rajas of Mayurbhanj also accepted the British Paramountcy and the Colonial structure of administration enjoying freedom in internal matters.

As early as December 1803 the letter of Colonel Harcourt and John Melville, the Joint Commissioners for the affairs of Cuttack province had set the tone of British relation with Mayurbhanj. The letter dated 5 December 1803 stated,

> "Morebhunge being one of the Principal tributary territories to the province of Cuttack we consider it highly important to proceed with great caution in any arrangements relating to it."

This spirit of mutual respect continued to pervade in showing special respect to the Rajas of Mayurbhanj. Whenever the Sanad was to be renewed or a Khilat was bestowed upon the Chief of Mayurbhnaj the Company was unequivocally proclaiming the special status due to the Chief. Among the 26 Tributary States of Orissa Mayurbhanj was accorded the highest position of honour.

In 1867 after suppressing the tribal uprising in Bamanghaty the then Superintendent of Orissa Feudatory States and the Commissioner of Orissa Division Mr. T.E.Ravenshaw as a friend of the new Raja Krushna Chandra Bhanj Deo advised him to modernize the State administration. The Maharaja did not let him down because he followed the advice in letter and spirit. Since then till his premature death in 1882 the Maharaja introduced English education in the State and a well documented recorded administration. He introduced reforms in Judiciary, Revenue and Public Works Department and encouraged education not only in the State, but also in Orissa Division, because of his financial support the Cuttack school could become a College and it was Commissioner's concern for the improvement of the Division.

Maharaja Krushna Chandra set the trend of the State administration leaving it to the successor to follow faithfully. During the time of Sreeram Chandra Bhanja Deo, along with his enlightened Dewans bestowed upon the State people the benefits of several welfare measures like efficient administration, local self Government, Public Health, Charitable dispensaries, Irrigation facilities, two hundred schools for boys and girls, hostels stipends and scholarships for aspiring students, a Teachers' Training School, railways and highways for easy communication, exploitation of mineral and forest wealth and industrialization. One can imagine the emergence of Mayurbhanj as the most progressive state when Maharaja Sreeram Chandra was invited to adorn the Presidentship of the inaugural session of the Utkal Union Conference in 1903 which was the first united forum to project Oriya nationalism. Having gone round the World to study the miracle of changes brought in by science and technology in Europe, United States of America and Japan, the Maharaja urged upon the Oriya speaking people to pursue western education and adopt scientific method of agriculture. He mooted the idea of sending meritorious Oriya students abroad for further studies. He was a visionary whose reign heralded the beginning of a new era. But as the Providence decided otherwise, he died in a tragic accident in 1912 at an early age of 42 only abruptly putting an end to the development and welfare schemes.

The two sons of Sreeramchandra Bhanj who ruled Mayurbhanj successively were Maharaja Purna Chandra (1920-28) and Maharaja Pratap Chandra (1928-47). They were well educated, widely traveled, endowed with the qualities of head and heart and a liberal outlook. Both sponsored wide ranging reforms pushing the state further in the path of modernization. Maharaja Purnachandra restored peace and order in the Tribal dominated Sub-division of Bamanghaty, provided electricity and drinking water at Baripada, introduced election system in the Municipality, setup the Department of Archaeology for conservation and excavation of ancient monuments, extended railways to Talbandh, gave financial aid to numerous institutions in and outside Orissa, gave funds for the publication of Oriya Encyclopedia and provided electricity for the Ravenshaw College.

Maharaja Pratap Chandra Bhanjdeo (1928-1947) was not born to be a King, but the death of Maharaja Purnachandra by Tetanus infection in Bombay catapulted him to the throne. Like his brother he was an ace pilot, well educated, lover of sports and music and a staunch believer in democratic values. He came at a crucial time of history when the British Paramountcy ended, India achieved her freedom, the country was partitioned, peasants movement in the shape of Prajamandal reached its crescendo and the Princely states had to be integrated with Orissa. As a good administrator he selected his Dewans with care and discretion, managed the state efficiently with their advice, initiated bold democratic measures to evolve a representative Government in a limited scale. During the World War-II there was scarcity of essential consumers items which had to be properly distributed through Control system and he devoted time to do the job himself in a fair and equitable manner. He revived Chhau Dance, started an Aviation Department, established a High Court, Praja Sabha, Kendra Parishad, Cooperative Societies and the Mayurbhanj State Bank to promote trade and industries. A Venadium factory was setup at Bahalda. He introduced the first Decennial Census, a Budget Manual, a State Gazette and regular Industrial cum Agricultural Exhibitions. A Law Reporter was regularly published for the High Court and annual football tournaments were organized. He established elite officers club, public parks, public entertainment and renovated the old temple at Khiching. He modernized the Secretariat and appointed Public Relation Officer to project the activities of the State Government. He was a practical man knowing fully well the grave situation that would arise after the withdrawal of British Parmountcy. He did not hesitate to read the writing on the wall and before Sardar Patel asked him to sign the Instrument of Accession on 14 December 1947 he had already transferred the power of State Governance to the Prajamandal Ministry of Saratchandra Das on 9 December 1947, opting for himself the role of a constitutional monarch. No other ruling Chief of Orissa states had the fore sight and moral courage like that of Maharaja Pratapchandra. His clarity of understating the events of his own time made him an outstanding statesman.

A pertinent question may arise here. Was the transfer of power on 9 December to the Popular Ministry a clever ploy to prolong his dynastic rule amidst great political catastrophe for all ruling Princes? It is difficult to explain. But one thing which may absolve the Maharaja from any ulterior motive was his departure from Baripada for good. He neither came back to the Palace nor interfered in the affairs of the Government. He chose to live in Calcutta involving himself in private business enterprise. Though he did not succeed either in Tea Plantation in Shillong and Guwahati or minor Tool factory in Calcutta, he left Baripada for good. He took the end of British Paramountcy and the Princely system in his stride and accepted silently the end of the thousand year old Bhanja rule over Mayurbhanj.

Maharaja Pratap Chandra will go down in history as a ruler who believed in democracy. During the last decade of his rule he sincerely tried to share administration with the people. It was not possible for him to think of universal adult franchise because the people of his state were not ready yet. He maintained good relation with the Prajamandal leaders and never adopted a policy of confrontation with them. He even sent his two sons to work as manual labourers in constructing an irrigation project and it was appreciated by the Prajamandal as a noble gesture.

He had no dissent against the merger of Orissa. In fact he had liberally contributed to the Utkal University's Corpus Fund and was its first Pro-Chancellor. He had taken Premier Saratchandra Das with him to Cuttack on the day other rulers signed the merger document and presented Sardar Patel the real situation in Mayurbhanj. Why Sardar Patel did not insist for signing the document of merger is a difficult puzzle of history. Ten months later Maharaja took the Premier to New Delhi to sign the Instrument of Merger on 17 October 1948 handing over the State to Indian Union.

Mayurbhanj was a small principality with limited natural resources which was no comparison to Baroda, Mysore, Jodhpur or Hyderabad. That the Maharaja was not against integration with the adjacent province was clear in 1947 when he declined to join the Eastern States Union with Patna and Kalahandi. His letters to the Raja of Dungarpur and Nawab of Bhopal clearly explained his stand. He was rather evaluating the strength of the people claiming popular Government.

With a hindsight it may be said that the legacy of the Bhanja rulers was one of liberalism and benevolence. This was in contrast to those of Talcher, Ranpur and Dhenkanal. Critics point out that there was no college in Mayurbhanj, though financial support was extended to college outside the state. The Maharaja gave priority to Primary and Secondary education, but not collegiate. The apprehension of producing unemployed youth was probably a deterrent. But the people of Mayurbhanj were, by and large, happy under the Bhanja rule.

The rise of Prajamandal during the rule of Maharaja Pratap Chandra is an enigma. If the state administration was benevolent and welfare oriented, what factors helped the emergence of Prajamandal?. The rise of Prajamandal in Mayurbhanj was a direct outcome and fallout of the Congress movement in Balasore. Saratchandra Das, the leader of the Prajamandal movement called himself "Sarat Gandhi". He was a Congress worker having been baptised and experienced, in the civil disobedience movement. He started political activity with village reconstruction programme and through propaganda against untouchability. His area of activity was small, it was limited to Betnoti area. Nationalism, at that time was a wild fire, catching the imagination of the students and farmers. The number of elites in Mayurbhanj was not much. The lawyers joined the national movement in large number. Though the Maharaja wanted to share administration with the people, his choice of persons was limited.

The absence of feudal practice in Mayurbhanj can not be denied, so also the social status of the Sardar and their henchmen. Their method of collecting revenue through Pradhans was probably unpopular in a state where the people were extremely poor. The exploitation of minerals and forest products did not percolate down to the common men improving their economic condition. The abolition of Paikari system was a factor which created deep grievance and created new leaders like Baikuntha Nath Sadual who strengthened the hands of Sarat Gandhi. It was the Congress wave which swept across Mayurbhanj through Balasore which created an anti-Maharaja stir. The transfer of power in 1947 was more on account of the Maharaja's willingness to handover in preference to bloodshed. He was committed to prevent violence and bloodshed at any cost. Having taken the Prajamandal movement stoically, he was prepared to transfer power with a sense of detachment. The rule of the Bhanjas came to an end in 1947 because monarchical rule everywhere else in the country came to an end. Like the withdrawal of the British, withdrawal of dynastic rule was historically imperative. The people as a whole wanted a change of Government and social order.

The Prajamandal Government remained in power for eleven months during which their achievements were quite praise worthy when viewed from the odds against which they worked. The Ministry had no previous experience in running administration. It abolished the much despised Sardari system and regularized the jagir lands of the Paiks by giving them Patta for their ancestral holdings. In order to give power of governance to the people it established village sabhas. Though the Prajamandal was affiliated to the All India States' People's

Conference and aimed at abolishing the feudal social order and extension of democratic institutions and practices, the new Constitution which it set down to draft was a time taking process. It could not be completed with in the short period of tenure in office. The root of the Prajamandal was not deep in the Tribal dominated Bamanghati and Panchpir Subdivisions. Its support came from the limited number of urban elites. Under their pressure the Government of 'Sarat Gandhi' adopted welfare measure like higher education and secondary education by establishing a college, many schools and one Girls high school which benefited the middle class. It neither setup Industries nor a technical institute for vocational training of the tribals. The relaxation of Forest and Excise Rules were populist measure which had no impact on economic progress. Before 1947, the Prajamandal was preoccupied with counterpropaganda against the Prajamangal Party of Harischandra Das, but after taking over the state Sarat Gandhi's Government had to confront the malicious propaganda of the Congress Government of Orissa and the Socialist leaders like Surendra Nath Dwibedy and Giris Chandra Roy who assiduously tried to create a Pro-merger atmosphere to sabotage the desire of Popular Government to remain as a separate entity. It was a crisis for survival. 'Sarat Gandhi' was shaky in his office, because of lack of internal cohesion and absence of wide popular support. The tribals were rallying under the banner of Mayurbhanj Adibasi Sabha with Sunaram Soren as their emerging leader whose point of focus was elsewhere. The tribals having an inborn suspicion of the 'Dikus' could never extend unconditional support to the Prajamandal Government. Sarat Chandra Das being a 'Diku' himself could neither be a substitute of the Maharaja, nor of Sunaram Soren as he neither spoke a tribal language, nor extensively toured the tribal areas to endear himself to the Santals, Kols or Bhumijs. As a leader he was neither dynamic nor potential enough to deliver the goods. Sarat Gandhi never faced Harekrushna Mahtab, the young and dynamic Prime Minister of Orissa seeking his, cooperation because he was aware of the price he would be asked to pay. His performance in New Delhi before the State Ministry was quite pathetic. The result was a foregone conclusion. Mayurbhanj was predestined to merge with Orissa sooner or later.

The demand of the Popular Government and the tribals of Mayrubhanj to remain a separate unit under the Indian Union is not difficult to explain. Mayurbhanj had a distinct geopolitical identity since long. It was politically and economically a viable state and it remained independent till 1803. In the British period the state remained independent under its Rajas who enjoyed internal autonomy. The non-extension of the Gandhian freedom movement in to Mayurbhanj helped it to maintain its exclusion from the national mainstream. Had it been extended to Mayurbhanj, the people would have developed identical aspiration and hopes like the British administered areas. The absence of the movement kept Mayurbhanj and the Garjat people separate in many ways. The people remained separate in two watertight compartments as two separate entities. This separate identity was at the root of their desire, to remain separate from the Orissa province. The people of Mayurbhanj having been ruled by benevolent rulers did not wish to sacrifice good administration and to remain under an unfamiliar Congress Government.

The Prajamandal was keen to keep Mayurbhanj separate from Orissa without taking in to consideration the socio-economic consequences. Mahtab was seriously pursuing the goal of unifying all the Oriya speaking Feudatory States with Orissa Province so that a Greater Orissa would be created. Since the visit of the Cabinet Mission to Delhi, he was moving in the Congress circle to create a lobby for that. He was also keeping the States Ministry informed of his dream scheme giving enough justification in favour of the same. The escape of Mayurbhanj from the dragnet of Sardar Patel in1947 must have been a great disappointment as the Premier Feudatory State remained excluded. Thereafter, the news papers of Cuttack (Prajatantra and Samaj) maintained regular editorial campaign to demoralise Sarat Chandra Das and to create a vigorous public opinion in favour of merger of Mayurbhanj with Orissa. The Prajamandal could not counter the above campaign as there was no newspaper published from Baripada. His only saviour was the States Ministry who was not likely to be helpful.

The separate existence of Mayurbhanj without viable economic support or moral support from any side was quite frustrating. The decision of Sarat Gandhi to call ' Prajamandal' as Mayurbhanj State Congress was another wrong move because the State Congress openly remained sub serviant to Mahtab's leadership. The erstwhile Sardars who were opposed to Prajamandal for the latter's antifeudal stance joined the State Congress strengthening the hands of Mahtab. In addition, Bidyadhar Mohapatra, the second Minister in Sarat Das Government not only joined the State Congress, but also differed from certain policy decisions of the Premier. The Ministry was divided and its weakness was an advantage for Mahtab's pro- merger campaign. The internal pressure for merger with Orissa gradually mounted. As the Government of Sarat Chandra Das failed to tackle the situation precipitating a crisis of great magnitude, Das was forced to discuss the issue of merger with the Government of India in August 1948. Sensing the coolness of the States Ministry whose Spokesman V P Menon advised him to merge with Orissa, Das returned home with a broken heart. He discussed the issue with the Vyavastha Parishad and in a statement humbly submitted what V P Menon had suggested. Menon had told him that separate entity of Mayurbhanj was neither possible nor desirable and that Mayurbhanj should merge with Orissa for the grater cause of India. Menon had also explained him the dangers and difficulties of separate existence away from the main part of the body politic, i,e, Orissa. Das also advised the members to go in with Utkal for linguistic homogeneity. Mayurbhanj accepted merger with Orissa on 17 October 1948 when the Maharaja signed the Instrument of Accession in New Delhi. Though Das was present on the spot his signature was not desired essential. The matter was finally settled with one condition, that instead of straight away joining with Orissa, it would be wise to keep Mayurbhanj under the Indian Union for a short period before handing it over to Orissa. That was agreed upon.

While the Prajamandal Government was in power (November 1947 to November 1948) keeping Mayurbhanj separate, the problem of Sareikela and Kharswan cropped up. The Chiefs of these two Oriya speaking Feudatory States had signed the Instrument of Merger at Cuttack on 14 December 1947 making it clear for the Orissa Government to take over the administration. Both states were clubbed together to form a district of Orissa Province. But suddenly, the Adibasi Mahasabha of Jaipal Singh took recourse to an armed rebellion demanding merger with Bihar. In January 1948 the Adibasis were encouraged to resort to an armed rebellion in response to the call of Jaipal Singh. The tribals of Singhbhum and some antisocial elements of Tatanagar took part in the violent demonstration. The rebels surrounded the Government offices, residence of the officers and paralysed the administration completely. The two rulers of Sareikela and Kharswan reversing their earlier decision of 14 December 1947 instigated the tribals to break away from Orissa. There was intelligence report that some Politicians of Bihar actively encouraged the revolt. Although the Government of Orissa took expeditious steps to curb violence through prompt deployment of military police there was unnecessary bloodshed and death of the Adibasis. The roads to Sareikela and Kharswan passed through Mayurbhanj. In view of her differences with Orissa Government the rebel leaders thought that Mayurbhanj would not allow any troop movement though her territory. Soon after the restoration of law and order, the Government of India appointed a Tribunal to enquire and report whether the powers delegated to the Government of Orissa by the Notification No III- IP dated 23 December 1947 by the Government of India, Ministry of States should be continued to be vested with that Government or whether those powers should be transferred to the Government of Bihar.

The above Tribunal could not meet for adjudication. But in a tripartite meeting held with the representatives of Bihar and Orissa Governments and V. P. Menon in New Delhi it was decided that;

> "On account of the situation of Sareikela and Kharswan as the island territories of the Singhbhum district, it was impossible for those states to the efficiently managed by any Government other than that which was responsible for the administration of that district." The Government of India, therefore, decided that these two states should be transferred to the Government of Bihar.

(Government of Orissa's Memorandum submitted to the States Recognisation Commission, 1955, p. 26)

On 18 May 1948 the notification was issued by the Government of India under section 3 and 4 of the Extra Provincial Jurisdiction Act, 1947 cancelling the previous notification of 23 December 1947. With effect from 18 May 1948, the states of Sareikela and Kharswan formed part of the Singhbhum district of Bihar.

The loss of Sareikela and Kharswan for Orissa was probably on account of weakness in political leadership. But it had a direct impact on the tribal people of Mayurbhanj. In Mayurbhanj the Adibasi Mahasabha of Sunaram Soren was deeply opposed to merger with Orissa. They initially wanted a unification of all the tribals under one administration. The accession of Sareikela and Kharswan with Bihar as a result of armed revolt worked like a heady tonic for the Adibasis of Mayurbhanj. They, therefore, resolved to follow a similar course of action to breakaway from Orissa after they came to know about the decision of the Government of India. Their delegation to the States Ministry was told categorically about this by V.P. Menon. The Adibasis under Sunaram Soren were now instigated by Rev. L. Bhawan and Jaipal Singh decided to strike. With Sunaram Soren and Ramchandra Majhi as their leaders they declared Bamanghaty Sub-division as independent unit with headquarters at Rairangpur. The road leading from Baripada to Rairangpur was either cut off or blocked by large stones and trees at several places to prevent troop movement. At strategic places the armed Adibasis staged the standard of revolt. They engaged school students as spies to bring advanced information and sacrificed a Forest Ranger before their Goddess seeking her blessings for success. They planned to kill as many Dikus as possible. The rebellion spread from Bamanghaty to Panchpir Sub-division creating panic among the non-tribals. Thousands of armed Adibasis entered Baripada town holding demonstration and public meetings. There were ladies, children, musicians, drummers and colourfully attired rebels who shouted "No merger with Orissa, but with Bihar".

Baripada town had never witnessed such spectacle. The Government of Orissa decided to take firm action when inspite of all persuasions the rebels did not return to the villages. With the help of armed military police firing had to be ordered at Kuldiha, Gunduria, Gitilata, Chandi Khamal, Bangriposi, Rairangpur and many other places. There was heavy casualties among the rebels. At last, law and order was restored and there was a sigh of relief among the non tribals. Due to police action and imposition of punitive taxes, the tribals got scared preferring to flee to the jungles. The Government initiated judicial proceedings and did not show any leniency.

But, slowly, there was a change of heart in the Government circle. After much bloodshed a soothing touch was essential for improving the relationship between the new administration and the Adibasi people. VS Mathews, the Collector established personal rapport with the rebel leaders negotiating for reconciliation. He persuaded Harekrushna Mahtab, the Prime Minister of Orissa to visit Mayurbhanj, talk directly to the Adibasis, show sympathy and understanding and urge upon them to join the political mainstream. It was a matter of political expediency to withdraw criminal cases for minor offences. Mahtab took steps to open a branch of the National Congress in Rairangpur area under the name of Adibasi Congress to enroll as many Adibasis as possible and to make them join the national mainstream. He was successful in his scheme as was seen in the General election of 1952. The Congress became popular among the tribals and their leaders got elected with Congress ticket. There was no further snag in the integration of Mayurbhanj with Orissa.

Mayurbhanj was made a district of Orissa province with effect from 2 January 1949.

During the period under review (1882-1949) Mayurbhanj had undergone rapid Socio-political and economic changes far ahead from other Princely States of Orissa. From an inaccessible mountainous and undeveloped state, it became the most vibrant, progressive and modern State in Orissa under good governance of its Rajas. An educated elite society had gradually emerged. These seven decades were important for the spread of education, better roads and communication, provision of modern health, electricity and drinking water facilities, reformed land revenue system, due rights to properties, freedom of expression and movements, setting up of an independent judiciary ensuring the Rule of Law, modern Secretariat with recorded administration, availability of Cooperative Society and Bank, absence of caste system, free entry to temples, exploitation of natural resources, equitable distribution of essential articles, free access to the Ruler and a society free of tension. These facilities were available earlier under an aristocracy which was enlightened and benevolent. That the people of Mayurbhanj even today cherish the happy memories of Bhanja rule has its own historical justification.

Appendices

ANNEXURE-I: Chronological

Treaty and Engagements signed between the Chiefs of Orissa and the East India Company in 1803-04

Raja Balabhadra Bhanja, Raja of Killah Kanika in the Soobah of Orissa, engage faithfully and correctly to abide by this engagements entered into by me with the Honourable East India Company as contained in the following clauses, to wit;

Clause-I: I will always hold myself in submission and loyal obedience to the Honourable East India Company aforesaid.

Clause-II: I will continue to pay, without demur, to the said Government, as my annual Peshkas or tribute 84,840 Kahuns of Cowrees in three installments, as specified herein below :

Clause-III: I will on demand to that effect, cause any person who is an inhabitant of the Soobah appertaining to the Honourable Company aforesaid, and who may have fled and come into my territory, to be forthwith arrested and delivered over to the Government.

Clause-IV: Should any person who is a resident in my territories, commit a crime within the limits of the

Mughalbandi, I hereby engage on demand to that effect, to cause such person to be arrested and delivered over for trial to the Government authority. Moreover, I further bind myself in cases where I may possess any claim or demand on one who is an inhabitant of Mughalbandi, not of my own authority to enforce such claim, but I will notify the same to the constituted authority and will act in accordance with such orders as may issue from him.

Clause-V: I engage that whenever the troops of the Honourable Company's Government shall pass through my territories, I will direct the people of my Killah to supply, to the extent of their capability, all russad and supplies, which shall be sold at fair prices. Further, I will, on no manner of pretext whatever stop or detain, or offer any let or hindrance to, any subject of the Honourable Company's Government, or to any other person whatever who may be proceeding by land or water with goods or orders, or with any Parwana on the part of the Government, through my boundaries, and will ensures natives taken care that no loss or mischief shall befall such parties in life or goods.

Clause-VI: In case any neighbouring Raja or any other person whatever shall disobey the said government, I engage, on demand and without demur, to depute a contingent force of my own troops with the forces of Government for the purpose of rebuking and chastising such rebel and bringing him under the subjection of the aforesaid Government. Such contingent to receive only rations agreeably to the previously current practice, so long as they shall be present.

These shall be the installments of my Peshkas :

In the month of Cheyt	-	28,840 Kahunas
In the month of Jeyt	-	28,000 Kahunas
In the month of Asar	-	28,000 Kahunas
		84,840 Kahunas

Dated 2nd November 1803

Saban 6th, 1211 Umlee.

The Kabol-Namah granted by the Honourable East India Company to the Raja of Kanika runs as follows :

We Lieutenant Colonel George Harcourt, Commanding the victorious troops of the Honourable East India Company and Commissioner of the Soobah of Orissa and John Melville, Commissioner of the same, appointed by the most Honourable the Marquis of Wellesley, Governor-General, for the settlement and pacification of the said Soobah, do, on behalf of the East India Company, execute this acknowledgement as set forth in the following paras to Raja Balabhadra Bhanja, of Kanika, in the said Soobah of Orissa.

Clause-I: The annual Peshkas payable by the Raja for his Rajajee of the said Killah, as fixed in the perpetuity at 84,840 Kahunas.

Clause-II: No further demand, however small, shall be made on the said Raja or received from him as nuzzur, supplies or otherwise.

Clause-III: The Government of Honourable East India Company, it is well known, is ever gracious to those Rajas who are always loyal and obedient to them, and constant in the imperial administration of justice to all its subjects alike, and, therefore, in like manner extends the same impartially to the Rajas, such as have been indicated above and seeks always their prosperity and peace. Therefore, any just representation or complaints made to the Government by the said Raja of Kanika will meet with a decision in accord with justice.

Dated 2nd November 1803 Sd/-G.Harcourt

Commissioners

Saban 6th, 1211 Umlee J.Melville

ANNEXURE-II

List of the States with their Area, Income and Tributes*

Sl.No	Name of the States	Area in	Income sq.miles	Tributes paid to the British Government		
1.	Athgarh	168	1,44,435	2,800	-	0-0
2.	Athmallik	730	1,64,122	480	-	0-0
3.	Baramba	142	93,504	1,397	-	15-5
4.	Bamara	1,988	5,19,265	7,500	-	0-0
5.	Baud	1,264	3,30,991	800	-	0-0
6.	Bonai	1,296	2,09,441	2,700	-	0-0
7.	Daspalla	568	1,37,982	661	-	7-11
8.	Dhenkanal	1,463	5,02,944	5,009	-	0-9
9.	Gangpur	2,492	5,54,511	10,000	-	0-0
10.	Hindol	312	94,186	551	-	3-11
11.	Kalahandi	3,745	6,32,180	16,000	-	0-0
12.	Keonjhar	3,096	7,75,775	1,710	-	1-3
13.	Khandapara	244	2,26,297	4,211	-	8-8
14.	Mayurbhanj	4,243	28,22,675	1,067	-	11-9
15.	Narasinghpur	199	1,08,471	1,455	-	8-3
16.	Nayagarh	590	3,94,271	5,525	-	4-1
17.	Nilgiri	284	1,94,987	3,900	-	7-8
18.	Pal-Lahara	452	89,363	266	-	10-8
19.	Patna	2,399	8,61,953	13,000	-	0-0
20.	Rairakhol	833	94,027	2,000	-	0-0
21.	Ranpur	203	88,226	1,400	-	13-2
22.	Sonepur	906	3,38,037	12,000	-	0-0
23.	Talcher	399	4,47,086	1,039	-	10-5
24.	Tigiria	46	36,765	882	-	0-0
25		28,664	1,01,28,237	96,449	-	7-11

* General Review of Administration of the Feudatory States of Orissa for the year, 1930-31, p.29.

ANNEXURE-III

List of Orissa States with their population, Classification and the Name of the Chiefs*

Sl.No.	Name of the States	Name of the Chiefs	Population 1931 Census
'A' Class			
1.	Mayurbhanj	Maharaja Pratap Chandra Bhanja Deo	8,86,745
2.	Patna	Maharaja Rajendra Narayan Singh Deo	5,66,943
3.	Kalahandi	Braja Mohan Deo, O.B.E.	5,13,675
4.	Keojhar	Balabahadur Narayan Bhanja Deo	4,60,647
5.	Gangpur	Biramitra Pratap Sekhar Deo	3,56,388
6.	Dhenkanal	Sankar Pratap Mahendra Bahadur	2,84,328
7	Sonepur	Maharaja Bira Mitroday Singh Deo	2,37,945
8.	Bamara	Bhanuganga Tribhuban Deb	1,51,259
9.	Nayagarh	Krushna Chandra Singh Mandhata	1,42,399
10	Baudh	Narayan Prasad Deo	1,35,248

'B' Class			
1.	Athgarh	Raja Srikaran Radhanath Babarta Pattnaik	50,148
2.	Athmallik	Kishore Chandra Deo Samanta	64,276
3.	Khandpara	Harihar Singh Mardraj Bhramarbar Ray	77,930
4.	Narsinghpur	Ananta Narayan Hari Charan Mahapatra	40,882
5.	Baramba	Narayan Chandra Birabar Mangaraj Mahapatra	46,689
6.	Bonai	Indra Deo	80,144
7.	Daspalla	Kishore Chandra Deo Bhanja	42,650
8.	Hindol	Bahadur Naba Kishore Chandra Mardraj Jagadeva	48,897
9.	Nilgiri	Kishore Chandra Mardaraj Harichandan	68,598
10.	Rairakhol	Bira Chandra Jadumani Deo	35,715
11.	Talche	Kishore Chandra Birabara Harichandan	69,631
'C' Class			
1.	Pal-Lahara	Raja Manipal	27,975
2.	Ranpur	Birabara Krushna Chandra Singh Narendra Mohapatra	47,713
3.	Tigiria	Banamali Kshetria Birabara Champupati Singh Mohapatra	24,840
4.			46,43,436

ANNEXURE-IV

Some Leading Persons who influenced the contemporary events of Mayurbhanj

Bhanj Deo Sriram Chandra

Sri Ram Chandra Bhanj Deo was born on the 17th December 1871. He was barely 11 years of age at the time of the death of his father Krushna Chandra Bhanj Deo. Hence the State came under the Court of Wards and P.Willy was appointed as its Manager. In December, 1882. Sri Ram Chandra assumed control over the State in 1892. He combined in him on the one hand the vision of a philosopher and an idealist, and on the other the shrewdness and practical wisdom of a lawyer, a legislator, philanthropist and a man of affairs. His administration was far ahead of his times; hence the status of Mayurbhanj rose to that of one of the best governed States in India. He patronized 'Utkal Prava' Oriya weekly literary journal, liberally financed the spread of higher education and Medical studies in Orissa, presided over the first meeting of the Utkal Union Conference in 1903. He appointed as his State Pleader, Pandit Gopabandhu Das who subsequently became one of the greatest leaders of Orissa. Sri Ram Chandra tried to bring up the administration of the State on British India level was honoured by an audience by His Majesty the King Emperor in London when he made a trip to England via Japan and America. Besides he was vested with the hereditary title of Maharaja by His Majesty the King Emperior in Delhi Durbar of 1911. He died on 22nd February 1912 by a shooting accident.

Bhanj Deo Purna Chandra

Maharaja Sri Ram Chandra was succeeded by his son Purna Chandra Bhanj Deo, but owing to the minority of the Ruler the State came under the administration of the Court of Wards. He was formally installed on the Gadi on the 13th November 1920. Like his father he was an enlightened and generous Ruler and although he ruled for 8 years, his period saw manifold development in the State. Besides, for services in connection with the First World War he was granted a permanent salute of 9 guns on the 1st January, 1918 and accordingly he visited France and England after the great war. He was appointed as A.D.C. to H.R.H. the Prince of Wales, during his visit to Patna. For the cause of learning he had contributed Rs.1 lakh for the Ravenshaw College. He died on 21st April, 1928.

Bhanj Deo Pratap Chandra

Purna Chandra Bhanj being childless was succeeded by his younger brother Pratap Chandra Bhanj Deo. In 1930-31 he was admitted to the Chamber of Princes as a full member by His Excellency the Viceroy under Act 2(ii) of the Constitution of the Chamber of Princes. During his time the State published the State Gazette (fortnightly), Mayurbhanj Chronicle and Bhanja Pradeepa, (Oriya) literary magazines. He was the first Pro-Chancellor of Utkal University. To provide political freedom to the people he organized the Praja Sabhas, Mayurbhanj Kendra Parishad and finally formed the prajamandal Ministry and transferred all his powers in the hands of the Ministry. Thus he proved himself to be every inch a democrat.

Das Sarat Chandra

He was born at Ambjora near Betnoti in Mayurbhanj district in the year 1891. At the age of 16 he passed Matriculation from Patna University. During 1920-21 he formed a voluntary organization named "Sevadal" to help the people from influenza fever which was very common then. In 1926-1930 he represented Orissa at the All India State's Peoples' Conference. After that he engineered the movement against the authoritarian rule of the Rajas. In 1932 he joined the legal profession but gave up and formed the 'Pragana Samiti' under his presidentship to serve the people. Later the

Pragana Samiti became the Praja Mandal. From the beginning up to 1947 he was the President of Mayurbhanj Praja Mandal. In 1947 he was selected to the Orissa and Chhatisgarh Council and was the Vice-President. In 1947 when the Ministry was formed under the aegis of the ruler he became the Prime Minister. He was so popular among the people that he was known as 'Sarat Gandhi'. He was rightly called the father of Mayurbhanj Praja Mandal.

Dash Prasanna Kumar

He belongs to Betnoti of Mayurbhanj district. When he was a student of High School he became sympathetic to the Praja Mandal Movement at Nilgiri which was a neighbouring State of Mayurbhanj. He personally had collected some funds and sent that to Nilgiri Praja Mandal Organisation. Giving up his study he joined the Mayurbhanj Praja Mandal in the year 1940. From 1941 to 1947 he served as the Secretary of Mayurbhanj Praja Mandal. Later when the Praja Mandal was identified with Mayurbhanj State Congress he served as the Vice President of Mayurbhanj State Congress. Besides he was elected to the Orissa and Chhatisgarh Council as a member and served as the Assistant Secretary of the Council. He also served as a member of the Mayurbhanj Constituent Assembly. By his able leadership and discipline the Praja Mandal became successful in establishing its long cherished goal that was the Responsible Government under the aegis of the Maharaja.

Dash Harish Chandra

He belongs to Baripada and the brother of Ram Chandra Das the Superintendent of Police, Mayurbhanj State. He was serving in the Palace. He was opposing the Praja Mandala movement and organized a parallel organization named "Praja Mangala", being backed by the Ruler. But the Mangala was outwitted by the Praja Mandala which ultimately formed the Ministry. Then he founded the Mayurbhanj District

Congress, a parallel organization with Mayurbhanj State Congress and favoured the merger of Mayurbhanj with Orissa.

Mahapatra Bidyadhar

He belongs to Baripada. He was the first graduate of Mayurbhanj State. He was a member of the Constituent Assembly. He was one of the three Ministers of the State during the popular Government under the aegis of the Ruler. As a Minister he was in-charge of (1) Revenue, (2) Law, (3) Health and Local Self Government.

Naik Maheswar

He belongs to Galusahi Village of Mayurbhanj and completed B.L. degree. He was a member of the Mayurbhanj Constituent Assembly and later became one of the three Ministers of Mayurbhanj during the popular Government.

As a Minister he was in charge of (1) Development, (2) Pubic Works, (3) Education, (4) Supply and Transport, and (5) Commerce and Labour. He was opposing the merger of Mayurbhanj with Orissa.

Pradhan Gaura Mohan

He was born in 1913 and belong to the village named Belanpur near Betnoti in Mayurbhanj district. While he was reading in High School he gave up study and joined the Balasore District Congress as a member. He had taken active part during the Non-Cooperation Movement and was imprisoned twice. When the Praja Mandal movement started in Mayurbhanj he joined that and became one of the leading figures. After the success of Praja Mandal he served as a member of the Constituent Assembly and later he became the Secretary of Mayurbhanj State Congress. In 1948 he was the editor of the Magazine "Desa Sevak".

He was a prolific writer. He has composed a booklet named "Maa ra daka" full of revolutionary songs. Some of its were sung as the opening song of the Praja Mandal meetings. Besides he was a very good and renowned practitioner of Aurvedic medicines.

Sandil Ghasiram

He belongs to Rairangpur. While he was reading in High School in Tata he joined the movement started by Jaipal Singh and gave up study and worked for the upliftment of the tribals. He was a member of the Constituent Assembly. He was a tribal leader during the Tribal Movement of 1948-49. For it he was arrested and imprisoned. Later on he was elected to the Orissa Assembly and served as a member of the Rajya Sabha.

Soren Sunaram

He belongs to Bahalda of Mayurbhanj State. He completed the law degree. He was a member of the Constituent Assembly. During the merger of Mayurbhanj; he became the leader of the Adivasis who opposed the merger with Orissa. He was using garlands of boiled eggs, green vegetables and a jacket made of Tiger skin. He was in favour of the merger of Mayurbhanj with Bihar. After the merger with orissa he was elected to the Orissa Legislative Assembly and served as a Cabinet Minister. He is recognized by the tribals as their guide, philosopher and leader.

Singh Jaipal

He was born in Takra in Ranchi district of Bihar. From childhood he remained in England and passed M.A. He established matrimonial relation with Lord Sinha family of Bengal. He returned to India after independence and joined as a lecturer. Then he joined as an officer of Burma Shell. During this period he worked for the upliftment of the tribals of Bihar and formed the 'Adivasi Mahasabha' under his Presidentship.

ANNEXURE-V

Excerpts From:
Mayurbhanj Merger Agreement

Agreement made this 17th of October 1948 between the Governor General of India and the Maharaja of Mayurbhanj.

Whereas in the best interests of the State of Mayurbhanj, as well as of the Dominion of India it is desirable to provide for the administration of the said state by of under the authority of the Dominion Government.

AND whereas the Maharaja has accepted the advice given to him.

It is hereby agreed as follows :

Article-1

The Maharaja of Mayurbhanj hereby cedes to the Dominion Government full and exclusive authority, jurisdiction and powers for and in relation to the Governance of the State and agrees to transfer the administration to the Dominion Government on the 9th Day of November 1948 (herein after referred to as the said day).

As from the said day the Dominion Government will be competent to exercise the said powers, authority and jurisdiction in such manner and through such agency as it may think fit.

Article-2

The Maharaja shall continue to enjoy the same personal rights, privileges, dignities and titles which he would have enjoyed had this Agreement not been made.

Article-3

The Maharaja shall with effect from the said day be entitled to receive from the revenues of the State Annually for his Privy Purse the sum of Rs.3,36,500/- - free of all taxes. This amount is intended to cover all the expenses of the Ruler and his family, including expenses on account of his personal staff, maintenance of his residences, marriages and other ceremonies, etc., and will neither he increased nor reduced for any reason whatsoever.

The Government of India undertake that the said sum of Rupees 3,36,500/- shall be paid to the Maharaja in four equal installments in advance at the beginning of each quarter from the State Treasury of at such other Treasury as may be Specified by Government of India.

Article-4

The Maharaja shall be entitled to the full ownership, use and enjoyment of all private properties (as distance from State Properties) belonging to him on the date of this agreement.

The Maharaja will furnish to the Dominion Government before the 17th day of November, 1948 as inventory of all the immovable property securities and cash balance held by him as such private property.

In any dispute arises as to whether any item of property of the Maharaja or State Property, it shall be referred to a Judicial Officer, qualified to be appointed as a High Court Judge, and the decision of that Officer shall be final and binding on both parties.

Article-5

All the members of the Maharaja's family including the Maharani Saheba, Yubarani and Dowager Maharanis shall be entitled to all the personal privileges, dignities and titles enjoyed by them whether within or outside the territories of the State, immediately before the 15th day of August 1947.

Article-6

The Dominion Government guarantees the succession, according to law and customs, to gaddi of the state and Maharaja's personal rights, privileges, dignities and titles.

Article-7

No enquiry shall be made by or under the authority of the Government of India and no proceedings shall lie in any court in Mayurbhanj, against the Maharaja, whether in a personal capacity or otherwise, in respect of anything done or omitted to be done by him or under his authority during the period of his administration of that State.

Article-8

(1) The Government of India hereby guarantees either the continuance in service of the permanent members of the Public Services of Mayurbhanj on conditions which will be not less advantages than these on which they were serving before the date on which the administration of Mayurbhanj is made over the Government of India or the payment of reasonable compensation.

(2) The Government of India further guarantees the continuance of pensions and leave salaries sanctioned by the Maharaja to members of the Public Services of the State who have retired or proceeded on leave preparatory to retirement before the date on which the administration of Mayurbhanj is made over the Government of India.

Article-9

Except with the previous sanction of the Government of India, no proceedings, Civil or Criminal, shall be instituted against any person in respect of any act done or purporting to be done in the execution of his duties as a servant of the State before the day on which the administration is made over to the Government of India.

Article-12

1. Mayurbhanj should be treated as a District and its geographical entity should be maintained.
2. It should be treated as a separate constituency by itself for election to Central Legislature.
3. An Advisory Body should be formed but of the present Legislative Assembly of Mayurbhanj which will advise the Government of Orissa on matters relating to Mayurbhanj generally and the backward classes particularly.
4. The spirit of local laws, rules, regulations, customs and usages should be respected, as far as possible.
5. All commitments of previous administration should be honoured.
6. The Reserve Fund of Mayurbhanj together with its interest should be expensed in consultation with the above mentioned Advisory Body in Mayurbhanj and on specific projects conductive to the benefit of its people.
7. A fund should be created by special contribution from the Center and from the Government of Orissa for the benefit and amelioration of the backward classes of the State. This fund should be administered with the advice of the Advisory Body.
8. Special Grants given by the State Administration for specific purposes (i.e. Maharaja Shree Ram Chandra Water Supply Fund, Maharaja Shree Ram Chandra Chair of Sanskrit Learning and Language in the Banaras University etc.) should be continued.
9. All other funds existing for specific purposes (i.e. Maharaja Purna Chandra Memorial Scholarship Fund, Maharaja Krushna Chandra Chikita Mandir Fund donated by the Late Routrai Saheb for adding a male ward to Baripada Hospital addition of Tuberculosis ward to Baripada hospital, etc.) together with interest accured thereon should be applied for these purposes. The schemes drawn for utilization of the funds should be carried out.
10. The objective of developing the newly started Maharaja Purna Chandra College in to a First Grade residential College in Takatpur garden should be carried out.

11. Existing institutions and installations should be maintained in their entirely and their equipments should not be removed. If it is found necessary to dispose of any equipment it should be sold and the sale proceeds should be credited to the Reserve Fund mentioned above.

12. Debottar including Debottar ceremonials should be maintained as at present as well as religious ceremonial which are now being celebrated at State expenses.

13. A guarantee of security and continuity of services of permanent State Servants and payment of adequate compensation pension, leave etc. in the event of their discharge.

14. Non-victimisation or harassment of State Servant or others for past acts, views and loyalties.

15. A guarantee that those Sate Servants who will be entitled to retire on pension within the next three years must not be discharged but allowed to earn their pensions in the regular manner.

16. A guarantee that State Servants who have been engaged for a specified period without any provisions for notice on either side for termination of their service may be paid compensation in the shape of salary for their un-expired portion of their terms in the event of their discharge.

17. Endeavour should be made to avoid immediate transfer of State Servants outside Mayurbhanj without their consent. But if the transfer is made the State Servant concerned should get the same scale of pay as Orissa Officers of the same status.

18. The length of service, status and not merely the pay in State Service should be the criteria on in determining the status or pay of State Servants vis a vis Officers of that class in Orissa Service or service in any other area.

19. Considering the percentage of backward classes in Mayurbhanj a certain weightage in the Provincial legislature as well as a minimum representation in the Orissa Cabinet should be ensured, as far as possible.

SUPPLEMENTARY LIST OF TERMS

1. Mayurbhanj should continue to receive the present quota of controlled goods.
2. Arrangement should be made for Orissa High Court of Judicature of move in Circuit to Baripada where excellent facilities for accommodation exist.

In confirmation where of Mullath Kadingi Veliodi, Secretary to the Government of India in the Ministry of States, has appended his signature on behalf and with the authority of the Governor General of India and Flight Lieutenant Maharaja Sir Pratap Chandra Bhanj Deo, Maharaja of Mayurbhanj has appended his signature on behalf of himself his heirs and successors.

Sd/- PRATAP CHANDRA BHANJ DEO
Maharaja of Mayurbhanj

Sd/- M.K.VELLODI
Secretary to Government of India
Ministry of State

Dated New Delhi the 17th day of October, 1948

ANNEXURE-VI

MEMBERS OF THE MAYURBHANJ ADIBASI SABHA

Sunaram Soren	-	President, Mayurbhanj Adibasi Sabha
Mahendranath Murmu	-	Vice President, Mayurbhanj Adibasi Sabha
Shyamcharan Hansda	-	Kendra Office Secretary, Mayurbhanj Adibasi Sabha
Sundar Mohan Hembram	-	Councillor, Mayurbhanj Adibasi Sabha
Ghasiram Sandyl	-	State Commander, Mayurbhanj Adibasi Sabha

Ramchandra Majhi	-	President, Bamanghati Subdivision
Surendra Nath Singh	-	President, Sadar Subdivision
Har Devsingh Tiriya	-	Vice-President, sadar Subdivision
Dhyan Chandra Tudu	-	Secretary,Sadar Sub-division
Karunakar Hembram	-	President, Panchpir Subdivision
Nilamani Sakhyal	-	Vice-President, Panchpir Subdivision
Baidhar Tudu	-	President, Kaptipada Subdivision
Harmahan Tudu	-	Vice-President, Kaptipada Subdivision
A.Pankaj	-	All State Organizer
Jadav Hansda	-	Vice-President
Baj Hansda	-	Working Committee member, Similipal Pargana
Kunu Singh, K.	-	Working Committee member, Mantri Paragana
Bharat Hansda	-	Workings Committee member, Muruda Pargana
Sangram Hansda	-	Working Committee member
Kalicharan Tudu	-	Working Committee member, Baghda Pargana
Shankar Marandi	-	Working Committee member, Sub-division
Harishchandra Soren	-	Working committee member, Sub-division
Raghunath Hansda	-	Working committee member, Sub-division
Lalmohan Murmu	-	Working committee member, Bamanghati subdivision
Ramdayal Murmu	-	Scretary, Kaptipada subdivision
Nisamani Tripathy	-	Organiser, Baripada
Ram Hari mahali	-	Organizer, Udala
Gopinath Singh Sandyl		
Jai Narayan Singh Babu		
Purna Chandra Bag Julia		
Raghunath Jirae		
Promod Kumar Ghose		
Bidyanadhar Nayak		
Kande Pingua		

ANNEXURE-VII

NOTIFICATION

The 16th December, 1948

No.3297 - Mr. V.P. Menon, C.S.I., C.I.F., Adviser, Ministry of States, Government of India, delivered the following speech at a public function held in the Mayurbhanj Assembly Hall, Baripada at 11 A.M. on the 16th December, 1948.

By Order,
T.N.SARAF,
For Secretary,
Home Department

"Your Highness and Gentlemen,

I am grateful to you for coming this morning to this meeting. This is an important occasion in the history of Mayurbhanj State. I came here to announce The decision of the Government of India relating to the future of the State. As you are all aware, the administration of the State was taken over by the Central Government on the 9th November, 1948 and Mr. Rege was appointed as Chief Commissioner of Mayurbhanj. The reason why the State was taken directly under the Central Government was that there was a certain difference of opinion as regards its ultimate destination. The Chief Commissioner has now had ample opportunity to study the situation and to gauge the public opinion.

Before I announce the decision, I shall try to state briefly the attitude of the Hon'ble the Deputy Prime Minister so far as Mayurbhanj State is concerned. When he went to Cuttack to induce the Rulers of the Eastern States to integrate their States with Orissa and Central Province respectively, the Maharaja of Mayurbhanj was one of the invitees to the Cuttack Conference. He, like his father, was ready to do anything in the interests of the country and was prepared to sign a merger agreement if Sardar Patel desired him to do so. At the same time, His Highness pointed out that since he had granted responsible government to his people, it was only democratic that the popular Government should be allowed to continue. (I may mention that His Highness' father, as you are all aware, was a great democrat. It was he who for the first time in India established a Council for the State. He again reorganized the Tenancy system when this reform was not even thought of in the Provinces). In view of the opinion expressed by His Highness, Sardar told him that the future of the Mayurbhanj State should be considered separately and he left the matter there. Subsequently the states Ministry went on with the policy of integration of States and we reached a stage when we had to take a decision about Mayurbhanj. Sardar again sent for His Highness and the Premier of Mayurbhanj. Both he and myself discussed the question with them as well as with the Adibasi leaders who had also come to Delhi. His Highness and the Premier were convinced that the integration of the State was in the best interests of the people of Mayurbhanj. He signed the merger agreement with the full approval and concurrence of his Ministry and the Government of India. So far as His Highness is concerned, his responsibility is finished.

The second stage involves the decision as to which Province the State should go. It is surrounded on three sides by Orissa and it has contact with Bihar only in the north. All the representative opinion which the States Ministry had gathered recommended that the State should go to Orissa to which it geographically, culturally and to a large extent, ethnologically belongs. This was the opinion passed by an independent Tribunal which investigated the question of amalgamation of Oriya people in one Province. The Government of India could have taken a decision on the basis of the views expressed to them by the majority of the representative bodies, but the Hon'ble the Deputy Prime Minister thought that further investigation was needed to find out exactly what some of the Adibasi leaders wanted as their views alone sounded a discordant note in the State. I may point out even among the Adibasi leaders there is no unanimity of views on this question. We entrusted the task to our Chief Commissioner. After careful investigation he has recommended that this State should go to Orissa. The main arguments which have been advanced by the Adibasi sabha leaders for integration of Mayurbhanj with Bihar are contained in the memorandum which was presented by them to Sardar Patel. If I may say so, every argument they used in the memorandum could with equal force be used for integrating the State with Bengal. I need not go into detail about these arguments, but I must say that they have no real substance in them. It is said that if the state is merged with Orissa it will be difficult to get justice. If this means that the people will have to go all the way from here to Cuttack to appeal to the High Court then I can tell them that the Orissa High Court might sit in Circuit in this area. The other Courts of Justice will be maintained intact as they are at present. Take again the argument that by integrating with Orissa the people will not get adequate employment as Bihar is an industrial Province and Orissa is not. On the basis of this argument the labour from Madras cannot go to Bombay and a Bombay labourer cannot go to Bengal; the whole conception is wrong. There is nothing to prevent, even if the State is integrated with Orissa, labour going from one Province to another. Take the instance of Assam, labourers in the Tea Estates do not belong to Assam but they come from neighbouring Provinces. It is also argued that Mayurbhanj should merge with Bihar as it is a richer Province than Orissa. I have no hesitation in declaring that Orissa has a future as good, if not better, than any other Province in India. We have now just started the Hirakud Dam on Mahanadi. When the three stages of Mahanadi project are completed, there will be enough electricity for industrialization of the Province and water for irrigation; the Province of Orissa could be converted literally into a paradise.

This country with all its resources belongs to the people of India. Viewing the Mayurbhanj question not from the position of any particular party and considering the interests of the State as a whole, there can only be one decision and that decision is that the State should be amalgamated with Orissa. This is what the Hon'ble the Deputy Prime Minister has decided. The policy which the Central Government would always follow and which is enjoined upon them by our revered leader, Gandhiji, who championed the cause of all down trodden people not only in India but throughout the world, is that the poor man's lot should be bettered. That policy means that there should not be any poverty in this country. That policy means that there should not be any sickness which can be prevented by human efforts. That policy means that every body must have equal opportunity. If that policy is adopted the Adibasis should have no fear that they would be exploited by anybody. After all for centuries they were hoping for a chance and that chance is now coming to them. The very purpose of my coming here is to carry the message of my Minister to them that their interests are safe in his hands. The Government of India will see and the Orissa Government will see that the lot of Adibasis is improved and that every fair chance is given to them. In a peaceful atmosphere we can work up everything to the best interests of the poor people who never had a chance in their life. But meaningless agitation will lead this country nowhere and we shall not achieve the objects we have all in view. I, therefore, appeal to you to bend all your energies to constructive efforts and to make the lot of the poor man better than what it is today. The real leader is not the man who can address large public meetings but the man who can do something for the betterment of his fellowmen. Tested by that standard the Adibasi leaders, have failed in their duties. If they bend their energies with the help of the Orissa Government and the Central Government, there is nothing which they can not achieve for their people. The institutions which have been started by His Highness and by the late Government in the State will be maintained intact. The Orissa Government will take in hand as soon as possible schemes which will benefit the people. It is the intention of the Central Government to which the Orissa Government have agreed that your present Chief Commissioner should stay in this place and he would see to it that the schemes are formulated and put into operation as soon as possible. In your Chief Commissioner you have got an administrator of great experience and wide sympathies. His only object is to improve the lot of the poor man. His reports on labour conditions in India would testify to his intentions.

My Minister has considered every aspect of the case and has taken this decision after very careful thought. If his decision would have in any way militated against the best interests of the people of Mayurbhanj, he would never have asked you to accept it. I, therefore, appeal with all the sincerity at my command that this decision of Government that the State of Mayurbhanj should be integrated with Orissa from the 2nd January, 1949, be accepted by the people of Mayurbhanj and that they should work in the best interests not only of Mayurbhanj but of the Orissa Province as a whole.

ANNEXURE-VIII

Census of Mayurbhanj State, 1931:
Volume II: Tables
by Mahammad Laeequddin, B.A., Census Officer, Mayurbhanj State, Table-VI: Religion

This Table shows the distribution of the population by five main religions viz-Hindus, Muslims, Christians, Animists and others. The Hindu population in this table has been sub-divided. Into `Tribal Hindus'. `Caste Hindus' and `other Hindus'. The term Animist' has been used to devote those tribals who did not return Hinduism as distinguished from tribal religion as their religion. `Others' include Sikhs, Buddhists, Jains, Brahmins, Kumbhi Patias and Aryans.

A list of Castes comprising (1) Tribal Hindus (2) Caste Hindus and (3) Other Hindus is appended over self.

I. Tribal Hindus

1. Amata (Amat, Amath)
2. Bathuri (Bathudi)
3. Bedea (Bedia, Bejea)
4. Bhanj Puran
5. Bhuinya (Bhuinyan)
6. Bhumij
7. Dharua (Dharua, Dhalua)
8. Cond
9. Gunju (Ganju)
10. Jhara (Jhora)
11. Kandh (Kawar)
12. Kaur (Kawar)
13. Kharia (Khadia, Kheria)
14. Kisan
15. Kol (Ho, Kolha)
16. Kora (Kuda, Kura, Kara)
17. Kurmi Mahtoo Kurmi Kshatriya)
18. Lodha (Nidha , Lodh, Nadh)
19. Mahali (Mahli)
20. Mankria (Mankdia)
21. Munda
22. Oraon (Uraon)
23. Puran (Tamria)
24. Rajuar (Rajwar)
25. Santal (Santhal, Saonthal, Saontar)
26. Tamria (Tamuria, Tamria)
27. Ujia.

II. Caste Hindus

Total 38 Caste Lists

III. Other Hindus

Total 66, Other Caste Lists.

Agreement with TISCO

This Indenture made the first day of one thousand nine hundred and ten between The Maharajah Sri Ram Chander Bhanj Deva feudatory Chief of the Mourbhanj State (hereinafter called "the Lesson" which expression shall where the context so requires or admits include his successors in office and assigns) of the one part and The Tata Iron and Steel Company Limited a Company registered Office at Navsari Buildings Horn by Road Bombay (hereinafter called " the Lessee" which expression shall where the context so requires or admits include its successors and assigns) of the other part Whereas by a Prospecting License date the Twenty-second day of September One thousand nine hundred and five and made between the Lessor of the one part and Dorabji Jamsetji Tata Rattonji Jamsetji Tata and Ratanji Dadabhoy Tata (hereinafter called "the Licensees") of the other part for the consideration therein mentoned the Lessor did thereby grant and demise to the Licensees the sole right and License (subject to the conditions thereinafter contained) to enter upon any place or places within the territories of the Lessor and to mine quarry bore dig search for win and work all or any iron lying or being within under or throughout the lands of the Lessor without any interruption claim or disturbance from or by the Lessor or any other person or persons whomsoever and to do such other acts and things as are therein mentioned for the term of three years from the date of the Lincense renewable as thereinafter provided and it was by the now reciting Prospecting License further provided that on the determination of the Prospecting License so granted to them as aforesaid the Licensees should be unconditionally entitled to demand and obtain a mining lease over any areas not exceeding twenty square miles in extent without restrictions as to dimensions in the spirit of the terms and conditions provided for by the Government of India by their Resolution No. 18-17-2 Department of Revenue and Agriculture dated Simla the Twentieth day of May One thousand eight hundred and ninety-nine for the grant by the local government of mining leases in British India subject to the further and other terms and conditions already approved and agreed upon between the parties to the now reciting Prospecting License and which were annexed thereto and whereas the Licensees deposited with the Lessor as security in respect of such license the sum of Rupees five hundred and whereas by a Memorandum dated the Twenty-nine day of November One thousand nine hundred and seven (which is endorsed upon the hereinbefore recited Prospecting License and is signed by the Lessor and the Diwan and Deputy Collector of the Mourbhanj State and also by the Licensees and two of the Directors and the Agents of the Lessee) it was declared that the transfer of the said Prospecting License to the Lessee was sanctioned by letter No. 2038 E of the Twenty-first day of September One thousand nine hundred and seven and addressed by the Secretary to the Chief of Mourbhanj to the Licensees and the Lessee was recognized as the holder of the said License and was entitled to all the benefits there under and whereas the Licensees and the Lessee have prospected certain of the land belonging to the Lessor and the Lessee has in terms of the sai Prospecting License requested the Lessor to grant to the Lessee a mining lease in manner and on the terms and conditions hereinafter contained now this indenture witnesseth that in pursuance of the said Prospecting License and in consideration of the rents and royalties hereinafter reserved it is hereby agreed and declared as follows:

1. The Lessor hereby demises to Lessee all that area or tract of land called or known by the name of the Gurumaishini Hill situate in nowpara pirh Bamanghatti sub-division Mourbhanj State and containing by admeasurment five and

one quarter square miles or thereabouts (and which said area or tract of land is shortly described in the schedule hereunder written and is particularly delineated and described in the map or plan there of hereunto annexed and is hereinafter to as "the demised land" unless otherwise designated) for the term hereinafter mentioned together with the liberties powers and privilages hereinafter specified.

2. There shall be included in the said demise the following liberties powers and privileges to be exercised and enjoyed by the lessee, namely:-

(a) To search for mine quarry bore dig win work raise make merchantable carry away and dispose of all or any iron ore lying under or throughout the demised land.

(b) For the purpose aforesaid or in connection therewith to enter upon any of the demised land to cut clear any timber undergrowth and brushwood rom all places required for the construction of works or for mining. Operations but subject within a reserved forest to such conditions regarding the use of fire that may be prescribed by the Lessor's forest officers and also to cut and any timber which shall be required for structural and other such purposes provided that no timber shall be cut from any existing forest reserved by the Lessor except in places required for the construction of work or for mining operations as aforesaid and that no timber shall be taken from any Protected forest without the customary payment in accordance with and at the rates for the time being prevailing and provided for in the State forest Rules and Regulations and further that all such timber to be selected and purchased as aforesaid shall be cut and taken away strictly in accordance with such rules and regulations.

(c) To make and use any drains or water courses for clearing the iron ore from any water which may flow or accumulate in or near the mines.

(d) To appropriate and use for any purpose connected with the working of the said mines the water in or upon the demised land and to impound the same in reservoirs or otherwise for the purpose of working the said mines in demised land.

(e) To bring erect and make in upon or over the demised land all such workmen's house sheds erections buildings and structures steam and other engines boilers plant machinery furnaces conveniences chattels effects tram-roads rail-roads and other roads and works as shall be necessary or convenient for effectually raising the said ore and working the mines contained in the demised land and for exercising the several liberties and powers herein granted and for providing for the housing, feeding and other necessities of the Lessee's employes.

(f) For the purposes aforesaid and for all other purposes connected with the due and proper management development searching for mining and working of said iron ore and disposing of the produce thereof to make maintain and develop in upon or over the demised land all such pits shafts levels drifts culverts and other works and conveniences as may be necessary or convenient and also below the surface of such lands to make erect and use such further levels drifts tram and other ways and such machinery and other works as may be necessary or convenient for searching for mining or working the said mines and for ventilating and draining the same.

(g) Within the demised land to dig get surface clay and make and burn bricks and tiles and to erect brick-kilns and lime kilns and burn lime and to dig and get sods earth and rubbish for building and repairing any houses and buildings to be built and repaired but for no other purposes.

(h) Within the demised land to quarry and get stone sand gravel and other building road and tramway materials and to use the same for the purpose of the buildings structures roads and works hereby authorized but not otherwise.

(i) The exclusive right within the demised land of mining for iron and operations associated with the same.

(j) The exclusive right within the demised land of operating for everything (except gold silver diamonds or precious stones) subject to the terms and conditions to be determined and agreed upon when the Lessee applies from time to time for mining leases for such purposes.

(k) Within the demised land to give to the Lessee the first offer of a mining lease for gold silver diamonds or precious stones.

(l) Within the demised land the right of excluding from any operations all parties except parties [subject to sub-clause (k)] connected with the mining for gold silver diamonds and precious stones.

(m) Generally to do all lawful acts and things within the said area which shall be convenient or necessary for winning working getting carrying away making merchantable and disposing of the iron ore upon in or uner the demised land.

3. There are excepted and reserved out of this demise the following

(a) All mines and minerals other than iron and iron ore subject nevertheless to the right granted to the Lessee under sub-clause (j) of clause 2 hereof to apply to the Lessor for mining leases for other purposes except for gold silver diamonds or precious stones and subject also to the Lessee's rights under sub-clause (k) of clause 2 hereof.

(b) Liberty for the Lessor or his lessees or tenants or other persons authorized by him (subject nevertheless to sub-clause (k) of clause 2 hereof) to search for sink work get raise carry away and dispose of gold silver diamonds and other precious stones and for such purposes to sink drive erect make and use all such pits shafts adits drifts waterways airways buildings railways tramways and other roads engines machinery and other works through across or under the demised land and the levels and workings of the Lessee as shall be necessary or convenient with full right for such purposes as aforesaid of ingress and regress over any of the surface lands for the time being occupied by the Lessee Provided that this liberty shall not be exercised in such a way as to obstruct hinder or prevent the Lessee from working getting and disposing of the iron ore hereby demised to the best advantage and provided also that fair and proper compensation shall be paid by the Lessor to the Lessee for all loss damages or injury which the Lessee may sustain by reason or in consequence of the exercise of the said reserved rights and privileges to work for gold silver diamonds and precious stones.

4. The said premises shall be held by the Lessee from the first day of July one thousand nine hundred and ten for the term of thirty years (determinable as hereinafter provided) with the privilege of renewal for a further term of thirty years subject to the same conditions in all respects as those obtaining at the time of the expiration of the first period of thirty years and the royalty for the further term of thirty years shall be fixed at five annas per ton of ore and the Lessee shall commence working for iron ore within two years from the date of these presents and shall thereafter carry on such working effectually in a proper skilful and mining like manner unless prevented by unavoidable cause.

5. The Lessee shall pay the following rents and royalties during the said term unless previously determined as hereinafter provided, viz:

(a) For all such land within the area of this demise as is at the date hereof assessable under the rent Law of the said State a yearly surface rent equal to the rent assessable at the date hereof on such land.

(b) For all such land within the area of this demise as is unassessed under the said Law at the date hereof a yearly surface rent at the rate of Rupees fifty per square mile.

(c) For the first five years of the said term a royalty of one anna per ton for each and every ton of iron ore mined and raised up to one hundred and fifty thousand tons annually and one half anna per ton for all further quantities over and above one hundred and fifty thousand tons.

(d) For the second five years of the term a royalty of two annas per ton of iron ore mined and raised upto one hundred and fifty thousand tons annually and one anna per ton for further quantities over and above one hundred and fifty thousand and tons.

(e) For the third five years of the said term a royalty of three annas per ton of iron ore mined and raised up to one hundred and fifty thousand tons annually and one and half anna for further quantities over and above one hundred and fifty thousand tons.

(f) For the remaining period of fifteen years of the said term a royalty of four annas per ton of iron ore mined and raised up to one hundred and fifty thousand tons annually and two annas per ton for further quantities over and above one hundred and fifty thousand tons. Provided always and it is hereby agreed that an annual minimum royalty calculated on fifty thousand tons of iron ore shall be paid in any case in every year as an annual minimum or dead rent so long as the mines remain unconnected by railway with a main line but if and when a connecting railway shall be constructed the annual minimum or dead ret shall after the same shall have been completed ready for traffic be calculated and paid upon one hundred and fifty thousand tons the intention being that in respect of such annual minimum or dead rent the Lessee may in every year work and raise from the mines such a quantity of iron ore as at royalties mentioned in sub-clauses ©, (d), (e) and (f) of clause 5 would yield or pay for that year a royalty equal in amount to the said minimum or dead rent.

A ton shall be taken to mean a gross ton of crude iron ore or iron stone as it is won from the ground and before being subjected to any manufacturing process and it shall be taken as a weight of 2240 ibs.

6. The Lessee to the intent that the obligation may continue throughout the term hereby created hereby covenants with the Lessor as following:

(a) To pay the said rent and royalties either into the State Treasury of the Lessor at Bapalda or into the Bank of Bengal in Calcutta to the credit of the Lessor such rents to be paid by two equal instalments on the first day of January and the first day of July in each year for the half-year immediately preceding at one of the places aforesaid and within thirty days after the first half-yearly payment of the said rents commencing from the date hereof or a proportionate part thereof to be paid on the First day of July One thousand nine hundred and ten and the said royalties shall be ascertained on the said First day of January and the First day of July in each year and be paid within tirty days thereafter at either of the palaces aforesaid but the said sum of Rupees five hundred, deposited by the Lessee as aforesaid shall be accepted and retained by the Lessor on account and in part payment of said rents.

(b) Subject as hereinafter provided to well and truly measure and weigh or cause to be measured and weighed the whole produce which shall be mind and raised as aforesaid of iron ore for the purpose of ascertaining the royalties payable in respect thereof and the Lessor or any persons appointed for that purpose on his behalf shall be permitted to be present at any time to check and inspect such measuring and weighment provided always and it it is hereby agreed that in respect of all iron ore dispatched by rail from the said mines the weight of iron ore as shown in the railway receipts shall for the purpose of calculating royalties be deemed to be the correct weight of all such iron ore as may be dispatched by rail and the Lessee shall not be required to measure or weigh or cause to be measured or weighed such iron ore.

(c) To permit the Lessor or his agents with or without miners surveyors or other persons at all reasonable times to enter upon and inspect the premises hereby demised and every part thereof and for the purpose aforesaid to use free of charge all the pits or shafts now sunk or hereafter to be sunk in the demised premises or in the said lands and to have all necessary assistance from the miners workmen and others in the employment of the Lessee.

(d) To enter or cause to be entered in proper books of account to be provided and kept for that purpose (and which books shall at all reasonable times be open to the inspection of the Lessor or any office authorized by him in that behalf with liberty to take copies extracts or abstracts there from) true and correct entries of all iron ore won raises and dispatched from the said mines and premises hereby emised together with all such particulars of dates quantities and weights as shall be necessary or proper to be entered therein in the usual course of business.

(e) On the fifteenth day of every month at the Lessee's expense to make out and deliver to the Lessor or his agent a correct account in writing signed by some responsible office or servant of the Lessee of all iron ore won raised and dispatched from the said premises hereby demised and to verify such accounts by the production of books and vouchers (railway wagon challans, declaration notes or receipts being accepted by the Lessor as conclusive) and to furnish the Lessor with such other information and returns in respect of the aforesaid matters as her may reasonable require.

(f) To keep a muster roll or other statement which shall accurately show the number of persons from time to time employed on the such work which shall show the areas mined and afford good and sufficient evidence of the working of the mines within the demised land and which plans shall at all reasonable time be open to the inspection of the Lessor or any office authorized by him that behalf with liberty to take copies there from.

(g) Not to assign underlet or part with the possession of the demised premises or any part thereof without first obtaining the written consent of the Lessor provided that such consent shall not be unreasonably withheld.

(h) To conform to and observe the provisions of all rules and regulations for the time being in force promulgated by the Feudatory Chief for the time being of the Mourbhanj State provided they are not inconsistent with the terms and conditions of this lease.

(i) To make an pay reasonable satisfaction and compensation for all injury which may be done or occasioned by the Lessee in the exercise of the power granted to the Lessee by these presents and to indemnify the Lessor against all claims which may e made by tird parties in respect of any such damage or injury as aforesaid.

(j) To take and use all necessary precautions to ensure the safety of all workmen and others employed in the said mining operations from accidents of any kind or description and in the event of an accident or loss of life occuring the same shall be immediately reported by the Lessee to the sub-divisional officer of Bhamanghatti.

(k) To erect at their own expense and at all times maintain and keep in good repair and condition boundary marks and pillars according to the demarcation shown in the said map or plan hereunto annexed.

(l) To inform the Lessor immediately on discovery of the existence of any mineral oil or other minerals that may be found during the continuance of this demise.

7. At the end or sooner determination of the lease the Lessee shall deliver up the said premises and all mines (if any) which may have been made dug or sunk by the Lessee under the liberties hereinbefore contained together with all pits shafts water courses air gates levels and fixtures below ground level and which cannot be moved without causing injury to the said mines, in a proper and workmanlike state save in respect of any working as to which the Lessor may have sanctioned abandonment and except any mines which shall have been abandoned or disused in the ordinary and fair course of working the same.

8. The Lessor hereby covenants with the Lessee as follows:

(a) That the Lessor has good right and full power to grant this lease and that the Lessee paying the rents and royalties hereby reserved and observing and performing the several covenants and stipulations herein on the Lessee's part contained shall peaceably hold and enjoy the premises, liberties and powers hereby demised and granted during the said term without any lawful interruption by the Lessor or any person rightfully claiming under or in trust for him.

(b) That the Lessor will not permit or authorize any person firm or other company to search for work mine or get any iron or iron ore in any place or places within his territories or grant any prospecting license or mining lease to any such person firm or company for a period of three years from the date hereof and that the Lessee shall be entitled from time to time within the said period of three years to mark out further areas within the Lessor's territories not exceeding in the whole an area of twenty square miles over which the Lessee shall be entitled to demand and obtain from the Lessor a mining lease or mining leases at the same rents and royalties and upon the same terms and conditions as are hereby reserved and contained in respect of the premised hereby demised save and except that any such mining lease or mining lease shall not provide for the payment of any annual minimum royalty as an annual minimum or dead rent.

(c) That the Lessor will from time to time if and when required during the said term of thirty years or any renewal thereof grant to the Lessee mining leases of so much of the aforesaid area (not exceeding twenty square miles in extent in the aggregate) for working and obtaining mineral oil metals coal and other minerals or substances or things (other than gold silver diamonds and precious stones) upon such terms and conditions as may be agreed upon by the parties hereto and in the case of gold silver diamonds and precious stones the Lessor will not authorize any other person firm or company to search for work or get any gold silver diamonds or precious stones or grant any prospecting license or mining lease in respect thereof in his territories unless he shall have first offered to the Lessee by written notice on the same terms and for the same area a prospecting license or mining lease and the Lessee shall during three calendar months after the receipt of such notice have omitted or neglected to accept such license or lease.

(d) That the Lessor will not permit or authorize any person firm or other company during the said term of thirty years or any renewal thereof to search for mine work or get any minerals (except gold silver diamonds and precious stones but subject as hereinbefore provided) stones or other substances within demised land or carry on or permit or authorize any other person firm or other company to carry on any operations relating thereto or grant any prospecting license mining or other lease in respect thereof.

(e) That the Lessee shall not be liable and shall not be called upon to pay in regard to the demised premises or the occupation thereof by the Lessee or in respect of any buildings·or works erected or constructed thereon or in respect of any iron ore extracted there from or otherwise howsoever in connection with this demise any rates taxes or assessments of any kind whatsoever the payment of the rents and royalties hereby reserved being accepted by the Lessor in full discharge of all claim for other rates taxes or assessments whatsoever.

9. It is hereby expressly agreed as follows:-Should the royalty or rent reserved or made payable by this demise be not paid within two months next after the same shall become due as aforesaid the Lessor may enter upon the said premises and distrain all or any of the minerals or moveable property therein, and may carry away or detain them until the rent or royalty due and all costs and expenses occasioned by the non-payment thereof shall be fully paid: and if any royalty or rent remain at any time unpaid for six calendar months after the date on which it is due or in the case of any breach on the part of the Lessee of all or any of the provision of the premises comprised therein subject to the previous sanction of the Commissioners of the Orissa division.

10. Upon the determination of this demits by effluxion of time or under the provisions of Clause 9 or at any time within six calendar months thereafter the Lessee shall be at liberty to enter into and upon the said land sand to take and carry away for its own use all such iron ore as shall have been won got under the powers hereinbefore granted and (subject nevertheless to clause 7 hereof) the plant machinery boilers engines furnaces shafts utensils implements articles and things set up and used in or about the said lands mines and premises and all buildings sheds railways tramways and other works whether above or below the ground level. Provided that if the Lessor shall be desirous of purchasing all or any of the buildings or works above ground level set up or constructed by the Lessee and shall signify such his desire by botice in writing to the Lessee six calendar months at least before the expiration of the said term or if the said term shall be determined under the power of re-entry provided in clause 9 at any time within three calendar months after the determination of the said term the Lessee shall sell to the

Lessor all or any of the said buildings and works a price which shall be fixed or ascertained by taking the net cost of such buildings or works as date of construction and deducting there from for depreciation a sum equivalent to 2 per cent. Per annum on the net original cost.

11. It is hereby expressly agreed and declared that the native smelters at present working the ores of the State shall be allowed to continue and take their necessary supplies of such ores and charcoal from the lands and deposits within the area of this demits provided always that the ore so taken is to be used only for the furnace blown by native processes and furnaces now in the ownership of such native smelters as aforesaid.

12. The Lessee may determine this demise at any time during the said term by giving not less than twelve calendar months notice in writing to the Lessor terminating at any time of the year and upon the expiration of such notice and provided that the Lessee shall upon the expiration of such notice pay all rents and royalties which may be then due and payable by the Lessee this present lease shall absolutely which may be then due and payable by the Lessee this present lease shall absolutely cease and determine and become void but without prejudice to any right of action or remedy which shall have accrued to the Lessor or the Lessee.

13. If at any time during the continuance of this demise the said mines shall become destroyed or rendered substantially and permanently unfit for the purposes of this demise by fire tempest or flood or violence of any army or mob or other irresistible force this present lease shall at the option of the Lessee be void provided that if the injury be occasioned by the wrongful act or default of the Lessee or its servants the Lessee shall not be entitled to avail itself of the benefit of this provision and provided also that if this lease shall become void for or by reason of any of the causes aforesaid it should be without prejudice to the rights and

remedies of the Lessor under or by virtue of these presents for the recovery of any rent or royalty which may then remain unpaid or in respect of any breach which may have been committed of any of the covenants herein contained on the part of the Lessee.

14. If at any time during the continuance of this lease or after the termination thereof any question difference or dispute shall arise between the parties hereto or any person or persons or corporations claiming under them respectively concerning the amount of the rent royalties payable hereunder or the quantity of iron ore got in the demised mines and premises or concerning any compensation payable by the Lessor or Lessee hereunder or touching the construction of any clause herein contained or the rights duties or liabilities of the parties hereunder or in any other way touching or arising out of these presents the same shall be referred to the commissioner of the Orissa division for the time being whose decision shall be final.

15. Every notice requiring to be served hereunder shall be sufficiently served if forwarded to the person or persons for whom such notices are intended by registered post in a prepaid packet or left at his or their last known address or place or residence.

In witness whereof the Maharajah Sri Ram Chander Bhanj Deva feudatory chief of the Mourbhanj State hath hereunto set his hand and seal and the common seal of The Tata Iron and Steel Company Limited hath been hereunto affixed in the presence of two directors and the agents of the Company the day and year first above written.

Glossary

Adibasi	A tribal
Amla	A revenue clerk
Amin	Surveyor of Land
Avadhana	A village Teacher
Bazar	Market place
Begari	A feudal levy on luggage
Bethi	A feudal levy on labourer
Bhuyan	A tribal group
Bund	An embankment
Chprasi	A peon
Chaukidar	A village watchman
Chautha	A tribute paid to the Marathas
Chuar	A low cast tribal
Chuar Sardar	Chief of the low caste tribe
Dak	Mail service
Daroga	A Police Officer
Deslok	Local people
Dewan	Chief Adviser of the Raja
Dhol	A drum used by the Tribals
Dhomsa	A drum
Durbar	Royal Court
Farman	Order with authority
Gadi	Throne
Garjat	Feudatory State/Native State

Garh	Fort
Grain Gola	Paddy Store house
Hamara	Government store
Handia	A drink made of fermented rice
Hasilat	A land on which tax is collected
Hat	Weekly village market
Hatuas	Non-tribals of Bamanghaty
Hazat	Prison
Holi	A festival of colour
Jagir	Rent free land
Jungle	Forest
Kendra Parishad	Council
Kheda	An operation to catch elephant
Khelat	Royal felicitation
Killa	Fort
Kunwer	Raja of Sareikela
Lakhraj	Revenue free land
Machan	A platform on a Tree
Madal	A tribal drum
Magan	Feudal levy
Mahal	A revenue unit
Mahajan	Money lender
Makar	Harvesting festival
Nazar	A presentation
Niz	Own
Palatak	A fugitive
Patrani	Chief Queen
Patta	Document of ownership of land
Parwana	Warrant
Peshkush	Tribute
Paik	A peasant militia
Pradhan	Village Headman
Praja Sabha	Assembly of peasants/subjects
Raja	A King or Chief of a Princely State
Rani	Queen
Rasad	Feudal levy
Ryot	A tenant

Sabha	Meeting
Samiti	An association
Sardar	Chief appointed by the Raja to Collect land revenue/ Also the Head of the Tribal group.
Sardar	An Institution Centering a Sardar
Shikar	Hunting
Shikari	A Hunter
Shikar bethi	A levy collected for shikar
Sunnud/ Sanad	A grant/A Charter granting title
Tahsil	A revenue unit
Tahsildar	A revenue official
Tassar	Silken thread collected from silk worm
Thana	Police station
Tikayat	Crown Prince
Zamindar	Land lord

Bibliography

PRIMARY SOURCES

(A) Unpublished Government Document

Abolition of the Post of Political Agent, 522p, 1932.

Adoption of Sands and Right of Succession to Princes, Despatch of Lord Canning to C.Wood No.43A, 30 April, 1860.

Annual General Administration Report of Orissa Division 1870 to 1905 36 Vols. Calcutta/Cuttack.

Annual Administration Report of Orissa Division 1895-1912.

Annual Report on Administration of Bihar and Orissa 1912-1936, 25 Volumes.

Annual Reports of Resolutions of Mayurbhanj Raj Estate, Calcutta, 1895.

All India States Peoples Conference, files No.112, 127, 138, 206, 245.

Bihar and Orissa First Decennial Review 1912-1922 of the Administration and Development of the Province, Patna, 1923.

Board of Revenue, Bengal, Proceedings No.15.

Board of Revenue Records, Cuttack Volumes 64-99.

Bengal Review Proceedings No.29, 1815. Richardson to the Government.

Census of Mayurbhanj State 1931, Vol.I, Calcutta, 1937.

(Report by Mohammed Laeequddin)

(Report by Mohammed Laeequddin, 1932, vol.II)

(Table by Mohammed Laeequddin) Calcutta, 1937.

Census of India 1911 (Bengal, Bihar, Orissa and Sikkim), Part-I, by LSSO' Malley, Calcuta, 1913.

Census of India, 1931, Bihar and Orissa, Part-I & II, W.G.Lacey, Patna, 1932.

Change in the Designation of Orissa Feudatory States to Orissa States, 286, P.1932.

Chamber of Princes, Reforms No.76, 1928.

Congress Agitation and Policy in Respect of the Internal Administration of Indian States, No.647, Political, Secret, 1938.

Commission of Enquiry No.5-21, Secret Reforms, September, 1921.

Cooperation of Indian States to Civil Disobedience, 20 p (Secret)1932.

Creation of Separate Province of Orissa and its Relation ot the Feudatory States, 42, Special, 1931.

Deposition of Sri Amar Sigh in Sessions Trial, 1950, No.3M.

Direct Political Relations with the Viceroy to the States of Orissa, 72 P, 1930.

Dominion Status and its implication on Indian States No.24, Federation Secret, 1940.

Estern States Agency, Aboriginal Risings F.No.703 p, 1933.

Eastern States Agency, Administration Report, 1934, 6(2) F.O. 1934.

Feudatory States of Bihar and Orissa, List of Ruling Chiefs and Leading Personage, Calcutta, 1924 and 1929.

Final Report of theSurvey and Settlement of the Province of Orissa, 1890-1900 (Temporarily settled Areas) by S.L.Maddox, Two Volumes.

Final Report on the settlement of Bamanghaty Sub-Division, 1902-1906.

Files on All India States Peoples Conference.F. No.112, 127,138, 206, 245.

Foreign Department A-Political Proceedings, May, 1883 No.6-8, Management of Mayurbhanj State KWP Letter No.1306p, 7 (110p) and 8(1221)

Foreign Department, Pol. A, October 1881 (Simla Records) No.14-18, Letters No.19, 21, 28.

Foreign and Political Department, Honours, Government of India File No.183-H, 1927 (Question of the Grant of an Interview by His Excellency Lady Irwin to the Dowger Maharani of Mayurbhanj.

Foreign Political Department (Accounts) 1930.

Government of India F.No.311-4, 1930 and 77A 1930.

Foreign and Political Department, 1930, F.No.468p (Secret)

Foreign and Poltiical Department Honours 1925, 1926 (Visit of some RulingChiefs to Simla, 1926).

Federation of Indian States No.9, Federation, Secret, 1935.

Future of Small States No.18, Political Secret, 1944.

Form of Instrument of Accession be entered in to by Indian States on entry in to Indian Federation No.134, Reform Secret, 1932.

Government of Orissa, 1944, Special Section (Conf.) File No.141, Acc. No.2865 OSA (Garjat Sasan, A booklet by Sarat Chandra Das).

Ibid., Letter No.2162, SB from FHC Raynor, SP CID Special Branch to the Under Secretary, Government of Orissa 8 March, 1944.

Ibid., Letter No.2865 from S.J.Mozumdar, Under Secretary to the Government to the SP CID, Orissa dated 28 February, 1944.

Ibid., D.O.No. 1071, From the Chief Secretary to the Dewan of Mayurbhanj, dated 6 April, 1944.

Government of Orissa, Special Section, File No.313 (Conf.) 1943, OSA sub: Requirement of the Mayurbhanj House for housing the Utkal University Office.

Governor of Orissa Secretariat, 1949, File No.1, Acc. No.365, OSA.

Ibid., 1949 File No.8, Acc. No.364 OSA. Agreement made between he Governor General of India and the Maharaja of Mayurbhanj State.

Home Department Political F.18/1/37F/18/12/37 12 files Reports on the political Situation from Provinces, 1937.

Home Department Political XXXII-A(11)/49 Merging of Orissa States.

Home Department Pol. (1) Branch 1945. Release of H.K.Mahatab, Member Congress Working Committee.

Home Department (Political and War) for 1918 Pol. September. 153, Part B(a) Papers regarding the disturbance in Mayurbhanj State, 1917.

H.K.Mahatab's Catalogue File No.11, File No.2.

Indian Statutory Commission No.385, (Political) 1928.

Indian Statutory Commission No.200(5) 1929.

Khola Chithi (An Open Letter in Oriya) by Twelve Persons of Mayurbhanj, dated 4 January 1948.

Letter from Jawaharlal Nehru to Sarat Chandra Das dated 25 May 1940.

(B) Mayurbhanj Records (Collectorate Record Room, Baripada)

Administration of Mayurbhanj Amendment Notification 1949.

Annual Administration Reports of Mayurbhanj

1897-98	1903-04	1913-14	1914-15	1916-17
1920-21	1921-22	1927-28	1928-29	1929-30
1930-31	1931-32	1934-35	1935-36	1936-37
1938-39	1940-41	1941-42	1943-44	1944-45

Mayurbhanj Police Manual, 1945. Part-I &II

Mayurbhanj Audit Mannual, Mayurbhanj Accounts Code, 1940.

Mayurbhanj Income Tax Manual- 922. Mayurbhanj Income Tax Orders, 1941

Mayurbhanj PWD Code 1941

Mayurbhanj State Service Regulation relating to salary, leave, pension, and Travelling allowance, 1927.

Mayurbhanj Service Regulation, 1939.

Mayurbhanj State Mines Order,1937

Mayurbhanj Hat Regulation, 1945.

Mayurbhanj Forest Manual

Mayurbhanj Forest Act, 1943.

Mayurbhanj State Regulation I of 1932.

Manual of Rules for Medical and Public Health Department.

Manual for Stationeries

Mayurbhanj Law Reporter, 1944

Mayurbhanj Excise Act, 1945.

Mayurbhanj Settlement Manual, Vol.II, Mayurbhanj Mutation Regulation of 1910.

Mayurbhanj Finance Department, Budget, Estimates of Government of Maharaja

Mayurbhanj Manual of Budget Proceedure

Mayurbhanj High Court, 1936-37,1937-38. Mayurbhanj Law Reporter,Vol.II, III and IV, 1937-38.

Mayurbhanj Law Reports,Vol. II-1936

Mayurbhanj Law Reporter Dec., 1935, Sept. 1936, Dec. 1938, Dec., 1941, March, 1943,June, 1943, March, 1944, Sept., 1944,June, 1945, Sept., 1945.

Mayurbhanj State Council Regulation, Vol.II, 1905.

Mayurbhanj Prajasabha, Order 1938.

Mayurbhanj Regulations of 1906-1910.

Mayurbhanj Kendra Parishad Order, 1945.

Mayurbhanj Muncipal Regulation, 1905.

Mayurbhanj State Council, Powers and Constitution.

Mayurbhanj State Council RegualtionVol.II, 1905.

Mayurbhanj Cinematography Order 1940

Mayurbhanj State Regulation, I of 1932.

Mayurbhanj Motor Vehicles Order 1942.

Mayurbhanj Railways.

(C) Other Archival Sources

Mayurbhanj, Sareikela and Talcher Chief's demand for more power and appointment of a Committee to enquire their status, 56 Special 1931.

Mill's Minutes on Tributary Mehals of Orissa 1847.

Memorandum on Treaties, Positions and Status of the Feudatory States of Orissa, Acc. No.41, OSA.

Notes on the History of Mayurbhanj, 1930.

Origin, Rise and Consolidation of Indian States F.236 R(Confidential) 1930.

Order of Pratap Chandra Bhanjdeo dated 5 March, 1947 under Regulation II of 1908

Orissa Boundary Committee (O'Donnel Committee) Report, 1932.

Orissa Committee Report, 1931

Proceedings of the Legislative Assembly of Orissa 1946-1947, 1948, 1949.

Proceedings of the Mayurbhanj State Council 1892-1910.

Proceedings Bengal Judicial Civil No.34, 1805.

Proceeding Bengal Judicial (Civil) Nos. 18, 19, of 1807. No.29 of 1814, No.33 of 1839.

Proceedings of Bengal Judicial (Criminal) No.26, 1837.

Proceedings Foreign Department, Secret 1, 1884, No.39-40 (Simla Papers)

Proceedings of Foreign and Political Department 1930. Government of India File Nos. 179-R/30, 227 Pol/26 Question of the admission of the Maharaja of Mayurbhanj to the Chamber of Commerce.

Proceedings of the Informal meetings held in Delhi on February 1918 before the Viceroy, Secretary of States and certain Ruling Princes in Connection with Constitutional reforms

Proceedings No.7 Dr. Heyes, Deputy Commissioner of Singhbhum to the Superintendent of Tributary Mahals 21 April 1866 and No.6 T.E.Ravenshaw to Government of Bengal No.E, 24 April 1866.

Proceedings of Simla Conference, 1901 Question of establishment of direct Political Relation between the Government of India and Indian States who have their political relations at present conducted through Provincial Government No.200, Political 1930.

Quinquennial report on the progress of education in Orissa for the period 1937-42.

Quinquennial Administrative Report on Orissa Division 1901-05

Report on the progress of education in Bihar and Orissa for 1927-28 to 1942-43

Report on the Orissa States Enquiry Committee by H.K.Mahatab, L.M.Pattnaik and B.R.Mehta, 1939.

(D) Reports

Annual report on the administration of Bengal, 1895-1902.

Annual Administrative Reports,Bihar and Orissa 1911-12 to 1936-37.

Annual Reports on the Administration of the Feudatory States of Orissa, and Chhotnagpur for 1911-12 Ranchi.

Annual Report on Resolutions of Mayurbhanj Raj Estate, Calcutta, 1895.

A short summary of the administration of Bihar and Orissa, 1935.

Bihar and Orissa, First decennial Review 1912-22.

Board of Revenue Records, Cuttack, Vols. 64-99.

Constitutional Reforms in India, 1908.

General Review of the Administration of the Feudatory States of Orissa for 1922-23, 1923-24, 1924-25, 1925-26, 1936-47.

Geological Account of Orissa (Geological Survey)

Local Self Government Resolution reviewing the Reports on the working of the Municipalities 1926-27, 1929-30.

Memorandum Submitted by the Government of Orissa to the States Reorganization Commission, 1955.

Memorandum of Native States of India, 1907, Vol.I and II.

Memorandum on Native States of India, 1911, Calcutta.

Miscellaneous Report on Orissa Division, 1908-12.

Orissa-Report of Partially excluded area Enquiry Committee, 1938.

Proceedings of Utkal Sammelani 1903-1920.

Report on the Land Revenue administration of the Province of Bihar and Orissa, 1911-12, 1912-13, 1913-14, 1914-15, 1915-16, 1916-17 to 1935-36.

Report on the Orissa Administration Committee, New Delhi, 1933.

Report on the working of the Municipalities, Bihar and Orissa.

Report on the working of the Cooperative Societies in Bihar and Orissa for the year 1913-14.

Selections from the official letters and records relating to the History of Mayurbhanj Vol.I and II (1761-1767)

Selection from Nagpur Residency Record, Vol.I, 1799-1807, Nagpur, 1950, H.N.Sinha (ed)

Settlement operations in Panchpir 1931.

Speech of Hon'ble H.K.Mahatab, Prime Minister of Orissa in introducing the Budget estimate for 1948-49.

The Eastern States Union Constitution Act 1947

White Papers on Indian States, Government of India, Ministry of States, Delhi, 1950.

(E) Private Papers of Sunaram Soren

Gist of discussion with Mr. Julius Tiga, the Prabasi Secretary, Adibasi Mahasabha, Ranchi by the Hon'ble Premier of Orissa on 20 April 1949 at Rairangpur.

Letter No.233-Camp H.P. dated 23 April 1949 from the Assistant Secretary to the Premier Orissa to Julius Tiga.

Letter No.AM/542 28 May 1949 from Julius Tiga to the Premier of Orissa.

Letter DO.No.3826 HE, dated 20 July 1949 from H.K.Mahtab, Premier of Orissa to Julius Tiga

Letter No.3282 dated 11 December 1948 from Mayurbhanj State Secretariat to Sunaram Majhi.

Letter of Sunaram Soren to Jaipal Singh, President of the All India Adibasi Mahasabha in December, 1948

Letter to the Secretary, States Ministry from Sunaram Soren dated 06.09.1948.

Memorandum submitted by Adibasis of Mayurbhanj to His Excellency the Governor of Orissa dated November 1949.

Memorandum submitted for consideration by the Excluded and the Partially excluded area subcommittee to the Constituent Assembly Advisory Committee for the establishment of a separate Governor's Province of Jharkhand out of the Chhotanagpur division, the district of the Santal Pargana and suitable portion of the out lying tracts.

Memorandum submitted on behalf of the Mayurbhanj Adibasi Sabha to the Hon'ble Sardar Ballabh Bhai Patel on the question of the desirability of merging Mayurbhanj with the province of Bihar.

Memorandum submitted on behalf of the Mayurbhanj Adivasi Sabha to His Highness the Maharaja of Mayurbhanj State on 6 September, 1947.

Memorandum submitted to the Advisory sub-committee on Excluded and Partially excluded areas on behalf of the Mayurbhanj Adivasi Sabha dated 19 September 1947

Memorandum on behalf of the consumer Association Kolhan and Porahat, Singhbhum (Bihar) to the Advisory Sub-Committee Excluded and Partially Excluded Areas, Constituent Assembly, India for the Constitution of a separate province of Jharkhand.

Memorandum on behalf of the Adivasi sabha, Kharswan state before the Arbitral Tribunal opposing merger of Kharswan State with Orissa, Undated.

Memorandum on behalf of Maniki Association to the Excluded and Partially Excluded Area Sub-Committee of the Constituent Assembly's Advisory Committee New Delhi, Undated.

Memorandum submitted on behalf of the Vice President, Adivasi Sabha, Jamshedpur dated 1.5.1947 to 41 persons for a separate Jharkhand Province.

Minutes of the Meeting of Adivasi Sabha, Mayurbhanj at Baripada dated 2 November 1948 to 6 November 1948.

Pamphlet titled "Development of Mayurbhanj Affairs" dated 27.08.1950.

Pamphlet issued by the Mayurbhanj AdivasiSabha titled Mayurbhanj Adivasi O Mayurbhanja Misrana Samasya (Oriya) not dated.

Pamphlet issued by the Mayurbhanj Adivasi Sabha titled Mayurbhanj Adivasi Sabha (Oriya) October 1947.

Pamphlet issued by Sunaram Soren titled "What Mayurbhanj Wants" dated 5 July 1948, Baripada.

Pamphlet issued by Sunaram Soren titled "Soochana" (Hindi) dated October 1948.

Pamphlet issued by Mayurbhanj Adivasi Sabha titled 'Mayurbhanj Kanhiki Bihar re Misiba' (Oriya) Undated.

Pamphlet issued by Mayurbhanj Adivasi sabha titled Mayurbhanj Adivasi Sabha O Ehara Udaishya (Oriya) 1 July 1948.

Pamphlet issued by Sunaram Soren titled 'Misran Birodhi Prastab' dated 30 December 1947.

Pamphlet issued by Jaipal Singh titled 'Mayurbhanj Relief Fund' dated 17 February 1948, New Delhi.

Proceedings of the meetings of Mayurbhanj Adivasi Sabha dated 02.06.1946.

Proceedings of the meetings of Mayurbhanj Adivasi Sabha, Undated.

Resolution Passed in an emergent meeting of the Working Committee of Adivasi Sabha, Mayurbhanj State held at Baripada on 16 September 1948 under the Presidency of Sunaram Soren.

Resolution takes at the meeting of Adivasi Sabha on 30.10.1948.

(F) Gazettes and Gazetteers

Mayurbhanj State Gazette, Baripada 1936, 1937, 1938, 1939, 1940, 1941, 1942, 1943, 1944, 1945, 1946, 1947, 1948

Mayurbhanj State Gazette Krodapatra Part-V (Oriya)

Mayurbhnaj States Information Bulletin 1945, 1946

Santal Pargana District Gazetteers B, 1900-01 and 1910-11

The Extraordinary Mayurbhanj State Gazetteer (Baripada) 1938, 1947, 1948.

Bengal District Gazetteers (LSSO' Malley-ed) Balasore, Calcutta 1907

Birbhum, Calcutta, 1910

Cuttack, Calcutta, 1906
Kharswan, Calcutta, 1910
Midnapore, Calcutta, 1911
Puri, Calcutta, 1908
Saraikela, Calcutta, 1910
Singhbum, Calcutta, 1910
Orissa District Gazetteers (N Senapati etal.)
Bolangir, Bhubaneswar, 1968
Dhenkanal, 1972
Mayurbhanj, 1967
Puri, 1977
Sambalpur, 1971

(G) News Papers and Periodicals

Abua Jharkhand (weekly) Hindi and English, Ranchi, 1947-49.
Asha (weekly), Berhampur, 1914-36.
Mayurbhanj Krodapatra, Baripada, 1940-48
Odia O Navasamvad (weekly) Balasore, 1899-1921
Sahakar (monthly), Cuttack, 1930-36.
Samvadvahika (weekly) Balasore, 1872-1923.
The Samaj (weekly) (daily) Puri/Cuttack, 1919-1950
TheDesakatha, Cuttack, 1930-78.
The Gadjatvasini 1903-36.
The Mayurbhanj Pakhika Patrika, Baripada, 1879-1881
The Prajatantra (weekly/Daily) Balasore, Cuttack, 1931-39, 1943-49.
Utkal Darpana, 1879-1907
Utkal Deepika (Cuttack), 1869-1933
Utkal Hitaisini weekly, Balasore, 1881-1902
Utkal Prava, weekly, Baripada

ENGLISH NEWS PAPERS

Amrit Bazar Patrika, Calcutta, 1905-1949
Star of Utkal, Cuttack, 1905-1912
The Eastern Times, Cuttack, 1949-50
The Search Light, Patna, 1921-1934.
The Statesman, Calcutta, 1935-49.

(H) State Papers in Orissa State Archives

Annual Administrative Reports of

Athgarh,	1930-34
Athmallik,	1945-47
Bamra,	1930-39
Baud,	1920-32
Dhenkanal,	1936-45
Mayurbhanj,	1929-45
Nayagarh,	1939-40, 1942-43, 1945-46
Talcher,	1935-42
Tigiria,	1943-44

General Review of Administration of the Feudatory States of Orissa, 1936-47.

Memorandum of Native States in India 1907,Vol.I and II.

Proceedings of the Lieutenant Governor of Bengal, Judicial Department (Political) 1872-1910

Proceedings of the Lieutenant Governor of Bengal, Judicial Department (Civil and Criminal) 1814-1870

Report of the Evacuation of Hirakud Dam 1956

Report on the Land Revenue Administration of Bihar and Orissa 1824-25, and 1932-35

The Feudatory and Tributary States of Orissa Division and the Rules Applicable to them

The State Committee for Compilation of who's who of Freedom Workers in Orissa Sambalpur, Sundargarh, Kalahandi and Bolangir Patna 1969. Mayurbhanj, Keonjhar and Balasore Districts, 1970.

The Compilation of Talcher Prajamandal Itihas Committee,

History of Talcher Prajamandal, Calcutta, 1950

The Compilation of Dhenkanal Itihas Committee,

Dhenkanal, *Swadhinata Andolanara Samkhipta Itihas*, 1965

White Paper on Indian States (Government of India) Ministry of States, New Delhi, 1950.

(I) Journals and Proceedings

Bengal Past and present No.132, 1950

Bhanja Pradeepa, 1945-1947

Calcutta Review, ix-xvii

Desa Sevak (Oriya), 1948
Mahtab O Odisa, 1979
The Hirakhanda Samachar (Oriya weekly) 1946
Utkal University Journal, Bharati, Vol.I-VI
Indian Historical Quarterly 1937 and 1952
Indian Historical records Commission, 1938, 1939 and 1942
Orissa Historical Research Journal 1951-60
Mayurbhanj Chronicle, Baripada, 1935-1945

(J) Autobiography

Das Nilakantha, *Autobiography* (Oriay) Cuttack, 1963
Dash Prasanna Kumar, *Karmir Sadhana*, Bhubaneswar, 1994
Dwibedi, Surendra Nath, *Quest for Socialism*, Delhi, 1984
Mahtab, H.K., *Sadhanar Pathe* (Oriya), Cuttack, 1972
Mishra, Godavaris, *Autobiography* (Oriya) Cuttack, 1971
Pradhan, Patitpaban, *Muktipathe Sainik*, Cuttack, 1972

(K) Interviews

Bansidhar Raj, Peasant Leader, Udala
Bhaktabandhu Mahanta, Peasant leader, Karanjia
Bharati Das, Rotarian, Baripada
Bhagabat Parida, Betnoti
Bibhas Chandra Bhanjdeo, Cousin of the Maharaja, Baripada
Bibhuti Dash, Advocate, Cuttack
Binoy Sharma, Advocate, Baripada
Bimal Mukherjee, Advocate, Baripada
Brajasundar Rath, Social activist, Baripada
Binod Kumar Das, Rotarian, Baripada
Harekrushna Dash Advocate, Baripada
Kalakar Bhanj, Artist, Baripada
Purna Chandra Bindhani, State Photographer
Prafulla Chandra Hota, Advocate, Baripada
Prasanna Kumar Dash, Prajamandal Leader, Member Legislative Assembly and Speaker and Minister
Ramchandra Majhi Former Member of Parliament, Bahalada
Radhakrushna Bhanja, Artist, Baripada

Surendra Nath Dwebedi, Socialist Leader, Rourkela

Santosh Kumar Sahu, former member Orissa Legislative Assembly, Minister, Bhubaneswar and M.P.(R.S.)

Siris Chandra Hota, Senior Citizen, Baripada

V.S.Mathews, Former Collector and Chief Secretary, Orissa, Bhubaneswar.

Girish Chandra Sahu, Baripada, Ex-employee of Mayurbhanj state, Durbar Administration, and Orissa Government

Sudam Chandra Tipiria, Senior Citizen, Khalapada (Gadia) Moroda Block

Laxmidhar Dhal, Social Activist, Bad-Dhenkia,Suliapada Block.

Shatrughan Mohanta - Ex Chairman, Suliapada Block

Sushil Chandra Das, Karanjia

Gour Mohan Mohapatra, Former Advocate, Baripada

Kamini Kanta Pattnaik, Advocate,Cuttack.

(L) Some Relevant Files on Native States

Government of India, Ministry of States 'P' Branch

Group File No.12(108) p/48,
File No.12(49) p/48
File No.12(67) p/48-1948
File No.625 p/48-1948
File No.530 p/48-1948
File No.12(i) p/48-1948
Group II File No. 66 p/48-1948
Group III File No.42 p/48,Vol.II, 1948
File No.411 p/48-1948
File No.191 Political/1948 Serial No.1(46)

Government of India, Home Department, Political, Internal File No.34/2/43 (Poll-I) 1943.

SECONDARY SOURCES

Abhayanakar,G.A., *Problems of Indian States, Poona*, 1928.

Acharya Paramananda, *Studies in Orissa History, Archaeology* and Archives, Cuttack, 1969.

Aitchison, C.U. *A Collection of Treaties. Engagements*, and Sunnuds Relating to India and Neighbouring Countries, Vol.I and II, Calcutta, 1862.

Andrews, C.F. *India and the Simon Report*, London, 1930.

Banerjee, R.D. History of Orissa Vol.I and II, Calcutta, 1931, Reprinted Delhi, 1980.

Bakshi, S.R., *British Diplomacy and Administration in India*, New Delhi, 1971.

Bakshi, S.R., *Simon Commission and Indian Nationalism*, New Delhi, 1976.

Bose, S.C. *The Indian Struggle* 1920-1942, Bombay, 1991

Bose, N. *The Indian Awakening and Bengal*, Calcutta, 1976

Buckland, C.E. *Bengal under the Lieutenant Governors*, 2 Vols, Calcutta, 1901.

Cobden Ramsay, L.E.B. *Feudatory States of Orissa*, Calcutta, 1910

Coupland, R. *The Future of India*, Part III, London, 1944

Chanda, R.P. (i) History of Mayurbhanj, Calcutta, 1949.

(ii) *Selection from official letters and Records Vol.I* and II (Baripada) 1942

Chand Tara. *History of Freedom Movement in India*, Vols II-IV, New Delhi, 1972.

Choudhury, S. *Economic History of Colonialism*, New Delhi, 1979.

Chandra Bipan. *India's Struggle for Independence* (Penguin) 1989.

Chandra,B., Tripathi, A., and De Barun, *Freedom Struggle*, New Delhi, 1972.

Chopra, P.N., *India Major Non-Violent Movement*, New Delhi, 1982.

Choudhury Gopabandhu, *Gandhi O Utkal*, Cuttack, 1945.

Copperfield Sir Conrad, The Princely India I Knew, Madras, 1975.

Copland Ian. *The British Raj and the Indian Princes Paramountcy* in Western India, 1857-1930, Bombay, 1981.

Das, Durga, *India from Curzon to Nehru and After*, London, 1969.

Das, M.N.(ed), *Sidelights on History ad Culture of Orissa*, Cuttack, 1977.

Das, S.C. *Emergence of Modern Orissa*, Meerut, 1967.

Das, Banchhanidhi, *Essays on Mayurbhanj Chhau*, Bhubaneswar, 1994.

Dash, Prasanna Kumar (i) *Karmira Sadhana, Cuttack*, 1997 (ii) Mayurbhanj Mukti Samgramra Samkhipta Itihas, Cuttack, 1987.

Das, Purna Chandra, *History of Orissa Since Kalinga War*, New Delhi, 1992.

Directorate of Chambers, *The British Crown and the Indian States*, London, 1927

Das, G.S. *History of Freedom Movement in Orissa*, IV, Cuttack, 1957.

Dodwel, H.H., *Cambridge History of India Vol. V and VI*, Delhi, 1956 and 1958.

East India Company, *Historical Sketch of the Princes of India*, London, N.A.

Enquiry Committee *Report on Orissa States*, Cuttack, 1939.

Fitze, K. *Twilight of the Maharaja*, London, 1956.

Frasser, H.L. *Among Indian Rajas and Ryots*, London, 1912.

Fraser, Lovat, *India Under Curzon and After*, Sagar, NY

Ganguly, D.K. *Historical Geography and Dynastic History of Orissa*, Calcutta, 1975.

Gandhi, M.K. *Indian States' Problems, Ahmedabad,* 1941.

Ghosh, Sunit, *Orissa inTurmoil, Calcutta,* 1978.

Gopal, S. *British Policy in India 1858-1905*, Bombay, 1975.

Griffith, P.J. (i) *British Impact on India (London 1952)*, (ii) Modern India, London, 1965.

Government of Orissa, *A short Summary of Administration* of Orissa in 1936, Cuttack, 1937.

Habshawn, *Peasants in History*, Oxford, 1980.

Handa, R.L. *History of Freedom struggle in Princely State*, New Delhi, 1989.

Hunter, W.W., *Orissa I and II,* London, 1872.

Joshi, A. *History and Culture of Khijjingakotta*, Bhubaneswar,

Kar, P., *Indian National Congress and Orissa*, Cuttack, 1987

Kumar Shive, *Peasantry in the Indian National Movement*, 1919-1933, Meerut, 1979.

Lee Warner, (i) *The Protected Princes of India*, London, 1894, (ii) The Native States of India, London, 1910.

Low Sir Sidney, Indian States and Ruling Princes, London, 1921.

Mahtab, H.K. (i) *History of Orissa,cuttack, 1960,*

(ii) *History of Freedom Movement in Orissa*, Cuttack, 1957,

(iii) *Beginning of the End,* Cuttack, 1972,

(iv) *Sadhanar Pathe*, Cuttack, 1977.

Maddox, S.L., *Final Report on the Survey* and Settlement of the Province of Orissa 1890-1900, Calcutta, 1900.

Mazumdar, R.C. The *History and Culture of Indian People,* Vol.XI, Bombay, 1964.

Mazumdar, A.K., *Advent of Independence*, Bombay, 1963.

Mansergh (ed). *Transfer of Power.* Vols. I &II, London, 1971-1972.

Mojumdar, K. *Changing Tribal life in British Orissa*, Delhi, 1996.

Mehta, B.R. The *Congress Policy towards states*, Bombay, 1938.

Menon, V.P.l (i) The *story of the Integration of Indian States,* Madras, 1961.

(ii) *The Transfer of Power in India*, Delhi, 1957.

Mishra, P.K. (i) *Archaeology of Mayurbhanj*, New Delhi, 1997,

(ii) *Political History of Orissa*, 1900-1936, New Delhi, 1979.

(iii) *Evolution of Orissa and Her Culture*, Calcutta, 1984.

(iv) (ed) *Culture, tribal History and Freedom Movement*, New Delhi, 1989.

(v)(ed) *Comprehensive History and Culture of Orissa*, Vol.I and II, New Delhi, 1996.

(vi) Changing *Pattern of Political Culture*, Delhi, 2000.

Mishra, Prasanna Kumar, *Political Unrest in Orissa in the 19th Century*, Calcutta, 1983.

Mohanta, B. *Panchpir Praja Andolan*, 1978.

Mohapatra, J.N. *Orissa*, 1936-37 to 1938-39, Cuttack, 1941

Mahapatra,R.P. *Archaeology of Orissa* 2 vols. 1986

Mohanty, B. *Introducing Orissa*, Bhubaneswar, 1979

Mohanty Nivedita, *Oriya Nationalism*, New Delhi, 1982

Mukherjee, P., *History of Orissa VI*, Bhubaneswar, 1964.

Munshi, K.M. End of an *Era*, *Bombay*, 1957.

Narovanl, D.N. The *Indian States in the Federation of India*, Bombay, 1939.

Natarajan, L. *Peasants uprising in India 1850-1900*, Bombay, 1953.

Nehru, J. *Independence and After*, 1944.

Orissa *Legislative Assembly*, *Who is who*, Bhubaneswar, 1996.

O'Malley, L.S.S. *History of Bengal, Bihar and Orissa under* the British Rule, Calcutta, 1925.

Pannicker, K.M. (i) *Evolution of British Policy towards* Indian State 1774-1858, Calcutta, 1929 (ii) I*ntroduction to the study of the Relations* of Indian States with the Government of India, London, 1927. (iii) Indian States and the Government of India, London, 1932.

Patel, V., *On Indian Problems*, Delhi, 1949.

Patnaik, Sudhakar, *Samvad Patraru Odisar Katha* (Oriya), Cuttack, 1972.

(i) *Orissa State Legislature and Freedom Struggle*, New Delhi, 1979.

Patra, K.M. (i) *Orissa Under the East India* Company, New Delhi, 1971.
(ii) *Advanced History of Orissa*, New Delhi, 1983.

Patra, S.C. *Formation of the Province of Orissa*, Calcutta, 1979.

Phadmis, U. *Towards the Integration of Indian States* 1919-1947, Bombay, 1968.

Padhi, S.C. British *Relation with the Chiefs* and Rajas of Orissa 1803-1858, Calcutta, 1986.

Panda, A., Political *Evolution of Feudatory States* in Orissa, New Delhi, 2002.

Panda, H. *History of Orissa*, Cuttack, 1997.

Panda, A.K. Four *Hundred Years* of Orissa, Calcutta, 1987.

Panda, P.C. *British Administration in Orissa,* New Delhi, 1984.

Panigrahi, K.C. (i) *A History of Orissa,* Cuttack, 1984. (ii) Autobiography (Oriya), 1987.

Panigrahi Kalindi Charan, Autobiography (Oriya), Cuttack, 1923.

Patro, P.S.N. The Maharaja of Parlakhemundi,Ganjam, 1981.

Patnaik, Jagannath, Feudatory States of Orissa, Vol.I and II, Allahabad, 1988.

Patnaik, P.K. A forgotten Chapter of Orissa History, Calcutta, 1979.

Pradhan, A.C. A study of History of Orissa, Bhubaneswar, 1988. 9ed) People's Movement in Orissa During the Colonial era, Bhubaneswar, 1994.

Pradhan, S. (i) Agrarian and Political movements in the states of Orissa, New Delhi, 1986.

(ii) (ed) Orissa History, Culture and Archaeology, New Delhi, 1999.

Prasad, N. Paramountcy under Dalhousie, Delhi, NYA

Praharaj D.M. Tribal movement and political History of India, Nw Delhi, 1988.

Ramasusack, Barbara N. The Princes of India in the Twilight of Empire, Dissolution of a Patron-Client System 1914-39, Columbus, Ohio, 1978.

Rath, A.K. Studies on Some aspects of the History and Culture of Orissa, Calcutta, 1987.

Rath, Radhanath, History of Freedom Movement in Orissa State, Cuttack, 1964.

Rath, S.N. The *Development of Welfare State in Orissa,* new Delhi, 1977

Ray, B.C. (i) *Orissa under the Mughals,* Calcutta, 1981.

(ii) Foundations of *British Orissa,*Cuttack, 1960.

(iii) Orissa under the *Marathas, Allahabad,* 1960.

Raghavaiah, V. *Tribal Revolt* (1778-1945) Nellore, 1971.

Roy, M.K. Princely *States and the Paramount Power,* Delhi, 1981.

Sahu, N.K. (i) *History of Orissa* Vol.I, Bhubaneswar, 1964.

(ii) Orissa from *Earliest Times to the Present Day,* Calcutta, 1956.

(iii)(ed) New *Aspects of History of Orissa,* Sambalpur, 1970.

Sahu, Mishra and Sahu, *History of Orissa,* Cuttack, 1980.

Samal, J.K. (i) Orissa *under the British* Crown, Delhi, 1977.

(ii) *Princely States of Orissa, Allahabad,* 1988.

Sharma, J. (ed) India's *Struggle for freedom, Select* Documents and Sources, Manohar, 1977.

Sarkar, S.N. *Biography of Maharaja Sreeram Chandra Bhanjdeo*, Calcutta, 1918.

Sarkar, Sumit, *Modern India 1885-1947*, Madras, 1985.

Sardar Patel, My *Political Memories*, Nagpur, 1959.

Satapathy, S. and Choudhury, P.K. *Mayubhanj Sasan Samstha* O Bandobast (Oriya) Baripada, 1966.

Seal Anil, The *Emergence of Indian Nationalism*, CUP, 1963.

Sen, S.N. *Geography of Mayurbhanj*, Mayurbhanj, 1900.

Sitaramayya, P. History of *Indian National Congress*, Two Vols. Bombay 1944 and 1946.

Sinha, B.N. *Geography of Orissa*, new Delhi, 1971.

Singh, H.N. *Indian States and British India*, Benaras, 1930.

Singdeo, N. Singhbhum, *Sareikela and Kharswan through* the Ages, Calcutta, NYA.

Srivastav, B. *The art of Khiching*, Varanasi, 1986.

State Archive Publication, Towards Integration of Princely States of Orissa, Bhubaneswar, 1998.

Stirling, A. An *Account of Orissa Proper or Cuttack*, Geographical and Historical, Calcutta, 1904.

Sundari Sanou, A.N. *Indian States Register and Directory*, Madras, 1929.

Tiwari, A.N. *Reference Orissa, Bhubaneswar*, 1999.

Thorner, D. The *Agrarian Prospects of India*, Delhi, 1956.

Thompson, E. *Making of Indian Princes*, London, 1943.

Thompson, E. and Gorrat, *Rise and Fulfillment of British*, Rule in India, Allahabad, 1948.

Toynbee, G. A Sketch of the *History of Orissa from 1803-1828*, Calcutta, NYA.

Tripathy, S. *The Inscription of Orissa*, Vol.VI, Bhubaneswar, 1976.

Vasu, N.N. *Archaeological Survey of Mayurbhanj*, Calcutta, 1977.

Varada Chariar, N.D. *Indian States in the Federation*, Oxford Press, 1936.

Warner Lee, The Native *States of India*, London, 1910.

Wills, C.K. British *Relation with Nagpur States* in the 18th Century, Nagpur, 1926.

Wilson, C.R. *Early Annals of English in Bengal* Vol.I, London, 1895.

Index